Sports Card Collecting & Investing

by Geoff Wilson, Ben Burrows, and Tyler Nethercott

Sports Card Collecting & Investing For Dummies®

Published by: **John Wiley & Sons, Inc.**, 111 River Street, Hoboken, NJ 07030-5774, www.wiley.com

Copyright © 2024 by John Wiley & Sons, Inc., Hoboken, New Jersey

Media and software compilation copyright © 2024 by John Wiley & Sons, Inc. All rights reserved.

Published simultaneously in Canada

For general information on our other products and services, please contact our Customer Care Department within the U.S. at 877-762-2974, outside the U.S. at 317-572-3993, or fax 317-572-4002. For technical support, please visit https://hub.wiley.com/community/support/dummies.

Wiley publishes in a variety of print and electronic formats and by print-on-demand. Some material included with standard print versions of this book may not be included in e-books or in print-on-demand. If this book refers to media such as a CD or DVD that is not included in the version you purchased, you may download this material at http://booksupport.wiley.com. For more information about Wiley products, visit www.wiley.com.

Library of Congress Control Number: 2024932428

ISBN 978-1-394-22505-7 (pbk); ISBN 978-1-394-22507-1 (ebk); ISBN 978-1-394-22506-4 (ebk)

SKY10068229_022624

Table of Contents

Introduction

Welcome to *Sports Card Collecting & Investing For Dummies*. Maybe you're new to the hobby and need a road map to get started. Or maybe you've been a casual hobbyist for years and want to level up your collection. Either way, this book has what you're looking for.

Card collecting is a hobby that many sports fans interact with early on, even if only briefly. If you're reading this book, chances are you or someone you know has opened a pack of cards at some point in your life. The hobby has become more and more complicated over the years, however, and can be overwhelming for anyone new or those jumping back in after a break.

Beyond collecting, sports cards have also emerged as popular alternative assets for those looking to invest their money more creatively. While there are some fundamental differences between stocks and cards, the prices of cards can fluctuate daily just like stocks, sometimes drastically. And like stocks, some cards are considered blue chips — relatively safe, long-term bets — while others are like small cap stocks with huge risk and potential huge reward.

About This Book

The point of this book is to help you become a better collector. What that means is completely up to you. Each chapter features tips to get newcomers started and tricks that even the savviest hobby veterans may have missed over the years.

Designed for collectors of all kinds, this book takes complicated concepts and confusing terminology and delivers them in a way that's easy to understand and easy to implement. And remember, this book doesn't need to be read chronologically to be useful. You can skip from one chapter to the next, searching for what you need at that exact moment. Consider this a reference text. If you can't quite remember what something means, dive back in and find your answer.

Packed with everything from the history of sports cards to advice on navigating a constantly changing hobby, this book is meant to get you excited about collecting while giving you the tools to thrive.

How This Book Is Organized

This book is meant to give you the tools to become a savvy collector, even if you're starting from scratch. We explore the history of sports card collecting and its many eras while teaching you about the key sets, brands, and players that have defined the hobby over the last century.

You'll also learn the different ways to collect and how you can apply those to your own journey — ideally in a truly fulfilling way. With a little patience and a willingness to learn, this book helps you accelerate your journey from novice collector to seasoned veteran.

Part 1: Getting the Scoop on Sports Cards

The hobby has undergone countless changes since the earliest sports cards were collected back in the late 1800s. Basic tobacco cards have been replaced by an endless lineup of refractors and variations, and cards once fit for bicycle spokes now sell for millions.

Part 1 of this book explores the history of sports card collecting and the psychology behind why we collect. This part will also cover the rise in cards as alternative investments, iconic cards and collections, and what to do if you've rediscovered your old collection.

Part 2: Checking Out the Many Traits of Sports Cards

Gone are the days when an entire season might see just a single sports card release and each player may only have a handful of cards at most. In the Ultra-Modern Era, a variety of manufacturers produce dozens of products each season, and players have thousands of different cards. In Part 2, we cover the basics of card designs, the production process, product checklists, and the major differences between the major sports and their key releases.

Part 3: The Basics of Buying and Collecting

Collecting sports cards requires making at least a few purchases, and you'll want to do plenty of research before spending a dime. In this part, we cover how to decide what kind of collector you want to be. After that, we give you tips for building your collection according to your unique budget and goals. We also arm you with tricks for navigating card shows and making deals in person if you plan on getting out of the house.

Part 4: Flipping, Investing, and Turning a Profit

Buying and selling cards can be a great way to make money for those willing to put in the time and effort. Even if you're a collector more than an investor, selling cards can also be a great way to consolidate your collection and trade up into bigger and better cards. In Part 4 of this book, you learn how to use data to properly value your cards while developing the basics for flipping and investing to turn a profit.

Part 5: The Part of Tens

Part 5 is all about an easy read. In Chapter 17, you find unwritten rules that every new collector should know going in. In Chapter 18, we give you tips for building a great collection without going broke, and in Chapter 19, we show you the cards that will absolutely make you go broke — the best of the best the hobby has to offer — and tell you the interesting stories behind what makes them great.

Glossary

You'll find that the sports card hobby is filled with various abbreviations and odd terminology. Although we try to provide plenty of context around many of the terms used in this book, we've selected a number of items to describe further in the glossary. Refer to this section as often as you need.

Foolish Assumptions

To be accessible to as many collectors as possible, we won't assume many things about you. We do, however, assume some of these things are true:

>> You are brand new to the hobby and need help navigating it.

>> You've been a collector before and are re-entering the hobby after taking time off.

>> You're looking to make money buying and selling cards.

>> You're hoping to learn tips and tricks to make your collecting life easier.

Conventions Used in This Book

To help you navigate through this book, we use the following conventions:

>> *Italic* is used to emphasize and highlight new words or defined terms.

>> **Boldfaced** text indicates keywords in bulleted lists.

>> Monofont is used for web addresses.

>> Sidebars, which look like text enclosed in a shaded gray box, consist of information that's interesting to know but not necessarily critical to your understanding of the chapter or section topic.

Icons Used in This Book

This book is packed with so much information that sometimes we like to highlight specific items that are especially important. You won't want to miss these:

REMEMBER

This icon underscores a valuable point to keep in mind.

These are practical and immediate remedies for becoming a skilled collector.

This icon highlights common pitfalls you want to avoid.

This is detailed information you may find interesting but unnecessary when you're just getting started as a collector (or returning to the hobby after a hiatus).

Beyond the Book

Find out more about card collecting by checking out the bonus content at www.dummies.com.

You can locate the book's Cheat Sheet at www.dummies.com. Search for "Sports Card Collecting & Investing For Dummies" and you'll find handy hints and tips.

Where to Go from Here

This book is designed to give you the tools to be a great collector. But collecting sports cards is a hobby, and the reality is that *you* decide what being a great collector is. You aren't doing this right if you aren't having fun. Even if there's a more efficient or proper way to collect, having fun and enjoying this experience is the most important thing. Never forget that, as the adage goes, collect what you like.

Although this book is designed to cover as many aspects of collecting as possible, feel free to consume it as you need and to skip over parts as you want. If a chapter or part doesn't apply to you, skip ahead, and use your time elsewhere. Choose your own destiny.

If you're just getting started, feel free to begin in Chapter 1. If you're a savvy collector who wants to dive into investing, jump over to Part 4.

Now, dive in — wherever you like — and start reading. We hope you learn something, but more importantly, we hope you have fun.

1

Getting the Scoop on Sports Cards

How we fell in love with collecting.

Sports cards through the eras.

Chapter **1**

Sizing Up the Sports Card Craze

t's hard to narrow down when humans first started collecting things, but evidence suggests it could have been more than 500,000 years ago with the recycling of discarded stone tools.

There's evidence humans may have also collected things like shells in caves that date back 40,000 years, and of course, there's evidence that items were collected and placed in temples and tombs in regions like ancient Egypt.

Humans, it seems, have long been collectors of all kinds of things. Through the years, items like coins and other currency have gained additional worth beyond the original value, artwork from classic painters and sculptors regularly stars in the most exclusive auctions, and even classic cars are chased to fill garages of the rich and famous.

Today, it's fair to call sports cards some of the most popular collectibles, and the sales track record backs that up. Million-dollar sales for important cards have recently become a regular occurrence, and the popularity of cards sold through retailers like Target and Walmart grew so fast and furious during the COVID-19 pandemic that many stores were forced to limit sales to specific hours, if they didn't halt them completely. For some stores, the sales weren't worth the Black Friday–like chaos.

In this chapter, we explore why we collect sports cards and why the trend has gained popularity again in the 21st century.

The Psychology of Collecting

Humans have a long history of collecting things, but why do we do it at all? A research study investigating 500,000-year-old tools speculated that they were collected to preserve the memories of their ancestors. Another study in the 1980s found that some adults collect for reasons such as wanting to complete a series or creating a visually appealing display.

The research shows that sports cards seem to check all the boxes.

Why we collect sports cards

The different eras of sports cards are covered more in Chapter 2, but the Library of Congress considers the earliest known card to be one commemorating the Brooklyn Atlantics baseball team from the 1860s (see Figure 1-1). From there, sports cards have evolved from simple marketing materials during the tobacco era to luxurious items that feature high-end game-used memorabilia and autographs.

Regardless of their physical attributes, sports cards have almost always provided all the makings of a great collector's item. First and foremost, trading cards help chronicle the past. Most cards feature the player's stats from previous seasons and may even offer a short story about an important moment in their career. Want to reminisce about past seasons of glory? Take a trip down memory lane with a binder of cards, and you can easily lose hours.

The best cards are often visually striking, too. Iconic sets like the 1909–1911 T206 are beloved today more for their design than anything else (see Figure 1-2). Some are rare, but many can be easily found cheaper than you'd expect. Cards are then conveniently organized into numbered sets, just asking to be completed.

FIGURE 1-1: 1865 Brooklyn Atlantics card

FIGURE 1-2: T206 Ty Cobb PSA 7

What likely makes sports cards especially collectible, however, is their ability to bring fans closer to the teams and players they love so much, and this has only gotten stronger since autographs and game-used memorabilia were introduced during the modern era. According to a 2023 Statista study, 75 percent of Americans considered themselves to be sports fans, and buying a little piece of cardboard with a player on the front is an easy and gratifying entry point to demonstrating one's fandom.

A new (not really) kind of investment

The sports card hobby is typically associated with collecting cards for fun, but there is also a long history of using cards to make money as an investment. We cover more about buying and selling cards for profit in Chapters 14, 15, and 16. Although some collectors can almost be described as hobby purists — they buy and collect *strictly* as a hobby — a large percentage of the community regularly sells cards for a variety of reasons using a variety of methods.

It's also important to know that, despite what many collect-first hobbyists may argue, investing and selling for a profit is not a new concept introduced during the Ultra-Modern Era. Some of the most basic concepts within the hobby prove this is wrong, too, and you don't need to look any further than card shops and card shows. These businesses certainly may have been founded out of passion, but it's hard to argue that people are committed to that extent while losing money. Although selling cards as a business may be more prevalent today than in the 1970s, it's hardly a novel concept.

One could argue, however, that cards used as high-end alternative investments have increased in popularity in recent years. Again, savvy industry people have bought and sold cards for extreme profits for decades, but the introduction of cryptocurrency and the rise in other digital assets as investments have made investing in alternative assets more popular than ever before. For some, it's better to have a 1952 Topps Mickey Mantle on their desk than an Andy Warhol above their fireplace, and the definition of what is considered "art" has evolved to include more than what you'd find in the Louvre.

Getting Lost in the Cardboard. (It's a Good Thing.)

From the nostalgia and the fandom to the thrill of completing a collecting goal, there are so many reasons to collect sports cards. And one of the most fun things you can do with collecting is to get lost in it. If you've collected before, dive into a stack of cards and run wild with the stories and memories they bring back. If you're new to the hobby, consider going online and spiraling down a rabbit hole of stunning Instagram accounts and interesting YouTube videos. After all, that spiral is often what keeps so many collectors hooked.

Rediscovering your old collection

The sports card hobby is cyclical, both in its overall popularity and in how collectors individually participate. The hobby tends to go through phases of extreme popularity before dying down for one reason or another and reemerging later. For example, after a long run of popularity in the 1980s and 1990s, the hobby stalled after the Junk Wax Era — a period we cover more in Chapter 2. Decades later, the hobby exploded to arguably the height of its popularity during the COVID-19 pandemic because many were forced to spend more time indoors and stumbled upon their old cards.

Individual collectors experience cycles, too. Many are introduced to the hobby as children, and after years of collecting, they may take a break to pour their time and money into different things during their late teens and 20s. The disposable income that sometimes comes with mid-career success or introducing the hobby to their children can restart the cycle.

If you've recently rediscovered your collection, these next tips are just for you.

The lay of the land

Getting back into collecting can be extremely overwhelming if you've just dusted off your old collection. There's a chance that it's been years since you've looked through it, and some of the faces you once collected may have been mostly forgotten.

Depending on how long you've been away and whether you're still following the same sports and players you used to collect, you may need to read up on the game's current stars or do some research on some of your old favorites and how they panned out. You'll use this info to get organized later.

You can take two routes to determine the value of your old collection. First, you can put the time in yourself using data tools like our own Market Movers, which we cover more in Part 4. You can also look at completed auctions on marketplaces like eBay to see what something recently sold for. If doing it on your own isn't the best route for you, consider visiting your local card shop and asking if they'd help organize or appraise your collection. Some shops offer this, and some don't. The ones that do may still want an idea of what you have before dedicating time to it. Many will also only appraise your collection if you have a legitimate interest in selling some or all of it.

TIP

We cover how to properly value your cards more in Chapter 16, but it's important to know now that price transparency has come a long way in the last few years alone. Although magazines like the *Beckett Price Guide* ruled for decades, there's now a variety of tools you can use on your own.

The disappointing news for many collectors is that most cards, aside from the rarest copies of the best players of all time, aren't worth much. Unfortunately, those Hoops David Robinson rookie cards you stockpiled in 1989 won't be your ticket to early retirement (see Figure 1-3). Nevertheless, rare gems are rediscovered daily in old childhood collections. So, while the odds may be long that you're sitting on a goldmine, it can pay off big if you're holding something in high demand.

Get organized

Many who dive back into collecting often find that their childhood version of themselves didn't exactly follow the playbook for preserving the value of their cards. Whether it's poor organization or, even worse, poor storage practices, things often go wrong when the person running the show is 12. Now is either the time to fix things or give yourself a pat on the back for thinking ahead early on. If you're new to the hobby, consider this an opportunity to start the *right* way.

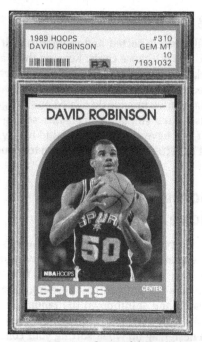

FIGURE 1-3: 1989 Hoops David Robinson PSA 10

Reorganizing may seem daunting, but many collectors look forward to it. We cover collecting for nostalgia purposes in the previous sections. This is where it comes into play. Ideally, you'll be sorting your old collection into new categories as you sift through it. Players that were once stars may now go in a "commons" box while some of those top prospects have now earned a penny sleeve and top loader. Organizing your old collection may be the most time-consuming part of the process, but there's a very real chance that it's the most fun.

If you're thinking about a collection reorganization, consider flipping to Chapter 8, where we cover the different types of collectors. It might be too early in the process, but there's no better time than now to sort your collection properly if you know you will prioritize a certain team, player, or sport.

Keep building or start selling

Once your old collection is sorted and reorganized, it's time to determine what to do with those cards. Keeping them all and just putting them back into proper storage, which we cover more in Chapter 9, is perfectly fine. You can continue building your collection on top of what you've previously owned or shift gears completely. This is also when you should consider selling cards you no longer want. If you have something in mind to buy, these old cards could be put to better use as a starter fund for your new collecting goals.

Tips for finding cards you will (or won't) love

We cover the different types of collectors extensively in Chapter 8, but you can start exploring all that's out there whenever you're comfortable or feeling inspired, if this is your first experience with the hobby. If you see something appealing, don't hesitate to do a little research and spiral down the rabbit hole with that card and others like it. If you're diving back in, you're bound to fall in love with a design again when sorting your collection, and we encourage you to explore whenever you're excited. Along with your old cards, below are a few places to get you started.

Card shops and shows

Searching for cards online will yield a much larger selection, but there's more than enough to get you started at your local card shops and card shows. Navigating card shows is covered more in Chapter 10, but one tip to know now is that they are great resources for things you haven't seen before.

WARNING

Be sure to keep a death grip on your wallet until you know exactly what you want to collect, how much those things should cost, and how much you can reasonably spend. If you wander into a card show like a babe in the woods, some dealers there will happily lead you to the slaughter.

If you see something cool, ask the dealer what they know about it. Card shop owners and card show dealers are often some of the most knowledgeable people in the hobby, and they are typically happy to share some info with you. Even if you aren't sure what you're looking for, feel free to visit these places early on to see what inspires you. Don't worry about specifics; simply allow your eyes to draw you to something exciting.

The web and beyond

Exploring the hobby online can really help you find your focus. We cover card communities in Chapter 11, but right now, you can just get lost in the photos. New and returning collectors alike will find a whole new world of cards once they get online. Whether it's Instagram or Facebook, there are collecting communities for just about every team and most of their key players. There will, of course, be plenty of collectors with tips for buying or selling stars like Tom Brady, but for every superstar, there will be someone with a shockingly good Seneca Wallace collection.

Chapter **2**

The Evolution of Sports Cards through the Decades

Like the sports they depict, cards have a long and complicated history with many twists and turns. Compared to their earliest iterations, sports like baseball, basketball, and football are nearly unrecognizable compared to today's versions. Cards are no different. Where increases in speed, power, and athleticism have completely reshaped how games are played through the decades, massive improvements to printing technology and new and unique creative concepts have turned sports cards into a billion-dollar industry.

In this chapter, we explore where sports cards started, how they evolved through the decades, and where the industry might be going from here.

Where It All Began

Based on its legend and record-setting prices, you might believe that the 1909–1911 T206 set, featuring the iconic Honus Wagner, is among the earliest sports cards created. You're right *and* wrong. Across the long history of sports cards, you could consider the early 1900s as some of the earliest cards. But to find the true start to the sports card hobby, we must go back even further to the mid-1800s.

Exploring the 1800s and the first cards

The format and spirit of today's cards weren't established until the mid-1900s, so there's minor debate about what's considered a sports card. At the time of this writing, the Library of Congress considers the earliest known sports card to have been produced in 1865. Celebrating the Brooklyn Atlantics' run of New York City championships in the 1860s, cards featuring the team were given out to fans as souvenirs. The design was considered a *visiting card*, or carte de visite, and featured a photograph attached to cardstock. Beyond sports teams, visiting cards saw a run of popularity as people put together collections of portraits featuring friends, family, and even famous individuals.

Cabinet cards

The 1860s also saw the gradual takeover of cabinet cards from visiting cards. Cabinet cards (see Figure 2-1) featured larger photographs and cardstock, making them ideal for displaying in, you guessed it, a cabinet. Cards from this era, as well as the tobacco era, were also often displayed in scrapbooks. As expected, the glue used to attach cards to the pages often had long-lasting effects, making finding cards in great condition extremely difficult years later. These cards also almost exclusively featured portraits, where the minor debate about sports cards comes into play. Do sports cards need to feature the sport being played, or does a portrait of an athlete count?

REMEMBER

It's worth noting that this period also saw an increase in cards featuring all types of subject matter. From animals and athletes to war heroes and presidents, cards featured interesting imagery, often as part of a promotional campaign. These types of advertisements helped lead the way into the tobacco era.

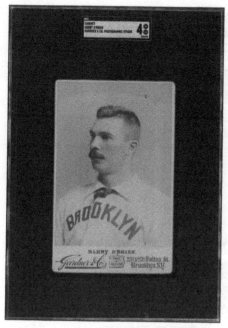

Courtesy of Heritage Auctions

FIGURE 2-1: 1888 Gardner & Co. Studio cabinet card

Tobacco cards

The tobacco card era is possibly the most famous of the sports card eras, featuring cards used as advertisements in packs of cigarettes. Much smaller than cabinet cards, tobacco cards actually served several purposes. Of course, they were collectors' items and motivated buyers to buy packs to complete their set. These cards also provided a stiff piece of cardstock to help support the cigarettes and prevent them from being easily crushed or destroyed.

The 1909–1911 T206 set (see Figure 2-2) is the most famous of the tobacco cards and holds tremendous value, especially in good condition. Important sets from the late 1880s even include brands that still exist today, like Allen & Ginter and Gypsy Queen (now produced by Topps) and Goodwin Champions (now produced by Upper Deck).

Courtesy of Heritage Auctions

FIGURE 2-2: 1909 T206 Honus Wagner, SGC A

REMEMBER

It's important to know that while cards like the T206 Honus Wagner are incredibly rare, that isn't the case for all tobacco-era cards. In fact, tobacco cards aren't difficult to find at all in most cases. They are, however, difficult to find in good condition. Low grades of many early tobacco sets can be purchased for a few hundred dollars, but you often see prices escalate significantly as the condition improves.

Pre-War and Vintage

The eras of sports cards are often broken down into large date ranges, with pre-war cards and vintage cards currently making up the largest range. Pre-war cards refer to cards made before World War I, while the term *vintage* becomes a little trickier.

TECHNICAL STUFF

As years pass, the meaning of what is considered vintage can change — we often see this with different eras of music. For this book, we consider anything prior to 1980 as vintage.

Colors, stats, and a sweet new hobby

While the cabinet cards of the late 1800s largely featured photographs with black, white, and cream colors, the early 1900s saw major improvements to the printing process that delivered vibrant colors. Along with tobacco products, cards began being used to promote products like candy and gum. In fact, many of the most iconic card manufacturers have roots as confectionery companies. Though mostly associated with cards today, Topps originally began when four brothers turned a struggling tobacco business into Topps Chewing Gum in 1938. Fleer may be best known to collectors as the creator of Michael Jordan's 1986 rookie card, but the company is also credited for creating bubblegum in the 1920s.

TECHNICAL STUFF

While working for the Frank H. Fleer Gum Company, Walter Diemer accidentally created bubblegum while tooling around in his lab during his breaks. Dubbed Double Bubble, Diemer's creation was made pink because it was the only food coloring available in sufficient quantity at the time. To this day, Double Bubble is pink. Thankfully, an earlier Fleer version of bubblegum, called Blibber Blubber, was scrapped before going to market because the concoction was so sticky that turpentine was reportedly needed to remove it from one's skin.

American Caramel and Cracker Jack

Often overshadowed by the T206 tobacco set, the 1909–11 American Caramel E90-1 is an important release in its own right. Featuring a similar design to the T206, the E90-1 had a much smaller checklist and was included in packs of caramel candy instead of cigarettes. Along with a rookie card for Joe Jackson, the set featured baseball heroes like Honus Wagner, Ty Cobb, Christy Mathewson, and Cy Young.

REMEMBER

You might know Joe Jackson as "Shoeless" Joe Jackson, whose name lives on in infamy because of his involvement in the 1919 World Series Black Sox Scandal. Jackson and some of his White Sox teammates were found to have colluded with organized crime figures to have thrown the series, giving the win to the Cincinnati Reds. The 1988 movie *Eight Men Out*, based on the book of the same name by Eliot Asinof, is about the scandal.

Soon after the American Caramel Company debuted, Cracker Jack (see Figure 2-3) joined the fray with a series of cards in 1914 and 1915. Best known for their bright red backgrounds, Cracker Jack cards also gave collectors a short biography on the back — cards from this era typically used the entire reverse for company promotion. Because they were packaged with the popcorn snack, cards were often found stained by syrup and sugar. A thin cardstock also made it difficult for cards to avoid significant damage in the packaging.

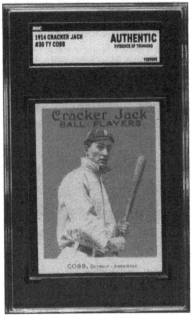

Courtesy of Heritage Auctions

FIGURE 2-3: 1914 Cracker Jack Ty Cobb, SGC A

1933 Goudey Big League Gum

Few releases are considered to have better eye appeal — even compared to ultra-modern products — than the 1933 Goudey Big League Chewing Gum set. Released as Americans were still battling the Great Depression, the set paired portraits and action shots with a beautiful lineup of colors. The 240-card set featured stars like Jimmy Foxx and Joe Cronin, as well as a missing Nap Lajoie (who was added in 1934).

Featured on card numbers 53, 144, 149, and 181, the Babe Ruth variations are some of the most recognizable cards in the hobby (see Figure 2-4).

Courtesy of Heritage Auctions

FIGURE 2-4: 1933 Goudey Ruth, PSA 4

The early Bowman, Leaf, Fleer, and Donruss entries

A variety of card sets were produced during the first half of the 20th century, but production slowed during World War II as paper and other materials became harder to produce. The first major baseball card release post–World War II came from Bowman in 1948, which featured a 48-card set with rookie cards from stars like Yogi Berra, Warren Spahn, Ralph Kiner, and Stan Musial. Founded in 1927 as Gum, Inc., the Bowman brand introduced trading cards in the 1930s, including the key Play Ball sets from 1938 to 1941, before halting production for World War II. The 1948 set featured black-and-white photos before Bowman added color to the backgrounds and team uniforms in 1949. Bowman used full color for the first time in 1950 and scored big in 1951 when it delivered full-color rookies for Mickey Mantle and Willie Mays.

Bowman remained Topps's primary rival during the 1950s until its final release in 1955. Topps acquired — and promptly discontinued — Bowman in 1956 before finally reviving the brand in 1989. Since 2000, Bowman has served as the primary brand featuring baseball prospect and rookie cards.

Shortly after Bowman released its 1948 set, confectionary company Leaf International issued its first sets of cards — this was also the first post-war set to feature cards in color. Despite Leaf's short stay in trading cards, 1948 Leaf Baseball is best known for featuring rookies for nine Hall of Famers, including Jackie Robinson, Stan Musial, Satchel Paige, and Warren Spahn. Leaf also produced football cards in 1948 featuring Sid Luckman and Bobby Layne, and boxing cards including Sugar Ray Robinson and Rocky Graziano.

TECHNICAL STUFF

It's important to note that Leaf International has no connection with Leaf Trading Cards, founded in 2010, or the Leaf name used from the 1980s into the 2000s.

It's not difficult to argue that 1986 Fleer Basketball is one of the most important sets of all time, though the brand began more than 100 years before as a confectionary company in 1885. Fleer debuted its trading cards in 1923, and the cards from that set remain extremely rare. Typically referred to as the *W515 strip card set*, it featured 60 baseball cards and 10 boxing cards. Fleer made its football debut in 1960 and covered the AFL rather than the NFL.

Fleer also helped lift the Donruss brand into the sports card market in the early 1980s. Founded in 1954, Donruss began making hard candies before diving into trading cards in the 1960s. The company would produce entertainment cards throughout the decade and eventually lucked out when Fleer sued Topps in 1975 over its exclusive baseball rights. After a judge ruled that Topps had illegally obtained exclusive rights, Donruss was able to produce its first sports set with 1981 Donruss Baseball.

The Donruss brand then took several twists and turns in the following decades that included a merger with Leaf International and an acquisition by Pinnacle Brands in 1996. Playoff later acquired

Pinnacle, which manufactured cards under the Donruss, Leaf, and Score brands. (Playoff acquired Score in 1998.)

Arguably, the biggest shakeup to Donruss came in 2009 when Panini acquired the Donruss Playoff brand to create Panini America.

1952 Topps and the modern sports card

For many, there is no set more important than 1952 Topps Baseball — and these collectors have a decent argument. This wasn't Topps's first set, though. Topps's first cards came in 1948, dubbed "Magic Photos," before introducing baseball cards with a limited set in 1951. The first full release in 1952 would go on to change everything.

TECHNICAL STUFF

The Topps Magic Photos baseball card set featured 252 sepia-toned cards, measuring just larger than today's postage stamps (7/8-inch x 1-7/16-inch). Of this massive set, just 19 cards depicted baseball players. The cards were "magic" because they were blank until exposed to sunlight, which developed the photo. The card backs included short trivia questions.

The 1952 set was larger than anything Bowman had done in both set size and physical card size. The 407-card checklist was much bigger than 1952 Bowman's 252-card set, and a larger card size was more in line with what collectors are accustomed to today. The combination of bright colors, team logos, and robust statistics on the reverse helped create the template for what we see today, and many collectors consider it the birth of what we consider the modern sports card.

The 1952 Topps Baseball set also features one of the most valuable cards of all time. Though it isn't his rookie card (that's his 1951 Bowman), the importance of Topps's 1952 release has made the #311 Mickey Mantle (see Figure 2-5) arguably the most iconic sports card ever. You can read more about Mantle's Topps debut in Chapter 19. Despite the set's importance, it wasn't a complete hit at the time. This set was released throughout the season in six series, and interest in it slipped toward the end of the baseball season. Sealed cases were dumped into the Atlantic Ocean to create warehouse space.

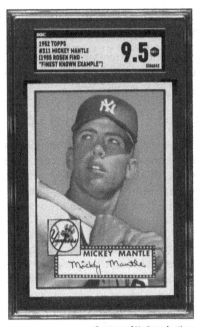

Courtesy of Heritage Auctions

FIGURE 2-5: 1952 Topps Mickey Mantle, SGC 9.5

TECHNICAL STUFF

Topps has often released cards in several series, with Series 1 released just prior to the start of the baseball season and the final series released at the end. Unfortunately for collectors attempting to build complete sets, getting their hands on those late-series cards was difficult because Topps printed them in smaller quantities. Some retailers didn't even stock cards from these late series; instead, they favored football cards, which rolled out at the end of baseball season. Those late-series cards are often called "short prints" and are usually considerably more valuable. If a star player happened to have their rookie appear in a late series — as The Mick's did in 1952 — that can drive values up. Topps Series 1 and Series 2 Baseball are extremely important sets today.

O-Pee-Chee and Panini make their debuts

The most popular sports card sets and manufacturers are often associated with companies in the United States, but Canadian confectionary company O-Pee-Chee has been an important brand for nearly 100 years. Most associated with hockey cards, O-Pee-Chee began producing trading cards in the 1930s and eventually partnered with Topps in the 1950s to distribute various sports cards in Canada that were nearly identical to the American Topps sets. O-Pee-Chee's most important set is typically considered its 1979 hockey release, which featured Wayne Gretzky's rookie (see Figure 2-6). The Gretzky rookie has both Topps and O-Pee-Chee variations, though hockey collectors often prefer the Canadian set, and the price reflects that. O-Pee-Chee was eventually sold to Nestle in 1996 and has been operated by Upper Deck since 2007.

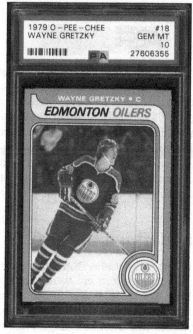

Courtesy of Heritage Auctions

FIGURE 2-6: 1979 O-Pee-Chee Wayne Gretzky, PSA 8

TECHNICAL STUFF

The O-Pee-Chee name is the Ojibwe word meaning "the robin," as referenced in Henry Wadsworth Longfellow's "The Song of Hiawatha". It's also the name of a Grand Bend, Ontario, summer cottage once owned by O-Pee-Chee co-founder John McKinnon (J.K.) McDermid. (The Ojibwe are Indigenous people of the Subarctic and Northeastern Woodlands.)

Many collectors associate the Panini brand with its explosive entry into the ultra-modern sports card market, but its debut into collectibles came in the 1960s with figurines. Founded in Modena, Italy, in 1961, Panini became known for its FIFA World Cup sticker sets starting in 1970. After decades of producing stickers, Panini entered the card market with Panini America in 2009 after acquiring Donruss Playoff and exclusive licensing rights to the NBA and later the NFL in 2016.

REMEMBER

As of early 2024, Fanatics's acquisition of licenses for the NBA, NFL, and MLB has jeopardized Panini's future in the hobby.

The Modern Era

While many credit 1952 Topps Baseball for introducing the modern card design, it was likely the modern era's innovations, creativity, and production that redefined what cards are still to this day. Where vintage cards typically featured simple sets of base cards, the modern era introduced widespread inserts, parallels, refractors, and other variations. The major changes to designs haven't always been considered positive, however, and the sports card hobby's massive surge in popularity and corresponding print runs in the 1980s and 1990s were also what nearly killed the hobby for good.

The sets that defined the era

It may seem hard to imagine decades later, but some of the most important sets during the modern era were met with extreme skepticism at the time. For some, it was an overall lack of popularity for the sport; for others, it was ridiculous-for-the-time pricing. The modern era saw a lot of changes, and not all collectors were excited about them. Below are a variety of sets that brought major innovations to the hobby during the modern era.

1986 Fleer Basketball

Arguably the most important basketball card set ever, 1986 Fleer Basketball was considered by many to be a flop at release. Simply put, the NBA wasn't nearly as popular then as it is today. In fact, Topps had stopped making basketball cards in 1981, and the hobby was without a major release until Fleer in 1986. Team sets from Star existed, but many collectors don't view those as regular releases. The hiatus for basketball cards also meant that 1986

Fleer was packed with both true rookies and the first cards for a host of Hall of Famers from Michael Jordan (see Figure 2-7) and Charles Barkley to Clyde Drexler, Patrick Ewing, Karl Malone, Hakeem Olajuwon, and Dominique Wilkins.

Courtesy of Heritage Auctions

FIGURE 2-7: 1986 Fleer Michael Jordan, PSA 10

1989 Upper Deck Baseball

Upper Deck's entry into the sports card hobby was nothing short of explosive and revolutionary (see Figure 2-8). Everything about the set was *premium*. They came on higher-quality cardstock with glossy photos and holograms on the reverse. Even the foil wrappers felt high-end compared to previous releases, which used waxed paper packaging called "wax packs." Of course, the strategy and higher price point missed the mark for some collectors, but the release raised the bar for other manufacturers to follow. It also didn't hurt that card No. 1 featured Ken Griffey Jr. — a card that has since become one of the most popular cards in existence and remains the most submitted card to PSA with more than 100,000 graded.

Ken Griffey Jr.   Randy Johnson   John Smoltz

Courtesy of Heritage Auctions

FIGURE 2-8: 1989 Upper Deck Baseball

1990 Upper Deck Baseball

A year after its entry into the hobby, Upper Deck raised the bar again with the first pack-inserted autographs. The first autographs debuted with "The Reggie" in a promotion that featured 2,500 cards signed and numbered by Reggie Jackson. The Upper Deck Baseball Heroes set even featured dual autographs with Harmon Killebrew on card No. 573 and Willie Mays on card No. 660 to match their career home run totals.

Before 1990, the only sports cards featuring autographs were hand-signed in person. Including signed cards in packs changed collecting, and today, most sports card sets feature autographs to chase.

1993 Topps Finest Baseball

Today's sports card hobby is dominated by parallels and refractors, and the craze all started with 1993 Topps Finest Baseball. In addition to the first refractors, 1993 Finest also featured the first use of chromium technology to give cards a unique shine.

TECHNICAL STUFF

Chrome cards have a shiny metallic look, while refractors use a special printing technique that causes them to refract light, creating a prism. Refractors are produced in various colors, with certain colors being rarer than others. Chrome and refractor cards are generally printed on thicker stock and are often valued higher than base cardboard cards.

1996 Press Pass Racing

Like the inclusion of autographs, many sets today feature cards with pieces of memorabilia, such as swatches of game-used jerseys and slivers of game-used bats. Often referred to as relic or memorabilia cards, some even include player autographs.

Relic cards got their start with 1996 Press Pass Racing. Featuring pieces of used tires from 1995, the 1996 Press Pass Burning Rubber set raised the bar for manufacturers and created a trend that has lasted decades.

2003 Upper Deck Exquisite Collection

If 1989 Upper Deck Baseball broke a price barrier for many with $1 packs' the 2003 Exquisite Collection (see Figure 2-9) shattered the ceiling. Originally priced at $500 for just five cards, Exquisite Collection was nothing short of shocking to the card community. Decades later, it seems like a steal. The 2003 release was very much a right place, right time product, and the ultra high-end set paired perfectly with one of the greatest rookie classes in NBA history. Featuring LeBron James, Dwyane Wade, Carmelo Anthony, and Chris Bosh, the set's Rookie Patch Autographs (RPAs) have become some of the most important cards in collecting history. At the time of this writing, one of James' RPAs is the most expensive basketball card ever sold at $5.2 million.

Great music, junk wax

For many, the modern era of cards is the best era. The vintage era created the foundation for sports cards, and the modern era built upon a strong start and shaped the hobby into what it is today. Unfortunately, for every Aerosmith and Tom Petty, there must be a Vanilla Ice or Wham! Often associated with important sets like 1986 Fleer Basketball and the introduction of refractors and pack-inserted autographs, the modern era also features the Junk Wax Era — and it nearly killed the hobby completely.

Few, if any, periods of time in the hobby were more harmful to collectors than the Junk Wax Wra, which is typically considered the middle-to-late 1980s and early 1990s. Things started off well enough — cards weren't hard to find, and shops and shows were all around. In fact, the Junk Wax Era was one of the most popular periods of collecting. The problem was that few people realized what was happening at the time, and the overall enthusiasm for the hobby was about to take a major hit.

Courtesy of Goldin Auctions

FIGURE 2-9: 2003-04 Upper Deck Exquisite Collection LeBron James Rookie Patch Autograph, BGS 9.5

A near-death experience

As popularity for the hobby surged, it was understandable that card manufacturers would want to increase print runs to meet demand. Unfortunately for collectors, manufacturers printed far beyond what was needed and greatly oversaturated the market with cards. With the market flooded, most cards from this era are nearly worthless. Not all Junk Wax Era cards are worthless, of course, but this period often sees prices that are especially low for even the greatest stars from the generation. In baseball alone, all-time greats like Greg Maddux, Randy Johnson, Ken Griffey Jr., Chipper Jones, and Derek Jeter have key rookies that can be found for just a few dollars.

REMEMBER

While many hobbyists collect strictly for fun, it still feels bad to know that many of their favorite cards from the time aren't worth anything. Even if the monetary aspect isn't important, it's not as fun to know that your key Randy Johnson rookie was just one of millions.

If you collect solely for the fun of collecting, don't let the shade thrown on cards from this era detract from your enjoyment. Many collectors still covet the cards depicting the heroes of their youth, even though they're not worth much on the aftermarket. The good news is that you can fill your home with 1980s and 1990s cards for very little money, especially if you don't give a rip about resale value. If you want to wallpaper your sports cave with Barry Bonds and Mark McGwire rookies, you can find them in mass quantities for next to nothing. You do you. Your collection is worth as much as it means to you.

Many collectors had also learned to keep their cards in penny sleeves and top loaders, so many of the most popular rookies from the era are also in near-mint or mint condition, which drives down the book value.

Many of the cards from even the tobacco era aren't especially rare, but finding them in great condition is difficult. Cards from the Junk Wax Era aren't generally rare and can typically be found in high grades, though gem-mint copies can be very tough to find because of centering and print defects as much as for how they were stored.

Years of work resulting in a nearly worthless collection was enough to drive millions of hobbyists away, and suddenly, a once-thriving industry seemed to be on life support.

The great rebound

With many collectors moving on to new things, the sports card hobby had to make serious adjustments to win them back. Really, the sports card hobby needed something for collectors to chase. In the aftermath of the Junk Wax Era, the 1990s proved to be a pivotal decade for the hobby. Luckily for collectors, a variety of sets delivered those key chases. As previously mentioned, 1993 Topps Finest Baseball introduced refractors to the hobby, and the debut of Topps Chrome in 1996 paired a new premium set with one of the most important NBA draft classes of all time.

With the rising popularity of basketball, collectors also saw the debut of SkyBox Basketball in 1990. The brand's creative designs and a commitment to chase cards in the '90s quickly made it a favorite among collectors, especially after its acquisition by Fleer in 1995. Two titans of creativity and innovation, Earl Arena and

Jean MacLeod of Arena Design, ran the show for Fleer/SkyBox in the second half of the '90s and revolutionized how we view cards. Using unique cardstock, ostentatious foil, die-cuts, and laser cuts helped fuse art and pop culture into the insert themes.

We won't get fooled again

Despite all the issues that the Junk Wax Era provided, the modern era still managed to revolutionize how cards were collected. After accepting the bare minimum for decades, collectors started demanding more from manufacturers. Base sets with minor design changes year after year were no longer good enough. To win over collectors, sets needed to have interesting designs, thoughtful themes for inserts, and autographs or memorabilia to chase. The value proposition needed to make sense.

The popularity of the sports card hobby saw a major slowdown as the manufacturers were forced into a course correction. Fleer and Upper Deck made a massive investment in memorabilia cards, though this was far overdone, and cards of even the biggest stars can often be found cheap today. Fleer would go on to halt trading card operations in 2005 before being acquired by Upper Deck. As companies like Fleer struggled, Topps continued to innovate in the late 1990s and early 2000s, and sets like Topps Chrome, Topps Finest, and Stadium Club have maintained value and popularity through the years.

The Ultra-Modern Era

There are so many ways to describe the Ultra-Modern Era of sports cards. You could argue that this period, which we consider as being from 2012 forward, has had the best lineup of high-end products ever. It's hard to tell for sure, but it wouldn't be a surprise to many if there were more collectors than ever during this era. Despite the variety of high-end cards and overall popularity, this period has also been marred by quality control issues, crime, a collapsing secondary market, and a variety of lawsuits between major manufacturers.

More than a sandwich

Any discussion about the Ultra-Modern Era must begin with Panini America. After an explosive entrance into sports cards in 2009, Panini spent the next decade-plus on top of the market. Panini secured exclusive rights to the NBA in 2009 and added the same for the NFL in 2016. Panini America's acquisition of Donruss Playoff in 2009 gave it access to multiple brands to get started, but some of the most important sets have been mostly new.

National Treasures, a spinoff from the Playoff brand, debuted in 2009 (see Figure 2-10) and has been arguably the most important set for rookie patch autographs since. Prizm — Panini's answer to Topps Chrome — was released in 2012 and has remained *the* flagship rookie card for basketball players. Flawless, another ultra high-end set, launched in 2012, and Panini added a chrome upgrade to the paper product with Donruss Optic in 2016.

Courtesy of Goldin Auctions

FIGURE 2-10: 2009-10 Stephen Curry National Treasures Rookie Patch Autograph, BGS 9

While Panini controlled the NBA and NFL markets, Topps maintained its hold on baseball. The explosive growth in basketball and football and a decline in baseball's popularity bled into the collectibles market, however, and many hobbyists shifted their attention toward something new. For the first time, baseball didn't seem like the runaway most popular sport in collecting.

The big boom

Panini America, Topps, and Upper Deck chugged along for years without much additional disruption. Card prices grew some, but sealed products weren't hard to find. After a decade of business-as-usual for Panini and the rest, the COVID-19 pandemic completely shifted everyday life, and the card market shifted with it. Government mandates kept most people indoors, while the Tax Relief Act in 2020 supplied additional disposable income. The pairing of extended time inside with extra cash to spend created a perfect storm for the sports card market. Many used the time inside to sift through their old belongings, and, as expected, old card collections resurfaced. Even *The Last Dance*, a documentary series about Michael Jordan and the Chicago Bulls released in 2020, is believed to have impacted collectors.

Record-high market

The reasons why the sports card market became so strong really don't matter. The only important thing is that the hobby saw explosive growth unlike anything ever before. Many savvy collectors and economic experts believed there would be a runup in card prices anyway, and the COVID-19 pandemic simply shortened the timeline.

Sports cards have a long history as alternative investments, which is covered more in Chapter 14, but their popularity has never been this high. The nostalgia, excessive free time, and additional disposable income all aligned perfectly with one of the most anticipated NBA Draft classes in years.

Zion Williamson (see Figure 2-11), considered by many to be the best basketball prospect since LeBron James at the time, was the top pick in the 2019 NBA Draft. Veteran collectors and new hobbyists alike swarmed to scoop up the next great player. Record-high prices for some of the hobby's most important cards quickly poured in, too. Collectors everywhere hoped to pull the next massive sale. Government stimulus checks were invested in sports cards, and the secondary market soared to new heights. An influx of hobby-related content creators also added fuel to the fire, and before collectors could blink, the grading companies were halting submissions because of overflow, and retail shelves were nearly always found empty.

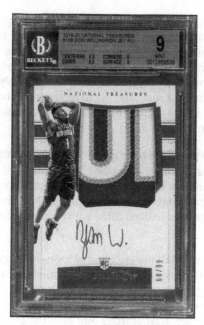

Courtesy of Goldin Auctions

FIGURE 2-11: 2019 Zion Williamson National Treasures RPA, BGS 9

The massive rise in popularity made it seem like prices would only ever go up, but that was not the reality. After months of record-high prices, peaking in early 2021, the card market slowly corrected. Card manufacturers ramped up production, and overall print runs soared. There appeared to be more collectors than ever, but prices regressed to pre-pandemic ranges in many cases.

Death by parallel and the Junk Slab Era

It's not hard to draw the parallels, no pun intended, between the rise in popularity during the COVID-19 pandemic and the runup before the Junk Wax Era. Many hobby experts don't believe print runs during the Ultra-Modern Era have reached what they were in the late 1980s and early 1990s, but collectors haven't felt any better.

As manufacturers attempted to meet demand, print runs increased, and parallels were suddenly substituted for "hits" across various products. Often considered autographs or memorabilia cards, "hits" have long been included in sealed products to provide collectors something to chase. There are only so many autographs and pieces of memorabilia to go around to begin with, and supply chain issues caused by the pandemic made creating "hits" harder than ever.

Many of the relics that were once game-worn turned into player-worn (not from any game), or worse, "not associated with any specific player, game, or event." To further compensate, products that previously guaranteed two autographs only delivered one, and those products were instead filled with a variety of numbered parallels.

TECHNICAL STUFF

Parallels and other variations are covered more in Chapter 4, but the key aspect to understand here is that parallels aren't all created equal. Adding another oddball color or design to a checklist to create another parallel isn't always a good thing. In fact, it's an easy way to create artificial scarcity and hide the fact that print runs have greatly increased.

THE JUNK SLAB ERA

Along with a massive increase in parallels, the Ultra-Modern Era has earned a reputation for its influx of graded cards. Grading is a fantastic and important part of the hobby that we cover more in Chapter 7, but not all cards should be graded. In reality, a very small number of cards deserve to be graded.

That concept wasn't always properly delivered to new collectors during this period, and the grading companies were met with more demand than ever as new hobbyists attempted to turn $20 cards into $80 cards with a PSA 10 label. PSA received such a substantial influx of cards in 2021 that it was forced to shut down submissions until reopening popular services in late 2022. As of this writing, seven of PSA's most graded individual cards overall come from the Ultra-Modern Era. This has resulted in many calling the years during and after the COVID-19 pandemic "the Junk Slab Era."

Violence, theft, and the retail controversy

The card manufacturers weren't the only ones who missed the mark during the COVID-19 pandemic. For all the mistakes the major companies made, it's not hard to point the finger at collectors themselves for causing so many of the hobby's woes. As the demand for cards continued to rise, so did the prices for sealed products on the secondary market. These prices rose so much that as retailers like Target and Walmart struggled to meet demand, collectors battled for the right to flip the products for massive profits on the secondary market.

Flippers lined up early in the morning as stores opened to purchase boxes. Even more sinister, some flippers paid store employees to ensure that they got the product when it was available. Store employees were even caught stealing these products. In some areas, flippers and their backdoor deals made it nearly impossible to buy retail products for retail prices. The race for profits, as expected, caused conflict between flippers, and in some unfortunate cases, violence resulted.

WARNING

Some unscrupulous collectors have perfected "pack searching," where they handle, pinch, squeeze — and sometimes, even weigh — individual packs to ferret out those containing hits. These shameless people often "search" every loose retail pack, leaving the packs unlikely to contain hits for unsuspecting buyers who think they have an equal chance of finding that Shohei Ohtani autographed jersey card they covet.

Eventually, the chaos caused by trading cards reached an apex in 2021, and some stores found it to be too much — some retailers halted sales of trading cards completely or limited sales to the customer service desk with purchase limits. Crime drastically rose at local card shops during this period, too, as thieves viewed these businesses as easy targets for guaranteed profits.

Where the hobby goes from here

As of this writing, the Ultra-Modern Era has largely been defined by record prices followed by record losses. There's the retail controversy, too, when many were driven by profits over passion.

The future of the sports card hobby remains unclear, but we know that Fanatics will be at the forefront. In a shocking turn of events, Fanatics swooped in and secured the exclusive rights to make trading cards for the NBA, NFL, and MLB in 2021 (those rights actually go into effect in 2025 and 2026 for the NBA and NFL) while leaving Panini America and Topps out in the cold. Without a background in trading card manufacturing, Fanatics acquired Topps in 2022 to handle the production before launching Fanatics Events to run card shows and Fanatics Live to handle live streaming and selling. Fanatics also acquired the marketplace PWCC in 2023.

Following an exodus of employees to the new Fanatics Collectibles, Panini America filed a lawsuit alleging that Fanatics had created a trading card monopoly. Experts have called Fanatics's moves similar to what Panini America pulled off in 2009, but lawsuits are difficult to navigate, and the outcome remains unclear. Regardless of any ruling on trading cards, Fanatics invested significantly in everything from memorabilia to future card shows with Fanatics Events. For better or for worse, Fanatics made a significant commitment to the collectibles space in 2021 and will be at the forefront of collectibles for the foreseeable future.

2

Checking Out the Many Traits of Sports Cards

Chapter **3**

The Anatomy of a Sports Card

A
t this point, sports cards have been produced for more than 150 years. Compared to the earliest iterations, today's cards are nearly unrecognizable. Once made from simple photos pasted onto a piece of cardstock, cards have changed and now come in all shapes and sizes and are produced using paper, plastic, cloth, wood, glass, and metal. Despite the materials and printing improvements, the spirit of what makes a sports card has remained largely unchanged even as the industry has evolved from a lineup of promotional items to a billion-dollar juggernaut.

In this chapter, you learn about the key design aspects that have defined cards through the decades and explore the production process from when the cards are printed to when they are delivered to your local card shop.

What Makes a Sports Card?

The simple answer to this question is pretty much any trading card that features a sport being played or an athlete. Unfortunately, that concept only covers the *spirit* of what a sports card is.

From a physical standpoint, sports cards have undergone nearly nonstop change since their earliest iterations to today's products. Improvements to the printing process have caused major adjustments while designers today continue looking for ways to innovate and produce something novel and creative. Greater access to athletes has allowed companies to include autographs and memorabilia, and the growing digital space now even allows you to carry around your collection in your pocket.

Major card designs through the years

Ultra-modern sports cards may look almost alien compared to the earliest releases, but the most basic concept has remained the same through the years. It's a photo attached to something solid for you to hold — it's not always paper or a square or rectangle, but it's solid. Usually.

Cabinet and tobacco cards

The first known sports card, at least if you trust the Library of Congress, arrived back in 1865 as a giveaway to fans celebrating a run of city championships for the Brooklyn Atlantics. We cover the different eras of sports cards more in Chapter 2, but it's important to know that most cards from this period were cabinet cards. Mostly just photographs glued to pieces of cardboard, they were large compared to today's cards and were typically displayed in, you guessed it, cabinets. The technology at the time meant that most photographs were black and white or cream in color.

Tobacco cards later arrived in the late 1800s and dominated the early 1900s as a popular form of advertising. In addition to motivating smokers to buy more packs while collecting the sets, these cards provided physical support to the cigarettes in the pack. This also meant that the cards were much smaller than the earlier cabinet cards and even today's cards. Early tobacco brands like Allen & Ginter (see Figure 3-1) or Gypsy Queen are still produced today under the Topps brand, and the sets often have "mini" variations that are similar in size to the early tobacco cards. Topps has even released 206 sets during the Ultra-Modern Era to give collectors a modern twist on the iconic T206 design. Early tobacco cards also introduced more vibrant colors still considered beautiful to many collectors today.

Courtesy of Heritage Auctions

FIGURE 3-1: 1887 Allen & Ginter Cap Anson, PSA 1.5

Vintage highlights

Prior to World War I, confectionary companies commonly produced cards to help market candies and gum. Fleer and Goudey were two of the most notable, with Goudey's 1933 Big League Gum cards some of the most visually striking. The 1933 Goudey set features beautiful portraits and vibrant colors. These cards also came on cardstock that was squarer in shape than the rectangular shape used by most tobacco sets.

Arguably, no set has been more influential in sports card design than 1952 Topps Baseball. Needing something special to compete with Bowman, a company we cover more in Chapter 2, Topps released its first flagship baseball set in 1952 with an all-new concept. Designed by Sy Berger, 1952 Topps Baseball was larger than previous Bowman sets and maximized the additional space. Marketed as "giant" baseball cards, 1952 Topps featured a color photograph feel (see Figure 3-2) and utilized the reverse for career stats (see Figure 3-3). Most card backs up to this point were used for marketing whatever confectionery or tobacco company was producing them, but Topps used this space to tell the player's story. To many, this was the birth of our modern sports card: bright designs, team logos, statistics, and a biography on the back. Plenty of differences exist between 1952's and today's cards, but it's hard to argue that Topps' flagship debut wasn't the foundation.

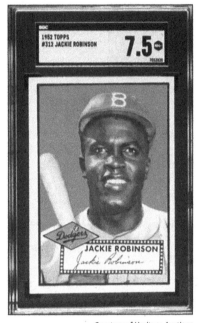

Courtesy of Heritage Auctions

FIGURE 3-2: 1952 Topps Jackie Robinson (front), SGC 7.5

The modern sports card

The modern sports card is where designs and materials get tricky. Did you think that all cards have four sides? Die-cuts would like a word. Do you think all cards are made of paper or cardboard-like material? Most, sure, but manufacturers have pushed the envelope with additional materials like acetate, cloth, wood, glass, and metal. Some of the most famous vintage cards are known for having vibrant colors with rich saturation, although ultra-modern cards often display a wide range of colored parallels and refractors.

FIGURE 3-3: 1952 Topps Jackie Robinson (back), SGC 7.5

And even those have evolved rapidly in recent years. The basic rainbow-like refractor is still a classic look for chrome cards, but companies like Panini and Topps have also delivered parallels with everything from mini basketballs and flowers to zebra prints (see Figure 3-4) and donuts. What's more, the companies utilize a wide array of prismatic effects to diversify the aesthetic of specific parallels. The traditional refractor effect is sometimes called the "true color" of a card, whereas there may be other effects like Wave, Scope, Pulsar, Prizm, Sparkle, Mojo, and many more. Some collectors have gravitated toward true colors, while many others love the variety and novelty of the various effects.

Modern sports cards are also where you'll find autographs and memorabilia. Some of the most important cards in existence feature on-card autographs and pieces of a game-used jersey.

Courtesy of Goldin Auctions

FIGURE 3-4: 2018 Lamar Jackson Zebra Prizm, BGS 10

REMEMBER

You can find more information about these types of cards in Chapter 4, but from a design standpoint, they have played a big part in, ideally, enhancing the design of a card. Sets like Upper Deck Exquisite Collection, Topps Dynasty (see Figure 3-5), and Panini National Treasures are all carefully designed to be complemented by multicolor patches and on-card autographs.

Though well-intentioned, the quality of a player's signature or the colors (or lack thereof) can also greatly detract from a card's eye appeal. Beyond just pieces of jersey, some relic cards may also feature other materials, including pieces of bats, gloves, shoes (sometimes cleats), hockey sticks, basketball courts, race car tires, and more. All of these are efforts to bring fans closer to the game in a real, tangible way.

FIGURE 3-5: 2020 Topps F1 Dynasty Max Verstappen, PSA 10

Making a first impression

For better or for worse, the front of a sports card is like a greeting from the card manufacturer. If a stunning photo or striking design is the equivalent of a bright smile, a clunky design or odd image equates to a limp handshake. You don't get a second chance to make a first impression with people; that concept isn't much different with sports cards.

Photos

You'll occasionally come across cards with cartoonish artwork and designs that are exceptions, but nearly every other card features actual photography. As the main selling point for most cards, an exciting action shot can make a card a must-own, especially if it captures something uniquely intrinsic to a particular player.

TIP

A popular example of cards that don't feature traditional photos is the Perez-Steele Hall of Fame Postcards set. Debuting in 1980 with Dick Perez's artwork, the set has been a favorite among autograph collectors due to its large design and bright colors.

Consider, for example, Michael Jordan soaring from the free throw line with his tongue out or David Tyree making "the catch" for the Giants en route to their upset of the Patriots. Similarly, photos featuring notable athletes other than those whose names are on the card tend to be popular, as with Kobe Bryant's 2008 Topps card featuring LeBron James guarding him (see Figure 3-6). A striking portrait has value, too — any tobacco era set shows that — though they are far less popular in today's hobby. Portraits in the early years of collecting were a necessity more than a design choice, and advancements in photography and technology have simply made capturing highlight-reel plays on a card easier than ever. Most sets strive for great photos, though products like Topps Stadium Club, Panini Luminance, and PhotoGenic feature the best of the best.

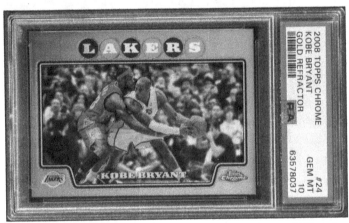

Courtesy of Goldin Auctions

FIGURE 3-6: 2008-09 Topps Chrome Gold Kobe Bryant, PSA 10

Great photography can also be the result of weird moments or Easter eggs. One of the most famous photos ever came from 1989 Fleer Baseball and the (in)famous Billy Ripken card. Before Fleer could fix the mistake, cards were printed that featured an extremely not-safe-for-work nickname on the knob of Ripken's bat.

TECHNICAL STUFF

The 1989 Fleer Billy Ripken "F-Face" card took on a life of its own. Not only did Fleer go through multiple "correction" iterations, each of which is considered a separate variation by collectors, but for years, Ripken (brother to MLB Iron Man Cal Ripken Jr.) claimed he didn't know that the colorful turn of phrase adorned his bat knob and that his teammates had pranked him. Years later, Ripken admitted he put the phrase on the bat knob as a joke but that he didn't intend to pose for the Fleer photo holding that particular bat.

Some cards also feature odd cameos in the background. Mark Jackson's 1990 Hoops card features him making a bounce pass, but the card is mostly known for featuring Lyle and Erik Menendez courtside in the background. The brothers gained notoriety after being convicted of murdering their parents in 1996. Similarly, Ja Morant's 2019 Chronicles card (see Figure 3-7) features rappers Young Dolph, Key Glock, and Crunchy Black, as well as actor Todd Bridges, and Leigh Anne and Sean Tuohy, who fostered former NFL offensive tackle Michael Oher, whose high school story is chronicled in the film, *The Blindside.*

Courtesy of Goldin Auctions

FIGURE 3-7: 2019-20 Panini Chronicles Luminance Bronze Ja Morant, BGS 10

Borders

Most sports cards, even dating back to the earliest sets, feature a border around the main photograph. Usually white or black, borders often create a nice contrast against the edge of the card. However, not all cards feature borders, with various sets opting for a "full-bleed" design. These cards skip a border and instead have the main photography stretch to the edge. Full-bleed cards can be some of the most stunning from a design standpoint, though they present different challenges when it comes to grading. We cover that aspect of full-bleed cards more in Chapter 7.

What's on the back?

The backs of cards have featured a variety of concepts throughout the decades. Some of the earliest cards simply featured a large advertisement for whatever manufacturer produced the card. Because cards from the late 1800s and early 1900s were often used to promote the sales of tobacco, gum, and other sweets, the backs were a prime space to feature the company's name and branding. Cards eventually began featuring notes and player statistics during the early and mid-1900s, though stats weren't kept as closely as they are today.

Later, once cards were marketed to kids rather than smokers, card backs included cartoons, fun facts about the player or league, and even scratch-off games. In the 1990s, manufacturers started adding a second photo to the card back, and today's cards sometimes include fantasy stats and projections and deep dives in Sabermetric stats, proving that most of today's cards are marketed at adults, not children.

TIP

As we discuss in Chapter 2, 1952 Topps Baseball featured extensive player notes and statistics across the back that helped usher in a new era of cards that collectors loved reading.

Art cards and custom cards

Looking for a new twist on iconic designs, Topps introduced Project 2020 in 2020. These cards saw artists apply their own creativity to previous designs. Topps then followed that up with Project70 in 2021 to celebrate its first baseball set in 1951 with a similar concept. These aren't sports cards in the typical sense, so they might be best described as officially licensed art cards.

Custom cards take the artwork concept a bit further but aren't licensed cards from manufacturers like Panini, Topps, or Upper Deck. The Ultra-Modern Era helped introduce a variety of high-end sets, though these, of course, don't feature every player. Some collectors have taken things into their own hands and have attempted to create high-end custom cards for players who might not have licensed cards. They may even attempt to apply classic or iconic designs to new players who were never featured in the original sets. Often created on commission for individual collectors, these custom cards have become increasingly popular during the Ultra-Modern Era.

WARNING

Many collectors accept customs as great additions to the space but only as part of a hobbyist's personal collection. Selling these cards at any scale will likely cause issues with the major manufacturers, the leagues, and the players.

Exploring the Printing Process and Product Configuration

The cabinet cards from the mid and late 1800s were largely created by pasting a photograph onto a piece of cardstock. And really, that's the spirit of what a sports card has been since the beginning — an image of an athlete attached to some type of supportive material. That process has, of course, changed through the decades as printing technology has improved, but this spirit has largely remained the same.

The materials that make sports cards

Cards are typically most associated with paper cardstock, and that's for good reason. Paper cardstock isn't the only material used, but from a volume standpoint, it's fair to say that nearly all sports cards are printed on some type of paper. The thickness of cardstock varies by set and the overall objective of the product. Flagship sets like Topps Baseball or Donruss Football are built for the most basic collectors and are printed on thinner cardstock to help accommodate that. These cards are light, easier to handle, and perfect for filling out binder pages with a complete set.

The type and thickness of the cardstock will often change as other elements are introduced. Memorabilia cards, for example, require a thicker card so that there is room for the material to fit inside. High-end cards are often printed on thicker or heavier cardstock to give the product a more premium feel.

TIP

It's worth noting that thicker cardstock isn't always better, and these cards can be more difficult to find in high grades because there is more surface area that can be damaged. This concept is covered more in Chapter 7.

Along with traditional paper cardstock, chromium paper is a popular material used to create some of the hobby's most striking designs and patterns. Chromium stock helps create ultra-popular refractor and prizm designs and is often slightly thicker and sturdier than traditional paper cardstock. Sets like Topps Chrome and Panini Prizm utilize a chromium finish.

WARNING

The earliest chromium products were prone to "greening" (or "hulking") discoloration, significantly impacting the eye appeal of cards. In addition, from the first years of use until now, the chromium stock cards often bend or bow significantly.

Canvas is another niche cardstock; canvas has a slight texturing and is featured in products like Panini Court Kings and some Topps Gallery cards.

Beyond the most common cardstock, materials like acetate or even cloth, glass, metal, or wood can be used. These materials all present their own quality control issues, however. Acetate cards have a history of "yellowing," causing the card to lose a lot of its original aesthetic appeal. Materials like glass or metal are extremely prone to scratches or other surface damage. These cards may come with a clear protective cover on the surface that can be peeled off after delivery.

One interesting fact is that the grading companies have been somewhat inconsistent in how they view the greening of chrome cards, the yellowing of paper cards, and the impact on their grade. One unfortunate fact is that some cards may get a Gem Mint grade only to experience this discoloration later, significantly impacting the eye appeal of the card and its value when trying to sell it. The good news is greening only seems to impact cards produced during the mid to late '90s.

Set size, hits, chases, and what makes a product

Beyond the material that makes a sports card, knowing what goes into making a set is important, too. We cover product configuration extensively in Chapter 4, but for now, we can cover the major aspects. The overall set size is one of the most important aspects, as some products feature base sets with 500 cards while others may only have 100. Some sets include a mix of rookies and veterans, whereas other products may only feature a very limited list of prospects, rookies, or veteran stars. Consider the size of the base set, the players included, and what types of parallels and inserts are available when making purchases. The major hits and chase cards may be the main targets for collectors who aren't hoping to complete the base set. Use checklists to see which kinds of autographs and memorabilia cards are also available. You should also examine the popular or rare inserts to make sure that the players and teams you're chasing are represented.

Outside of the overall characteristics of a set, collectors should closely examine what typically comes in each box. Some products guarantee hits like autographs or memorabilia cards, but others don't. Search for what is typically found in a single box break and then determine if the value proposition is acceptable for your budget. If a box doesn't offer an acceptable number of hits or chases for your budget, consider looking at a different configuration, if available, or simply look to buy singles on the secondary market.

REMEMBER

The most expensive products are often only offered in hobby box formats, but many of the most popular products have hobby boxes and various retail formats like blaster boxes or cello packs. Blasters are small boxes usually containing four or more packs of cards and are sold at retail locations such as Walmart and Target. Typically, cello packs contain more cards than standard packs and are wrapped in transparent packaging resembling cellophane. Some chases are also exclusive to certain configurations, so make sure you aren't buying cello packs when the parallel you want is only included in blaster boxes.

TIP

Hobby boxes are typically only offered directly from the manufacturer, through hobby shops, and from large trading card retailers. They are generally more expensive than retail products in stores like Target and Walmart but offer better odds at the top cards.

Studying box configurations and checklists is also critically important if you plan to invest long term into holding sealed products.

Understanding the Packout Process and Distribution

For many collectors, the process of opening packs and revealing the spoils is all that really matters. Cards have an interesting journey before they ever land in a hobbyist's hands, and that's important to know, too — at least if you want answers to questions like "Why isn't my card in perfect condition?" or "Why didn't I get my guaranteed hit?" In fact, nearly all the issues that collectors have with sports cards can easily be traced back to how cards are printed and packed and how they arrive at the local card shop.

From the printing press to sealed packs and boxes

Despite what critical collectors may argue, countless hours are poured into creating the typical sports card set. Results may vary, but an ideal release often features new concepts that stay true to the brand's core features — and sells extremely well, of course. Arriving at something that pairs those concepts and sees commercial success is anything but easy, however, and the process from design to packout is a difficult dance that needs to be carefully navigated.

Design

In an ideal timeline, a product's design is completed months before anything is printed. The process typically sees one or multiple designers assigned to an upcoming product. They'll research what has been done in the past and consider what's worked. The design process also includes selecting interesting photos and building out thoughtful insert sets that align in theme with the players featured. Designs must also include space for both sticker or on-card autographs and/or pieces of memorabilia that are inserted later.

Acquiring photographs can be more difficult than collectors realize, with manufacturers sometimes limited by what they can work with. An ideal photo might be an action shot, but it needs to have a high enough resolution to be used on a card. Whether the photo has been used before is something to consider. In some cases, limitations to what's available can result in photos being reused for multiple cards. A company like Panini America has even held events like rookie photoshoots to get a variety of early images for a draft's key players. After a product's design has been set and its digital assets are finalized, it can go to the printing press.

Printing

Modern technology has allowed cards to be printed in bulk, with higher quality images, and with unique designs like refractors and parallels. The modern process has the designs printed onto large sheets before they are cut into individual cards. Uncut sheets of key sets are extremely rare, with some realizing extremely high values on the secondary market. Once cut, individual cards are organized, randomized, and placed into packs.

Although some cards are simply printed and packed, cards that feature autographs or memorabilia may need to be assembled differently. Memorabilia cards, for example, may require the item to be cut and fit into one portion of the card before the front is placed on top, holding the memorabilia in place. On-card autographs need to be signed in person by the player and are most often signed at events or privately after receiving the cards through the mail (TTM). Additional handling of cards by the player can often make these cards more difficult to find in high grades.

Packout

Called the collation, the overall organization during the packout process is an extremely important part of any product. Because different configurations of products may feature different types of cards or guarantee a certain number of autographs or memorabilia, collation is important. Some sets have even featured a collation that results in specific sequences of cards. The iconic 1986 Fleer Basketball set is known to have consistent collation, resulting in collectors knowing they'll pull Michael Jordan's rookie card simply by the order of the cards in the pack before it.

Once organized, cards are sealed into packs, which are placed in boxes that eventually make up entire cases. Collation is important because pack odds tell collectors how often they can expect to come across something. A specific variation or parallel may appear once per blaster box, while an insert may only appear once per hobby case. These odds are important, and great products hit on these as much as possible.

It's worth noting that mistakes do happen. Many products will advertise a guaranteed autograph or memorabilia card on average. You'll likely get these hits, but it's not impossible to come up empty or even score more than one. Just remember, the next time you rip a box with one guaranteed autograph and you get two, someone else may be missing one.

A lesser-known fact about the printing process is that only so many facilities can make trading cards, so manufacturers may be required to share printing presses with competitors. Topps and Panini, for example, have been known to share facilities.

One final note is that the overall process of randomization and collation is something of a trade secret to the manufacturers. As of the writing of this book, this is not something they have been particularly transparent about, leading to a wide array of concerns and conspiracy theories from collectors, from general hit rates not matching pack odds to assertions that big-time breakers might be getting loaded boxes (boxes with the best cards inside). Fanatics has been taking strides to give the hobby more peace of mind by hiring independent auditors like Deloitte to provide assurances and to cover themselves legally.

Box breaks are covered more in Chapter 9, but it's important to know now that they are events where you can purchase specific types of cards from a box before a neutral party opens it. A common example is a team break, where collectors purchase the rights to specific teams before opening. Sometimes, you get the exact cards you want; sometimes, you get nothing.

The journey from manufacturer to storefronts

For many items, buying directly from the manufacturer is the best way to do it. Unfortunately for sports cards, it's not that easy. While some manufacturers do offer a limited number of products to be purchased directly online at release, much of the product in the sports industry is controlled by third-party distributors. These distributors are the middlemen between companies like Panini, Topps, and Upper Deck and the consumer. These distributors purchase products from the manufacturer in large quantities and then allocate them to smaller companies like local card shops or breakers.

Card shops and breakers can file an application to become direct dealers with the manufacturers, but the process is competitive, and some shops may go years without being approved. For many, working with distributors is the only option outside of buying products on the secondary market and marking them up even more. Even major retailers like Target and Walmart must work with third-party distributors. In these instances, employees from the distributors are the ones stocking trading card displays rather than the retail workers.

TECHNICAL
STUFF

Before we finish this chapter, it's important to know that Fanatics has created a major shakeup in the distribution of trading cards. Although companies like Topps and Panini America have previously relied on these distributors to deliver trading cards, as of this writing, it is expected that Fanatics will put its track record of major distribution to use with the trading card market, and these companies may have their business model put in jeopardy.

Chapter **4**

Understanding Product Checklists: Base Cards, Parallels, Inserts, and More

Tens of millions of unique sports cards have been printed since the very first cards were printed in the late 1800s, totaling hundreds of millions in circulation today. They come in all shapes, sizes, and materials, and unique cards are growing faster than ever.

For a little more context, the 1952 Topps Baseball set (see Figure 4-1) was released with a 407-card checklist. Considered one of the — if not *the* — most iconic sports card sets of all time, 1952 Topps Baseball featured red- and black-back variations for the first 80 cards, but that's where the variations ended.

Flash forward to 2022: Panini's 2022 Select Football has nearly 23,000 *unique* cards in its checklist. If you're wondering how that came to be, the answer is simple: variations and parallels. Although 1952 Topps Baseball featured that simple 407-card checklist of base cards, 2022 Select Football features base cards, short-printed variations, and dozens of color parallels and inserts for its entire lineup of players.

Courtesy of Goldin Auctions

FIGURE 4-1: 1952 Topps Willie Mays, PSA 8

Although variations of cards are nothing new — they go back about as far as the sports card itself — parallels and short-printed variations have ballooned the size of checklists since the first Refractor card in the early 1990s.

In this chapter, you learn how to navigate product checklists and separate simple base cards from valuable parallels and inserts while discovering the differences between the various types of autograph and memorabilia cards.

Learning How to Read (the Checklist)

The massive number of parallels and variations can seem intimidating at first, but the reality is that the majority are easy to spot. Some are certainly harder than others, but the process is typically straightforward. Before you go diving into a new set searching for something special, it's important to remember that you have two extremely helpful resources: the product checklist and the product information sheet.

Checklists

Gone are the days when a product's entire checklist could fit onto a single card included in the set itself. Arguably the favorite tool for set collectors at the time, those checklist cards were often included as the final card and featured the entire set, listed in numerical order. Today, you'll struggle to find a product that can pull off a checklist card; instead, you will need to rely on your search engine of choice to get you what you need.

Visiting the manufacturer's website is often the best start, though a variety of third-party sites also post full checklists with better organization and added context and analysis. A simple search for something like "2020 Panini Prizm Basketball checklist" will likely get you the right results. Include the manufacturer, product name, and release year with the word "checklist," and you're all set.

You'll immediately understand the product better once you dive into the checklist. Each checklist will be broken down into different categories that typically include base cards, inserts, autographs, and memorabilia. We go into more detail about identifying each of these categories later in this chapter, but it's important to know now what you should be looking for.

FINDING CHECKLISTS ONLINE

There are many online checklist resources available. Here are a few of our favorites (all of which are free):

- The Trading Card Database: www.tcdb.com
- The Cardboard Connection: www.cardboardconnection.com
- Beckett Media: www.beckett.com

You can find checklists and other resources through Beckett and the Beckett Magazines. Beckett is an indispensable resource even if you only use other data tools than its price guide.

The first section you'll want to find in a checklist is the base set. This set is typically the largest and includes the most common cards within each product. These cards are typically non-serial numbered and are generally less valuable than rarer variations. However, base cards often come with colored or numbered variations called *parallels* or *Refractors*, depending on the manufacturer. Panini, for example, typically calls these variations *parallels* or *prizms* — not to be confused with Panini's popular Prizm release— while Topps calls them *Refractors*. It's the same concept with different names.

TECHNICAL STUFF

In many cases, parallels show the same image on the front and have the same card number on the back as the base card but feature some design differences that allow them to stand out. These could be different backgrounds and borders or additional colors.

Inserts often take up the second-most space within a checklist and feature unique art that differentiates them from base cards. You'll find some of the sports card hobby's most iconic designs here. Again, we go into more depth with these later in the chapter. Inserts may also come with their own unique parallels similar to the base set.

Autographs and memorabilia are typically some of the rarest cards within a product and are often referred to as "hits."

When looking at the checklist, you'll want to pay close attention to the card and serial numbers, if applicable. Short-printed variations may have subtle differences in design or even in the player's photo, but you can sometimes tell by the card's number on the back. Serial-numbering, or the total number of cards printed in that variation, will be stamped on the card and is also a helpful way to identify a card.

TECHNICAL STUFF

For example, Trae Young may have a Bronze and a Gold parallel in one of Panini's sets. In some sets, these could be visually similar when holding them in person. The serial numbering can help here, however, with Bronze parallels sometimes numbered out of 249 while Gold parallels might be out of 10.

REMEMBER

It's important to remember that not all parallels and variations are numbered the same across all products and manufacturers. Red parallels are sometimes numbered out of 99 in Panini products but just out of 5 in Topps products. Similarly, Gold parallels are often numbered to just 10 in Panini products but have

50 copies in many Topps releases. These numbering sequences can also vary from year to year within the same products. Use the checklist to verify these types of differences.

Product information sheets

The product information sheet is the next resource collectors can dive into before examining a set. Often called the PIS document or sell sheet, the manufacturer sends these to stores and retailers that may carry the set and provide key details about the release.

These documents can often be found on the manufacturer's website or included in the product listing through an online retailer.

PIS documents often feature preview images of upcoming products and include details about elements that are new to the set. If an insert is debuting in that specific set, those details will likely be included in the sell sheet. The PIS document will also provide the exact box break and configuration details.

Box break details refer to what you can expect in a complete box of that specific product. For example, you can expect a hobby box of 2022 Panini Select Football to include two autographs, one memorabilia card, ten Silver Prizms, five other Prizms, six inserts, and one Zebra parallel per case.

REMEMBER

Box break details should be considered on average and not exact, meaning a 2022 Panini Select Football hobby box may only include a single autograph instead of two. It's also possible to receive more than the expected number.

The sell sheet also provides details for the product configuration. This refers to the number of packs and cards within a box. For example, 2022 Panini Select Football packs contain five cards each, packed 12 packs per box and 12 boxes per case. Using this breakdown, you can expect each hobby box to contain 60 cards.

This information can be critical to know before buying a product you haven't opened before. Many collectors associate sealed boxes with having a significant number of cards. A flagship release like Panini Donruss Basketball typically contains hundreds of cards in a hobby box, while more premium products may contain only a single pack of five to ten cards.

TIP

Collectors should find product configuration details especially helpful when dealing with high-end products. Panini's 2021–2022 Flawless Basketball contains just a single pack per box with only ten total cards. Topps's 2022 Dynasty Baseball release contains just a single card. All products aren't created equal, and understanding how much you're paying per card and how much those cards can fetch on the secondary market will make your collecting experience much better.

Spotting a Base Card and the Rainbow of Parallels

Sports cards as we know them have changed immensely over the years. Different shapes, sizes, designs, and colors have made their way into the hobby through the decades, but the base card has remained mostly unchanged in design and spirit since the early 1950s.

As we outline in Chapter 2, Topps's iconic 1952 release changed everything. The front featured colorful photos with a clear nameplate, and the back was covered in statistics and player notes. This has been the formula for the majority of base cards ever since. The designs vary by manufacturer, sport, and set, of course, but the objective of the base card has remained unchanged.

Identifying base cards

Base cards will be the easiest cards in the set to spot in almost all cases. These cards are typically the most common and feature the most recognizable layouts. There are no special colors or designs here. You can expect player action photos or portraits with a clear name and possibly a position and/or team. Some base cards feature a border around the image of the athletes, whereas others may have the photo stretch to the edges of the card.

Beyond the basic design, base cards are easily identified by the numbering on the back of the card and in the checklist. The base set starts with card No. 1 and is generally displayed with "1" on the back. If the design on the front of the card has you stumped, the numbering on the back often has the answer.

In many cases, inserts will use letters, numbers, or dashes to show the difference. As an example, Shohei Ohtani is card No. 17 in 2023 Topps Series 1 Baseball. The number on the back of this card is simply "17." Ohtani is also featured in insert sets like All Aces and Home Field Advantage, where his card numbers are "AA-11" and "HA-3." Although not a uniform rule, many inserts will have an abbreviation for the set name and a dash before the card number.

Spotting the many variations

Identifying the many parallels is where things can get tricky. The overall number of color-based parallels and Refractors has exploded during the Ultra-Modern Era, and it's possible to have variations that all seem similar within a release.

REMEMBER

The hobby's parallels and Refractor boom are discussed in Chapter 2. Remember, your checklist and sell sheet can do the heavy lifting here.

To better illustrate variations, we dive into the terminology and the key visual aspects of each.

Variations

"Variation" has become a catchall term that refers to just about anything beyond the original base card. If it's a short-printed version, that's a variation. Color parallel or Refractor? That's a variation. There are more specific terms to use, but when in doubt, *variation* is good enough.

TECHNICAL STUFF

A short print is a card printed in smaller quantities than other cards in the same set, making it more difficult to find and worth more (ostensibly anyway). At one time, short prints weren't necessarily intentional. Many short-printed cards were simply part of the last series or two produced in that set. A particular sport's cards — let's say, football — tend to sell more at retail during the football season. If the seventh and final series in a set was released in December, just as the regular season was wrapping up, retailers often stopped carrying football cards in favor of an in-season sport like basketball. A card manufacturer like Topps would print fewer Series 7 cards because the demand was lower. The back-end effect is that cards in Series 7 were harder to find, ratcheting up their value. Today, card producers intentionally produce certain cards in smaller numbers to give collectors something to chase.

Short prints are often simply called SPs, but cards printed in even smaller numbers — super-short prints — are called SSPs.

It's important to know that variations appear less often than base cards in most cases. It can be hard to know exact print runs, but the general rule is that variations are short-printed compared to base cards — even if they aren't serial numbered.

REMEMBER

It's also critical to know that those types of cards aren't the only variations. Photo variations (see Figure 4-2) are popular, especially in Topps products, and may include major or even small differences. These differences can have major implications on rarity and, therefore, pricing. While some products will have labels like SP or SSP near the card number on the back, others may have no indicator at all — you should assume there will be no indicator. If applicable, you can typically find information about the SP and SSP indicators in the checklist. It's especially important to do your research with checklists and PIS documents before diving into a product you're unfamiliar with. Super short-printed cards can be extremely valuable, and you'll kick yourself if you miss one.

Courtesy of Goldin Auctions

FIGURE 4-2: 2022 Topps Heritage Bo Bichette card back variation, PSA 8

Prizms and refactors

The difference here is in name only. Panini calls these cards *Prizms*, while Topps and Upper Deck call them *Refractors*. In each case, the card will have a different visual element than the original base card. As the two names aptly suggest, the cards have a prismatic rainbow shine (refraction), which is distinct.

It's important to know that while there are hundreds of different prizm and Refractor designs across the many different sets, there is also a generic prizm and Refractor. The most basic Refractor design from Topps and Upper Deck is simply called a *Refractor*. Panini's most basic prizm design is called a *Silver* (see Figure 4-3) or a *Holo*. These have been considered some of the hobby's most beloved and popular designs since their introduction in 1993 Topps Finest Baseball.

Courtesy of Goldin Auctions

FIGURE 4-3: 2013-14 Prizm Silver Giannis Antetokounmpo, PSA 10

Colors and designs

Beyond the basic Silver Prizm and Refractor, the rest of the parallel and Refractor lineup comprises various colors and prismatic effects. These are straightforward and apply an additional element to the base card. Popular colors include gold, red, orange, black, blue, green, and purple, although some iconic effects include color variations with exciting names like Atomic, Mojo, and Wave.

Some of these color variations have also earned hobby significance beyond the print run. Gold (see Figure 4-4) and Black parallels have become extremely sought after during the Ultra-Modern Era. In general, color matches — where the color of the parallel matches the player's uniform on the card — have become extremely popular across all sets and manufacturers.

FIGURE 4-4: 2020 Panini Gold Prizm LeBron James

TIP

With so many colors in production, it's important to refer to your checklist often when unsure of a card's color variation. As we state earlier in this chapter, check the serial numbering, if applicable, to help differentiate Bronze from Gold or Blue from Teal. When it comes to purchasing or selling a card, the difference between a Bronze and Gold could be hundreds, if not thousands, of dollars.

Alongside colors, design elements called prismatic effects make up many variations, and there is plenty of overlap with different naming conventions across the manufacturers. For example, Panini's popular Hyper parallel closely matches Topps's Prizm parallel.

The Ultra-Modern Era of cards has also introduced animal print designs as parallels. Patterns like the Zebra and Tiger parallels (see Figure 4-5) from Panini have become popular chases, though other designs like the Elephant were initially met with less enthusiasm. The non-numbered but super short-printed Peacock parallel is exclusive to Panini Mosaic products and is so elusive that many hobbyists don't even know it exists.

Courtesy of Goldin Auctions

FIGURE 4-5: 2018 Panini Prizm Tiger Stripe Luka Doncic, PSA 10

TIP

If you're wondering about collecting all the variations and parallels of a specific card, well, there's a term for that. "Rainbow chasing" has become a popular goal during the Ultra-Modern Era and involves collectors tracking down the entire lineup of variations for a specific card — from the base cards down to the 1/1s. We cover Rainbow chasing and other types of collecting more in Chapter 8.

Inserts and Design Madness

Although inserts have played a significant role in sports card collecting in recent decades, their origin can be traced back much further. What is considered an insert can vary by collector, though they are generally considered any non-base card — parallels, Refractors, or other variations of base cards aren't considered inserts either — within a set. Some collectors consider any autographs or memorabilia cards to be inserts, but others don't.

More history on inserts and their evolution can be found in Chapter 2, so we strictly focus on identifying characteristics here. From a design standpoint, if base cards are meant to be the meat and potatoes of a set, inserts are meant to be the milkshakes and apple pie.

What makes an insert

Broadly speaking, an insert is any card that is not part of a product's base set. Often featuring some of the most stunning designs in card collecting, inserts are subsets within the larger release that follow a specific theme around a group of players. These players are often the game's most elite and popular stars, and the theme typically fits their play style or personality. Many of the hobby's most beloved inserts are also some of the rarest cards, and it may require opening thousands of packs to find just one.

Panini's Downtown is one ultra-modern insert that captured the hobby's attention. Found in both Donruss and Donruss Optic sets, Downtown features top players with a backdrop filled with callouts to that player's city. For example, former New Orleans Saints quarterback Drew Brees (see Figure 4-6) stands in front of a backdrop featuring architecture resembling buildings in the city's famous French Quarter. Not all insert sets include these concepts, but the best often do.

Courtesy of Goldin Auctions

FIGURE 4-6: 2021 Panini Donruss Downtown, PSA 9

Embracing the design madness

Often made up of stickers, peel-offs, or even metal coins, the earliest insert sets didn't have the same level of design as those in the modern and Ultra-Modern Era. Topps competitors like Fleer, Donruss, and Upper Deck helped create a design revolution in the 1990s, and inserts were a major beneficiary. This will often make them easy to identify.

Savvy collectors can often spot 1990s inserts with a quick glance, usually because they are distinct and unique. Want to see Michael Jordan flanked by a flaming basketball? The 1996–1997 Flair Showcase Hot Shots set (see Figure 4-7) is right for you. What about an unauthorized brand crossover with Vince Carter and Dunkin Donuts? You'll love Dunk N' Go Nuts from 1998–1999 SkyBox E-X Century (see Figure 4-8).

Courtesy of Goldin Auctions

FIGURE 4-7: 1996–1997 Flair Showcase Hot Shots Michael Jordan, PSA 10

FIGURE 4-8: 1998–1999 SkyBox E-X Century Dunk 'N Go Nuts Vince Carter, PSA 10

Ultra-modern inserts haven't always stunned collectors with designs, but several have greatly impacted the hobby. Panini's Downtown, Color Blast, and Kaboom! (see Figure 4-9) are among the most sought after ultra-modern cards that sell incredibly well on the secondary market.

Inserts also change in design from year to year, though the name and theme may stay the same. One version of Optic Basketball's Splash! — a set that highlights the NBA's top shooters — will differ from the others, though it may contain many of the same players, which ideally promotes collectors tracking down their favorite insert sets year after year.

Courtesy of Goldin Auctions

FIGURE 4-9: 2019 Panini Kaboom Gold Patrick Mahomes, BGS 9

Thoughtful designs and themes have made inserts some of the most desired cards in the hobby. These subsets should be one of your first stops when diving into a new checklist. It's worth noting that inserts can also have their own parallels.

Chasing Autographs and (Maybe) Game-Used Memorabilia

Few feelings are better than opening a pack and finding autographed cards or memorabilia inside. These types of cards don't come often for many collectors. After all, it's a special experience pulling a card held by a professional athlete or one with a game-used jersey inside.

Unfortunately, this isn't always the case. That player may not have held your card, and the jersey inside may have never been worn in a game. The world of autographs and memorabilia is deceptive but can be easily navigated by savvy collectors.

Understanding authenticity

Before we dive into the different types of autographs and memorabilia, it's important to understand the authentication of these items. You can certainly trust an item's authenticity if you acquired it in person. Did you witness the player signing your card before handing it back to you? That works. Did they personally hand you an item as they ran off the field? You can accept that as authentic. However, the key is that *you* can accept that as authentic. Everyone else should insist on more substantial proof.

For your own collecting safety, you should be extremely careful when acquiring autographs or memorabilia — they are faked more often than anyone would like to admit, and no one wants a fake item in their collection.

For cards specifically, autographs guaranteed by the manufacturer are likely your safest bet. To find these, check the back of the card for the authentication notice. The guarantee will read something like, "The signing of all Topps autograph cards is witnessed by Topps representatives to guarantee authenticity."

REMEMBER

It should be noted that manufacturers make mistakes, too, but the safety here is that you'll likely be made whole by the company if a mistake is made. Autographs that a major grading service has authenticated are generally safe as well. Again, mistakes can happen, but reputable authenticators like PSA, JSA, and BGS stand by their work. You can read more about the grading companies and their standards in Chapter 7.

Cards that aren't guaranteed by the manufacturer or authenticated by a third-party grading company should always come with a certificate of authenticity (COA) for best results, but you still need to be skeptical. Not all COAs are legitimate, and collectors should research the company providing them. Does the company regularly host athletes and celebrities for signings? There's a good chance the COA is genuine. Can't find any trace of the company online? You may want to stay clear. A quick Internet search can also save a lot of hassle when dealing with questionable COAs. You don't need to be an expert to spot poor forgery attempts; many are out there.

Signed, sealed, and delivered

There are two types of autographed cards: on-card and sticker autographs. The former is more desirable, and the latter much less so. The good news is that both types can have significant value. That value will, of course, depend on the quality of the player, but the quality of the signature matters, too.

TECHNICAL STUFF

The quality of signatures when the first autographed card was inserted into packs back in 1990 was much different than today. This isn't exactly a knock against new athletes, either. Remember, education has shifted heavily online and uses computers more than ever. If students are typing on computers, they aren't writing in cursive. And if students aren't learning cursive, they probably aren't developing a great signature either. Today's athletes are also asked to sign significantly more cards than any athlete was asked to sign back in the '90s.

Keep that in mind when buying your autographs, but more importantly, look for the delivery method.

TIP

In addition to declining autograph quality, there has been a major rise in the use of redemptions by the major manufacturers. Basically an IOU, redemptions take the place of a physical card in packs and allow collectors to redeem a code to receive the physical card later. Unfortunately, redemptions aren't always fulfilled, and collectors are sent replacements for far less valuable or desirable cards — redemptions are often for high-end autograph or memorabilia cards. While not new to the Ultra-Modern Era, redemptions have never been more common and have become a major pain point for the collecting community.

On-card autographs

These are the most desirable and often most valuable autographs in the hobby. The term "on-card" is literal here — these cards have been held by the player and signed directly on the card. In addition to being more visually appealing, many collectors value the player having held the actual card.

On-card autographs are typically acquired in person by the collector, through the mail (TTM), or from the manufacturer. Autographs guaranteed by the manufacturer are likely your safest bet (see the earlier section "Understanding authenticity").

Manufacturers and grading companies all make mistakes, but you are at least given some protections in those cases.

Many collectors also enjoy having vintage cards signed in person. These autographs are almost always on-card. In these cases, anything being bought or sold should be authenticated by a third party like PSA, JSA, or BGS. Anything else should be bought at your own risk.

Acquiring autographs through the mail has been a common practice with collectors for decades. Before autographed cards were ever inserted into packs in 1990, collectors would track down addresses and send cards directly to athletes. Some would sign, and some wouldn't. You should seek third-party authentication if you aren't sure an autograph is authentic.

Autographed cards received through the mail should be carefully examined, as some athletes and celebrities use a stamp or autopen to sign. These are not authentic autographs and hold little value. Some secretaries have also been known to sign in place of the athlete or celebrity; people who sign in place of an athlete/celebrity are commonly called "ghost-signers." Ghost-signed items also hold little value and are not considered authentic.

REMEMBER

When grading on-card autographs, it's important to remember that these types of autographs require the card to be handled by the athlete. This additional handling is another opportunity for the card to be damaged and will impact the overall grade. Many high-end cards come in poor condition because of the sensitive card stock and the additional handling by athletes.

On-card autographs are also meant to fall within a specific space on the card. There is usually a blank area left on these cards, and autographs that are signed outside of this area can drop the autograph's grade from a 10 to a 9 or 8. Smudges and mistakes on the signature will also impact the grade.

REMEMBER

Remember that autographs don't need to be graded during the authentication process. Collectors may grade the card, just the autograph, or both. Excluding one of these is often done when either the card or the autograph may not receive a high grade. Also, some collectors are more concerned about the autograph's authenticity than the card's physical grade.

Sticker autographs

Like on-card autographs, the term *sticker autograph* describes exactly what you're getting. Where on-card autographs have been signed directly onto the card, sticker autographs have been placed on the card by the manufacturer. This process typically involves the card manufacturer sending the athlete a sheet of stickers (similar to clear labels) to sign. The stickers are then peeled and placed onto the card by the manufacturer.

Sticker autographs are considered less desirable for two reasons:

>> First, stickers are generally less visually appealing than on-card autographs. Often, the sticker is clearly visible, and many collectors find it less appealing.

>> Second, signing a sticker rather than the card itself is less personal. There is value for many collectors knowing that the athlete held the card, and sticker autographs don't include that aspect.

From a grading perspective, signatures must remain entirely on the sticker to receive the highest grade. Unfortunately, stickers are harder to sign than the space left for on-card autographs, and mistakes can happen. It's easy for the signer's pen to slip off the sticker, or the signer may feel the need to shorten the signature to fit into the space. Stickers can also be placed on the card crooked.

One advantage of a sticker autograph is that it requires less handling overall than on-card autographs — which means there's less opportunity for damage to the card itself.

Getting closer to the game (or your local retailer)

Much like the different autographs we cover in this chapter, you'll run across many nuances to the memorabilia cards in the sports card hobby. Unlike with autographs, the key nuances with memorabilia are less about how they are applied to the card and more about how they are classified.

The first game-used memorabilia cards surfaced in the mid-1990s, and since then, they've transformed card collecting altogether. Head over to an auction website, sort by the most expensive cards recently sold, and you'll almost always see a fantastic lineup of beautiful relics paired with autographs.

Cards with jersey swatches inside are the most common, though bats, gloves, sneakers, bases, balls, cleats, and more have all made their way into cards. Some NASCAR cards even have pieces of tires in them. Jerseys are generally the easiest to use because of their size, while items like sneakers require a much thicker card that is more prone to damage. Thicker cards and their grading are referenced more in Chapter 7.

Jerseys are also prime candidates for memorabilia cards because a single jersey can supply enough swatches to make hundreds of cards. The most desired cards feature pieces of a patch on the jersey. This can be a piece of the lettering from the player's name, part of the team logo, or even the most highly sought-after: the logo patch.

TECHNICAL STUFF

Logo, or logoman, cards (see Figure 4-10) include the MLB, NFL, or NBA logo patch from the player's jersey. These cards are exceptionally valuable and highly sought after by collectors.

Courtesy of Goldin Auctions

FIGURE 4-10: 2015-16 Panini National Treasures LeBron James logoman card, BGS 9

Also highly desired are pieces of jerseys with multiple colors. The better patches or jerseys usually correspond to lower serial numbering or a lower print run. The rarer the card, the better the relic in many cases. Unfortunately, collectors are more likely to find a single color, or even worse, the dreaded "napkin" card, which features a plain white jersey.

Memorabilia cards are often called jersey or patch cards — the distinction between the two is important. While many collectors may consider the terms to mean the same thing, "jersey" is often associated with pieces that feature a single solid color, while a "patch" card is of higher quality and features multiple colors from the player's jersey.

It's important to remember that not all memorabilia cards are created equal, even beyond the colors featured. The jersey piece's quality — especially its source — is extremely important. The following sections explain the various types of memorabilia cards and key details about each:

Game-used memorabilia — enjoyed by most

Game-used memorabilia is exactly what it sounds like. These pieces of memorabilia have been used in a professional game and are the most desirable in the hobby. On rare occasions, you may find stains or other markings indicating use, but most of the time, you'll need to take the manufacturer's word.

Speaking of their word, you'll usually find that on the card back. For example, "The enclosed game-used material is guaranteed by Panini America, Inc."

REMEMBER

It's noteworthy that mishaps happen here, just like with autographs. There have been instances where cards have been opened, and evidence has been found that the enclosed material couldn't possibly be from that specific player, team, or era. Things that tip off an incorrect piece of memorabilia can be the evidence that the number on the jersey was incorrect or a logo didn't match the correct season.

Some manufacturers and sets have gone as far as to indicate the exact game the material was worn, though these types of cards aren't common. Because of this, photo matching, or using markings and other clues to match material to an exact game or moment, has become more common — especially with high-end items.

One important — and frustrating — thing to remember about game-used memorabilia is the process behind acquiring it. Jerseys and other items need to be used in a game to qualify, which means that you may find it hard to find rookie cards with game-used memorabilia. It's certainly possible if the cards are near the end of that season's release cycle, but it isn't common. Panini's Flawless Basketball is a premium product released at the end of the NBA season (or even into the next year). So, some of the rookie memorabilia is game-worn and, therefore, more highly sought after. Game-used rookie materials are out there, but don't get your hopes up.

Player- and event-worn memorabilia — enjoyed by some

For years, memorabilia labeled as "player-worn" or "event-worn" was the least valuable in the hobby. "Not-associated memorabilia" has become more common, however, and some collectors of ultra-modern cards don't find player- and event-worn materials as awful as they used to — mostly because non-associated memorabilia is even worse.

Still, these materials are far less desired than game-worn materials. When a material is labeled as "player-worn" or "event-worn," it usually means that the item was worn by the player for a short time to create association. These can happen at manufacturer events or shows and signings that players are paid to attend.

With these types of materials, it's possible that the player simply slipped in and out of dozens of jerseys during an event to create the association. Players are sometimes instructed to wear larger jerseys than they normally would to create more cards. Players may also wear jerseys numbered 88 rather than their actual number because it takes up the most space on the jersey, creating more patches with multiple colors.

For most athletes, the player- and event-worn materials aren't as desirable, but as we cover above, sometimes, that's the best you may get with cards from a player's rookie season.

Not-associated memorabilia — enjoyed by few

This is the worst of the worst. Memorabilia that isn't associated (see Figure 4-11) means that it didn't come from the player on the front of the card — or possibly even any player *at all*. These cards can be spotted by verbiage on the back: "This enclosed officially licensed material is not associated with any specific player, game, or event."

Courtesy of Goldin Auctions

FIGURE 4-11: 2020-21 Panini National Treasures Patch Autographs Anthony Edwards, PSA 8

These types of cards are the least desirable in the memorabilia category and are outright despised by many collectors. Sure, the patch may be a beautiful three-color jersey with a number, logo, or player name — but is it worth anything if it never touched a professional athlete? That's the question many collectors ask themselves.

This doesn't mean that these cards can't be valuable at all. Supply chain issues caused extreme delays in production and the sourcing of memorabilia and autographs, and companies resorted to these types of cards during the COVID-19 pandemic. As outlined in Chapter 2, that period also saw a massive surge in the popularity of collecting. Several strong — at least at the time — rookie classes didn't always have access to game-used materials, and hobby stars like Zion Williamson, Ja Morant, Justin Herbert, and Joe Burrow had high-end cards produced with this type of memorabilia.

High-end products from hobby stars featuring not-associated memorabilia still sell for incredible amounts, mostly because the patch looked fantastic next to an authentic autograph. For some collectors, the origin of the memorabilia doesn't matter. Or they didn't pay close enough attention.

While many collectors will never buy anything other than game-worn memorabilia cards, others care far less. In fact, the hobby's explosion in popularity around 2020 also brought with it a rise in custom cards. These cards are made by individuals using pieces of authentic cards, but they often add in jerseys or other memorabilia. This memorabilia is typically not game-used, player-worn, or event-worn, but it adds some serious flair to the original card.

WARNING

A final note of importance: Always check the back of the card when bidding online. Some sellers, whether intentionally or accidentally, will list cards as "game-worn" despite the card saying otherwise. Send a polite message requesting a photo of the back if the seller hasn't included one. You can also cross-reference other sales of the same card to confirm its status. Unfortunately, most checklists will not include any information about whether memorabilia cards are game-worn, player-worn, or not associated.

Chapter 5

Different Sports and Their Nuances

Having journeyed through the historical evolution of sports cards, exploring their intricate composition, diverse types, and fascinating array of inserts, it might be tempting to plunge into a buying frenzy. However, there's a vital bridge between understanding cards at a surface level and embarking on a confident collecting and/or investment journey.

Sports cards, like the athletes they represent, exhibit a spectrum of nuances, differing significantly not just between sports but also among manufacturers. Although the overarching information we cover serves as a foundation, delving deeper into a specific sport becomes paramount due to its unique intricacies.

This chapter serves as a guide to propel you beyond the surface understanding. Here, we aim to equip you with insights into the labyrinth of manufacturers crafting cards for distinct sports, unraveling the mysteries of licensing, and spotlighting the standout players and products that dominate the landscape.

We've previously refrained from suggesting specific purchases, and our approach remains the same here. Although we reference a number of specific cards based on broadly accepted iconic status and sustained price history, we intend to empower you to decide what is right for your own collection or investment portfolio.

A common pitfall for newcomers lies in the assumption that principles applying to one sport seamlessly translate across all. Undoubtedly, similarities exist, yet the landscape is painted with myriad intricate differences. For instance, the allure of rookie cards unites enthusiasts across sports, emerging as the crown jewels of many people's collections. However, the specific rookies commanding fervent attention vary across the sporting realm. Many basketball and football aficionados also embark on quests for elusive inserts and rainbow chases, while baseball enthusiasts lean toward the allure of first prospect cards, autographs, and specific parallels with an established lineage. Conversely, hockey devotees prioritize distinct rookie cards while valuing game-used relics and autographs. This section endeavors to be a guiding compass, steering you through the maze of divergent preferences, emphasizing the need for a sport-specific lens in discerning coveted cards, and understanding the nuances that differentiate one collection from the next.

Basketball cards

NBA basketball didn't always bask in the limelight it commands today. An era lingered when skeptics whispered of a fading league until luminaries like Julius Erving, Magic Johnson, and Larry Bird took center stage. Then, a titan emerged whose influence transcended the sport itself: Michael Jordan.

Former NBA commissioner David Stern, orchestrating strategic maneuvers to catapult the game onto the global stage, played a pivotal role in changing the game. The collective impact revitalized basketball and reshaped the sporting tapestry in unforeseen ways.

Built on superstars and flash

Basketball is a superstar-driven league, and the spotlight gleams brightest on those occupying the top slots on a roster. Other players often struggle to command significant value in the sports card market. Championships, to some extent, emerge as the fulcrum for determining card value, evident in the lower values of celebrated legends like Charles Barkley, Karl Malone, Chris Paul, and James Harden, whose illustrious careers are bereft of a coveted championship. In contrast, players like Tony Parker and Manu Ginobili, etched in basketball lore for their championship conquests alongside the legendary Tim Duncan and the San Antonio Spurs, see price bumps to their cards for their dynasty. Although they are not the most expensive players, their cards would not hold anywhere near the value they do if it weren't for their championships.

While the Hall of Fame holds relevance, longevity and accolades assume paramount importance. Uniquely, basketball enthusiasts embrace a broader spectrum of players, often transcending team allegiances. In an era where many stars regularly change teams, many basketball fans and hobbyists focus on individual players rather than specific teams.

Hype and style of play also wield immense influence as guards and forwards often seize the limelight over the towering big men who live in the paint and dominate the boards. Despite Tim Duncan being the almost consensus greatest power forward of all time and in spite of having multiple championships, his cards don't even come close to Kobe Bryant in terms of price. While some of the most notable early players were centers (Bill Russell, Wilt Chamberlain, and Kareem Abdul-Jabbar), the big man's collectability has largely waned outside of exceptions like Nikola Jokic, Giannis Antetokounmpo, and Joel Embiid — who all feature skills beyond the traditional big man.

TECHNICAL STUFF

The sport's global appeal, particularly across East Asia, has significantly impacted card prices while fueling the fervor for basketball cards within the collector community.

Iconic basketball players

The earliest notable basketball cards date back to 1910, but the most notable early set is 1948 Bowman, featuring George Mikan's rookie card (see Figure 5-1). Don't let the simple (yet striking) design and the photo of a guy who looks more like a goofy accountant or biology teacher fool you.

Courtesy of Heritage Auctions

FIGURE 5-1: 1948 Bowman George Mikan, PSA 8

The most collectible athletes from the 1950s through the 1970s included stars like Bill Russell, Wilt Chamberlain, Oscar Robertson, Kareem Abdul-Jabbar, and Julius Erving.

TECHNICAL STUFF

These cards were not particularly popular at the time they were being manufactured, so print runs and overall population counts with grading companies are often very low.

The 1980s were really when all the magic began for basketball cards — no pun intended. There's a saying that every Michael Jordan card is a good card, and the first card for Larry Bird or Magic Johnson is one of the most iconic basketball cards of all time.

Other notable athletes from the 1980s include Kevin McHale, Hakeem Olajuwon, Karl Malone, Charles Barkley, Isiah Thomas, Patrick Ewing, Chris Mullin, Clyde Drexler, Dominique Wilkins, James Worthy, and David Robinson.

The 1990s were a period when everything changed in sports cards from a design and checklist perspective. Sets like 1992 Topps Stadium Club Beam Team and the 1993 Fleer Ultra Scoring Kings really put inserts on the map. Upper Deck was the first to include autographed cards in random packs in 1990, but the idea really took off when SkyBox began randomly inserting its Autographics cards into its products.

The '90s saw more than just new card concepts. It also introduced all kinds of new cardstock materials and technology, as we discuss in Chapter 3.

TECHNICAL
STUFF

Unlike prior eras, this is the first time we saw players featured with many different rookie cards, offering collectors unprecedented choice and variety while eliminating a clear-cut "rookie card" for any player.

The 2000s, though filled with numerous notable athletes (from all sports), was a decade when things really slowed down in sports cards. Overproduction in the '90s and some other snafus by the manufacturers led many collectors, especially investors, to lose interest (at least temporarily) in the hobby. If sports cards had a "dead ball era" over the last 40 years, it would be the 2000s.

TECHNICAL
STUFF

The most notable athletes with rookie cards from the 2000s include LeBron James, Dwyane Wade, Carmelo Anthony, Kevin Durant, and Stephen Curry. As with the '90s, these players have many different rookie cards, but Topps products tend to be the most widely sought-after and iconic rookie cards from a flagship perspective (ubiquitous, non-high-end).

The transition to Panini

From about 2009 until 2016, things looked bleak in general for Panini. It's hard to say definitively what started the renaissance for the sports card industry, but some agree that it began to pick up momentum, somewhat slowly, starting in 2017 and most notably with basketball cards.

And then, in 2019, the hype around Zion Williamson and Luka Doncic caused a surge in interest. Hobbyists couldn't find sealed retail products on shelves for the first time in the Panini era (and maybe ever). People would wait in line for hours just to get a chance at getting a box or two. Flippers coordinated with stockers to scoop all of the product as soon as it hit the shelves, and then resold it on the secondary market making massive profits. The combination of a few highly rated rookie classes, the stay-at-home orders during the COVID-19 pandemic, and other pop culture factors like *The Last Dance* documentary about Michael Jordan and the Chicago Bulls dynasty led to sports cards skyrocketing in popularity. For about 18 months, from early to mid-2020 until late 2021, the overall sports card hobby hit a fever pitch, with prices we may never see again.

TIP

We cover more about specific products from the Panini era in Chapter 6. Prizm, Select, and Donruss Optic tend to be considered the most iconic rookie cards for basketball. Some also argue that Hoops and Donruss are notable entry-level products, while National Treasures and Flawless dominate the high-end market.

TECHNICAL STUFF

From a price and accolades perspective, some of the most notable rookies from the Panini era are Giannis Antetokoumpo, Nikola Jokic, Joel Embiid, Luka Doncic, and Victor Wembanyama.

As of the publication of this book in early 2024, we're now on the cusp of the Fanatics/Topps era, with many modern hobbyists experiencing some combination of trepidation (about the loss of beloved Panini brands) and anticipation (with the return of so many beloved Topps products).

WNBA rises in popularity

The WNBA was founded in 1996, emerging as a seminal milestone in women's sports history. Created as an offshoot of the NBA, it aimed to provide a professional platform for female basketball players. The WNBA became a harbinger of change, spotlighting exceptional talent while challenging gender norms entrenched in professional sports. It paved the way for female athletes to display their prowess on a grand stage, fostering a new era of opportunities.

The first WNBA cards were produced by Pinnacle in 1997 in a can (yes, it looked like a soup can) with 10 cards. This product notably features WNBA legends such as Cheryl Swoopes, Cynthia Cooper, and Lisa Leslie. In 1999, Fleer took over the production of WNBA cards with products like Hoops, Fleer Authentix, and the ultra-popular Fleer Ultra.

Following Fleer's bankruptcy in 2005, WNBA cards were taken over by Rittenhouse Archives, known for producing collectible trading cards and particularly renowned for their licensed trading cards related to popular TV shows, movies, and comics.

Some notable WNBA stars include Diana Taurasi, Sue Bird, and Candace Parker (see Figure 5-2).

Courtesy of Goldin Auctions

FIGURE 5-2: 2008 Rittenhouse WNBA Candace Parker, PSA 9

Rittenhouse carried the licenses until 2018, when Panini took over. In 2019, Panini launched WNBA Donruss as well as Panini Instant cards. The WNBA Prizm set marked a new era for women's sports cards in 2020. Sabrina Ionescu is the most sought-after player from that 2020 rookie class, while some of the most popular cards from these Prizm sets have been veterans who didn't have many cards from the preceding 15 years.

Baseball cards

Baseball cards have the longest history, the most iconic cards, and the most expensive sales of any sport. Baseball cards immerse collectors in an ocean of history and a rich sea of stories, artistry, and captivating narratives — both remembered and forgotten. Vintage baseball cards represent the genesis of sports cards overall, creating a style steeped in heritage unlike any other sport. One could truly spend multiple lifetimes learning all there is to know about vintage baseball cards. The names Honus Wagner, Jackie Robinson, Mickey Mantle, and Willie Mays echo throughout the decades and from one century to the next, passing the torch to the likes of Ken Griffey Jr., Derek Jeter, Albert Pujols, and Mike Trout. Baseball is truly a sport with a style and a story of its own in the hobby.

The richest history

Statistical significance reigns supreme in baseball, where fans dive into a trove of traditional and advanced stats, adding numerous layers to player evaluation from the earliest days of speculation to the latter days of the Hall of Fame ballot. Hitters, especially those with home run prowess, command attention, though a well-rounded hitter can do the same. Unlike basketball, baseball collectors value versatile players, with their worth holistically measured by stats like Wins Above Replacement (WAR), reflecting comprehensive player contributions rather than focusing solely on a few offensive stats. Because of their general lack of longevity and sporadic appearances (they play far less often), pitchers almost never command the same price premium as the best hitters.

In baseball collecting, loyalty to a favorite team often harmonizes with an appreciation for player greatness across teams, fostering a blend of die-hard team and player collectors. It is common for baseball hobbyists to collect many players, not just those from their favorite team. Playoff success and championships have very little effect on baseball card values, except for short-term bumps right after the titles or as some value-added benefit with a player like Derek Jeter. But most of the value given to a player is attributed to his regular season performance over the years, and of all the sports, acceptance into the Hall of Fame affects baseball card prices the most.

Baseball was once the most popular sport in the hobby by a landslide, so much so that people often referred to the hobby as "collecting baseball cards" without much consideration for the existence of other sports. Yet, in recent years, the popularity of collecting basketball and football cards has rapidly grown, and that major gap no longer exists. Overall, Major League Baseball and the baseball card hobby are doing fine and should still be around for years to come, but the league will have to continue to take meaningful steps (as it did with the implementation of the pitch clock in 2023) to ensure that younger audiences with shorter attention spans remain interested in America's pastime.

Iconic baseball players

We cover the history of vintage baseball in Chapter 2, and we shed even more light on some of the sets in Chapter 6. Here, it's all about the icons who helped shape their own sports and paved the way for so many other sports in the future — not to mention critical efforts in civil rights and social justice. Baseball, more than any other sport, has the longest list of larger-than-life icons, almost too many to list in these limited pages. Because there are so many notable figures, we've limited our list of key players by era to the truly greatest of all time and those who command the greatest demand in sports cards. We're sure we were forced to leave off some notable players for brevity's sake, so don't hold that against us.

Pre-war

Any discussion about pre-war cards needs to start with greats like Ty Cobb, Honus Wagner, Tris Speaker, Walter Johnson, Christy Mathewson, Cy Young, and "Shoeless" Joe Jackson. Babe Ruth's rookie card is debated, though a common candidate is the ultra-rare 1914 Baltimore News "card," which sold for $7.2 million in 2023. Some people contest calling it a card since it was technically a team schedule and not a card.

Lou Gehrig's rookie card is found in 1933 Goudey, as is the ever-important Nap Lajoie, which was not included in 1933 and had to be requested via mail in 1934. Joe DiMaggio has a handful of cards that people consider rookies, ranging from 1936 World Wide Gum to a playful caricature in 1938 Goudey Heads Up and a striking black-and-white pose in 1939 Play Ball. Ted Williams, who many believe was the most gifted hitter of all time, also has his rookie card in 1939 Play Ball.

Post-war

We start the era once again with a bang with Jackie Robinson, Satchel Paige, Warren Spahn, Yogi Berra, and Stan Musial (see Figure 5-3) in 1948 Leaf, and Mickey Mantle and Willie Mays in 1951 Bowman. The entire 1952 Topps set could command its own chapter, if not its own book. One notable rookie from the set is Eddie Matthews. Hank Aaron and Ernie Banks rookies can be found in 1954 Topps, Roberto Clemente and Sandy Koufax in 1955, Frank Robinson in 1957, and Bob Gibson in 1959. The 1960s and '70s Topps sets featured rookie cards for Willie McCovey, Carl Yastrzemski, Pete Rose, Nolan Ryan, and Ozzie Smith.

Courtesy of Heritage Auctions

FIGURE 5-3: 1948 Leaf Stan Musial, PSA 3

Topps continued its stronghold into the 1980s with rookies for Rickey Henderson, Cal Ripken Jr., Tony Gwynn, Roger Clemens, Barry Bonds, Mark McGwire, and Greg Maddux.

In 1981, Topps introduced its first stand-alone Traded and Rookies set, which featured cards depicting midseason rookie call-ups and trades. These boxed sets were only available in hobby stores or directly from Topps mail orders. Because Topps cards often combined anywhere from two to four rookie players on a single card, rookie cards for notable players were included in that year's Traded and Rookies set. These extra rookie cards — often identified in print as XRCs — are more difficult to find than the multi-player rookie cards found in the base set, thus commanding higher resale values. Cal Ripken Jr.'s 1982 XRC and Doc Gooden's 1984 XRC are two such examples.

But in 1989, everything changed when Upper Deck began production and introduced arguably the most iconic card since the '52 Mantle, the 1989 Ken Griffey Jr. #1. Fresh-faced and smiling with the bat over his shoulder, this was the card everyone and their cousin wanted. With more than 160,000 copies graded to date — but fewer than 7,500 total gem mints across PSA, BGS, SGC, and CGC — it's a card that can range in price from just a few dollars to a high sale of $23,100 in 2021.

Other notable rookies from the 1990s include Frank Thomas, Chipper Jones, Pedro Martinez, Derek Jeter, Alex Rodriguez, and David Ortiz. While the 2000s had plenty of Hall of Fame–caliber players, the most notable rookies are truly some of the greatest of all time, including Miguel Cabrera, Albert Pujols, Ichiro Suzuki, Justin Verlander, and Clayton Kershaw.

As we move into the Ultra-Modern Era, everything begins and ends with Mike Trout, whose rookie cards are from 2011. Trout holds the record for the most expensive modern baseball card when his 2009 Bowman Draft Chrome Prospects Superfractor 1/1 in BGS 9 sold for $3.84 million in 2020.

Suffice it to say that Mike Trout's prospect and rookie cards have an incredible premium attached to them, including his 2011 Topps paper rookie card. One disappointing note is that Trout does not have a 2011 Topps Chrome rookie card or a rookie autograph. As such, hobbyists turn to Topps Finest and Bowman Sterling for those cards. There's a saying when opening modern products that "any Trout is a good Trout." His legacy in the sports card hobby proves that postseason success is somewhat irrelevant in baseball since Trout has only played in one playoff series to this point in his career.

The other notable rookies from the last 13 years include Buster Posey, Freddie Freeman, Bryce Harper, Mookie Betts, Aaron Judge, Shohei Ohtani, Ronald Acuna Jr., and Julio Rodriguez.

Football cards

Compared to baseball and basketball cards, football cards were long overlooked and far less popular — especially considering that football is by far the most popular sport in the United States. That trend has been changing in recent years, and football cards have been surging to new heights.

Super Bowl LVII in 2023, featuring the Kansas City Chiefs and the Philadelphia Eagles, saw an estimated 115 million people tune in.

Quarterback or bust

Much like the overall popularity of players in the NFL today, quarterbacks dominate the spotlight for football cards as the league has shifted heavily toward a pass-first strategy. In an earlier era, running backs shared more of a featured role in the offense and likewise shared the limelight of stardom. Because of a more pass-focused league, wide receivers can spur interest, yet their card prices tend to be sporadic and fleeting, driven by reactions to current performances. Despite the NFL having a 53-man roster, including 11 important players on both sides of the ball plus special teams, the quarterback is given an inordinate amount of credit for his team's success and is, likewise, given an inordinate amount of value fixation to his cards.

When it comes to Hall of Fame considerations, football falls between basketball and baseball in the HOF's importance for card prices. More tenured collectors tend to appreciate those who reach Canton. Championships significantly bolster a quarterback's prestige, often shaping how they are perceived within the hobby. Once again, championships may be inappropriately attributed to the field generals, even if they played poorly on the biggest stage. Take, for example, Peyton Manning — arguably the second-best quarterback of all time. He played in four Super Bowls and won two of them. Yet his stats in those four games don't even come close to mirroring his regular-season success year over year.

REMEMBER

We're not here to contend that the quarterback position is the most important position on any team, but there is something to consider when it comes to the massive premium placed on that position and whether it will remain that way in the future.

Fantasy football's influence has also been steadily infiltrating card collections in two distinct ways:

» First is the nature of football's week-to-week dynamics and its top-scoring fantasy performers. Fans are tuned in to the guys putting up the biggest stat lines and sometimes overreact to a particular player who may have been recently flying under the radar. This is especially true for backup quarterbacks who get spot starts. Of all the players within a given season, backup quarterbacks most consistently see short-term card price spikes.

» The other way fantasy football impacts the football card hobby is by fans developing an appreciation and attachment to players who helped them realize fantasy success. A growing number of people will even go out at the end of the season and pick up at least one significant card of every player who contributed to their fantasy success. We further note that some of the biggest fantasy stars of the 2000s have been gaining cult popularity on their most iconic cards, even if they only had three or four solid NFL seasons.

REMEMBER

Although it might be most felt in football, fantasy sports' impact on all collectibles has been massive. Some companies have even attempted to merge the two by allowing you to play fantasy football each week with digital cards. In general, collectors want to feel closer to the athletes they buy, and something like fantasy football can help create a deeper connection.

Although predominantly a North American game, football's international allure is steadily growing as the NFL has been moving games overseas and into different countries each season in an effort to expand its global footprint. It's a bit of a tough sell, considering that much of the rest of the world refers to soccer as *football*, but it has been slowly gaining traction, which can only mean good things for football cards overseas as well.

Iconic football players

The first notable football cards were from 1933 Goudey Multisport and featured Jim Thorpe, Red Grange, and Knute Rockne rookies. In 1935, National Chicle released its own set of 36 cards, most notably the famous Bronco Nagurski.

In 1948, Leaf featured many of the same players as Bowman but also notably Doak Walker and Chuck Bednarik. As with baseball, Bowman continued to produce sets until 1955, including the likes of YA Tittle, Lou Groza, Otto Graham, and others.

The shift into Topps started thereafter, with Lenny Moore, Bart Starr, Johnny Unitas, Jim Brown, Mike Ditka, Joe Namath (see Figure 5-4), OJ Simpson, and Walter Payton.

Courtesy of Heritage Auctions

FIGURE 5-4: 1965 Topps Joe Namath, PSA 9

Through the Junk Wax Era of the 1980s, there was an undeniable run of some of the greatest to ever play, including Joe Montana, John Elway, Dan Marino, Jerry Rice, Reggie White, Steve Young,

Bo Jackson, Barry Sanders, and Troy Aikman. Like the NBA, this was the decade when these players transcended from athletes to icons.

While the '80s feature some of the most immortalized names in NFL lore, the subsequent decades are certainly not without their star power. The 1990s are headlined by Peyton Manning, Emmitt Smith, Brett Favre, Marvin Harrison, Randy Moss, and Kurt Warner.

The 2000s started, quite literally, with the near consensus greatest of all time, Tom Brady. His 2000 Contenders Rookie Ticket Autograph is arguably the most iconic football card of all time, along with his 2000 Bowman Chrome. Stars like Drew Brees, LaDanian Tomlinson, Michael Vick, Aaron Rodgers, and Adrian Peterson highlighted the early 2000s, too.

Unlike with basketball, Topps continued making football cards until 2015. There was an overlap of three years, with Panini and Topps both making licensed cards from 2012 to 2015, creating some really unique rookie offerings for those years, albeit with somewhat shallow rookie classes.

The most important player of the Panini era is Patrick Mahomes, whose rookie cards can be found in 2017 products. His 2017 National Treasures Platinum Shield 1/1 RPA is purported to have sold, via private sale, for a football card record $4.3M in 2021. Other notable rookies from the last decade include Dak Prescott, Lamar Jackson, Joe Burrow, Justin Herbert, Trevor Lawrence, and Brock Purdy.

Hockey cards

In the realm of hockey card collecting, there's an inspiring stability that distinguishes it from other sports. The landscape is shaped by a passionate and collector-driven community, contributing to more consistent and less volatile card values.

A small but passionate fan base

Unlike other sports, the hockey hobby is predominantly geared toward collectors, with fewer individuals solely focused on investing for a profit. Enthusiasts are divided between their team allegiances and a diverse range of player collections, creating an interesting mix within the community.

Among hockey collectors, the value hierarchy is distinct. While top-tier players command significant premiums, the weight of championships and awards on card prices is notably lighter. The induction into the Hall of Fame does not necessarily elevate card values, which focus instead on sustained elite performance with one ultimate metric: goal scoring.

Note that emphasis lies not just on points but notably on players who score goals consistently. As such, it goes without saying that defensemen generally command less value than forwards, except in rare cases where they display remarkable goal-scoring abilities — instances seen historically with players like Bobby Orr and, more recently, with Cale Makar. Goalies generally command less value than skaters, except for exceptional players like Patrick Roy, Martin Brodeur, Dominik Hasek, and Carey Price, who have fervent fan bases. Some noteworthy milestones, such as 500 goals, 1,000 points, and 300 wins for goalies, catch the attention of collectors.

In terms of team association, the value spectrum skews dramatically. Toronto and Montreal hold a significant premium in card value. The prominence of these two teams overshadows the value potential for others like Arizona, Columbus, and Florida, as well as even for Canadian teams like Winnipeg and Ottawa. The remaining Original Six teams, including the Boston Bruins, Detroit Red Wings, Chicago Blackhawks, and New York Rangers, also have substantial fan bases and reasonable support in terms of card values.

Notably, Upper Deck stands as the exclusive licensed manufacturer of NHL cards, establishing a stable presence in an industry undergoing monumental shifts with the wave of maneuvers by Fanatics. Despite initial hype and speculation surrounding certain card releases, maintaining high value for players proves challenging — particularly those featured in Upper Deck's Series 1 and 2 Young Guns — without consistent and exceptional performance over time.

TIP

One cool tidbit is that Tim Hortons releases a set every year by Upper Deck, and it is distributed at all 3,500-plus locations, helping bring broad awareness at a grassroots level to hockey cards.

Iconic hockey players

As we mention in the first section about hockey nuances, this is a foundation of hobbyists who are as pure as they come in their preferences and focus. The first notable set of the pre-war era is the 1910 C56 Imperial Tobacco, the first hockey set showcasing pioneers and Hall of Famers, including Art Ross, Fred "Cyclone" Taylor, Édouard "Newsy" Lalonde, brothers Frank and Lester Patrick, and more. Rookies for Georges Vézina and Joe Malone came in 1911.

Key Hall of Famers like Howie Morenz, Aurel Joliat, Jack Adams, and Frank "King" Clancy had rookies delivered in 1923.

Venturing into the mid-century era, Gordie Howe has solidified his place on many hockey hobbyists' Mount Rushmore. The 1958 Topps release contains a compelling portrait of Bobby Hull with a striking green-and-yellow background.

Subsequent decades showcased the likes of Bobby Orr, Guy LaFleur, Ken Dryden, and Marcel Dionne. The Great One's — Wayne Gretzky — rookie card came in 1979 (see Figure 2-6 in Chapter 2). There were Mark Messier and Ray Bourque in 1980 and Mario Lemieux in 1985. Patrick Roy's rookie came in 1986.

While the cards are not nearly as expensive, the 1990s had no shortage of incredible talent. This marked the transition from O-Pee-Chee and Topps to Upper Deck Young Guns. Rookies from the decade include Jaromir Jagr and Martin Brodeur.

The early 2000s saw debuts for Alexander Ovechkin, Sidney Crosby, Patrick Kane, and Evander Kane. The most recent decade-plus has been highlighted by Connor McDavid — the modern-day Gretzky — and Connor Bedard, who is being hailed as "next up" from McDavid.

Other notable sports

While the big four sports largely dominate sports cards, they extend broadly well beyond those four.

Soccer

By a landslide, soccer is the most popular sport globally, with an estimated 3.5 billion fans. That said, soccer cards and stickers aren't nearly as popular as the other sports we cover. Part of the reason is that the culture of collecting cards hasn't taken hold entirely within the fan base. But a bigger portion seems to be attributed to a great number of other factors. Firstly, soccer has many different leagues, from the English Premier League to the Spanish La Liga, the German Bundesliga, the French Ligue 1, and the Italian Serie A.

Each of these leagues has teams of the highest caliber and many other teams that can barely compete. Soccer clubs, perhaps more than any other sport, are all about money and who can provide the biggest contracts and pay the biggest transfer fees. Many other countries also have their own smaller soccer leagues, including MLS in the United States. Soccer fans tend to be die-hard loyal to their clubs and to their countries.

Unfortunately for soccer cards, players tend to transfer to different clubs throughout their careers. Cristiano Ronaldo, for example, has played for four different clubs in four different leagues. And while most players only ever play for one national team, many countries are not competitive in FIFA international play. For example, Erling Haaland is one of the best young stars in the world, but he is from Norway and can never field a competitive team even for the Euro Cup, let alone the World Cup. The lack of club loyalty combined with inconsistent national team opportunities constrains the collectibility of players in many ways. Soccer also lacks meaningful statistics like other sports have developed.

Much like hockey, it's all about goals scored and, basically, nothing else. But in soccer, goal-scoring is even harder to come by. If a player averages one goal per match, they're doing well. The problem is that there aren't compelling and widely used statistics and measurables for some of the highest-impact players who don't score in volume. Ultimately, very few soccer players rise to truly distinguished levels of stardom like Lionel Messi (see Figure 5-5) and Ronaldo have seen. In that way, even if the popularity of soccer cards and stickers matched that of the sport, one wonders who the fans would actually gravitate toward with sustainable value over time.

Courtesy of Heritage Auctions

FIGURE 5-5: 2004-05 Panini Megacracks Lionel Messi, BGS 5

With that being said, soccer cards and stickers still very much have a place in the hobby. Those who enjoy this segment, much like hockey hobbyists, tend to be extremely dedicated and really like to research the available sets inside and out. Vintage soccer, in particular, is arguably the most complicated segment of sports cards. The cards go back, like baseball, to the turn of the 19th/20th century. What makes them so complicated is that they originate from all corners of the world, from France, Italy, and the Netherlands to Brazil and beyond. Some of these cards have also been incredibly hard to authenticate, with fakes unfortunately slipping past experienced graders. Die-hard collectors have even gone so far as to teach themselves foreign languages to communicate with people overseas to locate, ship, and authenticate rare cards and stickers that would otherwise rarely find their way here to the United States.

The most notable athletes for soccer cards include Pelé. However, as with Mickey Mantle, any Pelé is valuable and a good Pelé. Johan Cruyff, the greatest Dutch footballer of all time, has his key rookie in a striking red-and-white shirt with a green background in 1968 Palirex Campeoes Europeus de Futebol.

Other key soccer stars across the years include Michel Platini, Diego Maradona, Zinedine Zidane, Ronaldo, David Beckham, and Ronaldinho. Kylian Mbappe and Erling Haaland have been key hobby favorites in the Ultra-Modern Era.

Boxing and MMA

Boxing has a longstanding tradition and history within the United States as well as in many other countries all over the world. Jack Johnson is one of the most notable early boxers, especially his 1909 Ogden's Pugilists and Wrestlers and his 1911 Turkey Red. Jack Dempsey has early cards in the 1920s. Joe Louis and Sugar Ray Robinson highlighted the 1940s. Rocky Marciano has a key rookie from 1951. In the 1960s and 1970s, there are, of course, Muhammad Ali, Joe Frazier, and George Foreman.

The most feared boxer ever — Mike Tyson — and others like Evander Holyfield, Roy Jones Jr., Floyd Mayeather Jr., and Manny Pacquiao round out the 1980s and 1990s.

While combat sports and martial arts are as old as mankind, Mixed Martial Arts (MMA) gained popularity in the 1990s, most notably with the debut of Ultimate Fighting Championship (UFC) in 1993. There are far too many MMA fighters to name, though star fighters like Jon Jones, George St-Pierre, Anderson Silva, and Khabib Nurmagomedov have all had significant hobby followings.

While the overall greatness of Conor McGregor may be hotly debated, no one can contest that he's been arguably the most marketable UFC fighter in history, and his card prices command premiums. Ronda Rousey is the most well-known female fighter of all time and has rookies in 2013 sets.

Golf and tennis

If club memberships, cardigans, plaid sweaters, and etiquette suit your fancy, you're likely drawn to golf or tennis and the cards of the greatest athletes from these sports.

From the perspective of golf, no single athlete has transcended the sport and had iconic moments more than Tiger Woods. With 15 major championships and 82 PGA Tour wins, Woods reigns as one of golf's most decorated athletes. Beyond Woods, collectors have targeted golfers like Jack Nicklaus, Arnold Palmer, and Phil Mickelson.

For tennis, we have been graced with arguably the four greatest tennis players of all time over the last 20 years — Roger Federer, Novak Djokovic, Rafael Nadal, and Serena Williams. These four have been extremely popular among collectors, though — much like golf — there aren't many sets to choose from.

Serena Williams, bucking the trend of women's cards typically selling for significantly less than men's sports cards, holds the record for the most expensive sale of a tennis card with her 2003 NetPro International Series Authentic Apparel PSA 8, Auto 10 at $266,400 in May 2022.

Other notable tennis greats with popular cards through the years include Venus Williams, Pete Sampras, Andre Agassi, Björn Borg, and Martina Navratilova.

Racing

The Formula 1 segment of the hobby closely mirrors the sport itself: flashy, fast, wealthy, and serious about the sport. While small in number of collectors, the total dollars spent on some of the cards is no joking matter. The two most notable retired F1 drivers are Ayrton Senna and Michael Schumacher, and Lewis Hamilton and Max Verstappen lead modern drivers (see Figure 3-5 in Chapter 3).

The Formula 1 market got a massive boost in popularity in 2020 and 2021, and many attribute the rise to the Drive to Survive Netflix series, which documented the drivers and their teams. The hobby's popularity was at an all-time high, and many viewers became regular F1 watchers while collecting cards of their favorite drivers.

One challenge that the Formula 1 card market has faced is the fact that the quality of teams is extremely top-heavy. During the peak of F1's hobby popularity, only a handful of drivers and teams had a realistic shot at race wins. After years of Hamilton dominating the sport, Verstappen quickly took over and has dominated while driving for Red Bull Racing. The 2022 season, for example, saw Verstappen win 15 of 22 events.

Taking a left turn in the racing world, several key drivers from the world of NASCAR stand out. Richard Petty, also known as "The King," is the original great and holds the record for most wins with 7 NASCAR Cup Series championships and 200 race victories. Among hobby favorites are Dale Earnhardt Sr., Dale Earnhardt Jr., Jimmie Johnson, and Chase Elliott.

Despite regular releases from companies like Panini, NASCAR has remained a relatively small but passionate community.

Chapter 6

Key Manufacturers, Brands, and Products

N avigating the labyrinthine world of sports cards demands a nuanced understanding beyond the surface knowledge offered in Chapter 2, where we delved into the birth stories of renowned manufacturers and their best products. Although we're providing a somewhat long list of sets and variations from all the eras, we fully acknowledge that we will miss some and are forced to intentionally omit others for brevity. One of the most beautiful aspects of the sports card hobby is discovery, and we hope this section – more than anything – will inspire you on your journey toward discovering what you love.

Licenses make all the difference

In the world of sports cards, securing the right to depict leagues, teams, and players involves a process known as licensing. The framework of this practice revolves around negotiations and agreements between card manufacturers, leagues, and individual athletes, intricately woven to bring these collectibles to life.

Currently, Topps, Panini, Upper Deck, and others engage in extensive dialogues with the NBA, NFL, MLB, NHL, and more, vying for the exclusive rights to showcase logos, team names, and player likenesses on their trading cards. Yet, it doesn't stop there. These companies also forge alliances with player associations or individual athletes, securing permissions and sometimes navigating royalty payments to feature their images and names.

Exclusive arrangements aren't uncommon and are exemplified by Panini's former stronghold in NBA cards since 2010 and NFL cards since 2016, or Topps's longtime (and former) exclusive dominion over MLB cards. However, these partnerships aren't just verbal agreements but meticulously outlined contracts delineating production quotas, design parameters, and quality benchmarks. And the licenses are not cheap. Fanatics utilized its substantial investment capacity and robust financial position to acquire the licensing rights for MLB, NBA, and NFL, displacing Topps and Panini in the process. Following these licensing wins, Fanatics acquired Topps, strategically leveraging its established brand reputation to guarantee continuity and assurance for collectors within the industry.

Unlicensed cards

While licensed cards undoubtedly dominate the market, an intriguing facet lies in the realm of unlicensed cards, some crafted by the major manufacturers and others by entirely separate companies. In the instances where one of the big three (Panini, Topps, Upper Deck) makes an unlicensed set, constraints on utilizing league logos prompt creative workarounds, such as an athlete showcased not in their team's official attire but rather in street clothes or even uniforms that have been photoshopped so that team logos or names are not shown. Their cards may simply list the city name rather than the team's insignia.

Intriguingly, these productions circumvent licensing intricacies by striking deals directly with the players themselves, such as Upper Deck's Goodwin Champions, Panini's unlicensed baseball in flagship collections like Prizm, Optic, and Select, and Topps's occasional forays into the same. These ventures straddle the boundary between legality and innovation, offering collectors a unique angle that some (though fewer) people enjoy.

Leaf is known for creating entirely unlicensed products with a wide array of products, often with autographs and relic cards that can be had for a fraction of the price of licensed cards. Leaf was founded in 2010 by Brian Gray and has no affiliation with Leaf (the gum manufacturer) products from prior generations. Leaf has created products from many different sports as well as pop culture cards. The product designs are often compelling and flashy, featuring various autographs and authentic relics and memorabilia.

Though a manufacturer like Panini has previously made unlicensed baseball cards, Fanatics's acquisition of exclusive trading card rights for the NBA, NFL, and MLB could force the company toward this category in a larger way. Fanatics will take over licenses for the NBA and NFL in 2025 and 2026, respectively, so Panini's place in the hobby is unclear as of the writing of this book.

Key basketball card sets

We pretty much cover the world of vintage basketball sets in the player section of this chapter. It started with 1948 Bowman and transitioned into a mix of Topps and Fleer products over the years. Upper Deck burst onto the scene in 1990, and then the real design revolution began.

We first reference Arena Design in Chapter 2 for its work with Fleer and SkyBox, and we absolutely must mention it again here because its impact has been felt on the hobby ever since.

Fleer got things started with its 1993 Ultra Scoring Kings, most notably with Michael Jordan soaring for a dunk with bright pink lightning flashing behind him. Collectors from the 1990s loved cards with electricity, fire, or outer space involved. The 1994 Ultra set introduced Ultra Power, Jam City, and Power in the Key, and 1996 is known for the rare Rising Stars on canvas stock.

The 1997 release is when Ultra took it to the next level, with sparkling gold and platinum medallion parallels. Impressive insert designs like Court Masters, Star Power, Ultra Stars, Jam City, and Big Shots were hits.

When Fleer Metal debuted in 1995, it wasn't a highly regarded product despite its unique foil finish and distinct design. The most notable insert set from 1995 was Slick Silver. The amazing draft class of 1996 brought new life to Metal (and other products from that year) while featured in popular designs like Lenticular Molten Metal, Steel Slammin', and the rare Net-Rageous die-cuts.

Fleer Metal also had Precious Metal parallels, which were seeded 1 in 36 packs — not the toughest odds to find one, but it was much tougher to get a specific player when considering the expansive checklist. These Precious Metals were the precursors to arguably the most sought-after parallels of the 90s — 1997 Metal Precious Metal Gems (PMGs). These were not highly sought after in the '90s, but over time, a mix of nostalgia, hype, and general epiphany about their beauty has caused their popularity and overall demand to explode. Some of the most popular Metal inserts from subsequent years include Planet Metal, Platinum Portraits, Fusion, and Titanium.

Topps really took off with its own identity while coupled to the refractor craze, starting in 1993 Topps Finest and skyrocketing in 1996 with Topps Chrome. As we mention earlier, these products continue to be the foundations of Topps offerings to this day.

Other notable inserts from the '90s include E-X2000 A Cut Above, Flair Showcase Hot Shots (see Figure 6-1), SkyBox Z-Force Big Men On Court, E-X2001 Jambalaya, and SkyBox Thunder Noyz Boyz.

Courtesy of Goldin Auctions

FIGURE 6-1: 1996 Flair Showcase Hot Shots Michael Jordan, PSA 10

Upper Deck carved out its identity in the '90s, first by hitching its wagon to holograms, then to heavy foil and holofoil, and eventually to game-used memorabilia and autographs. As we moved into the 2000s, Upper Deck really took hold of the game-used memorabilia and autograph space with arguably the most important high-end basketball set ever created, 2003 Upper Deck Exquisite — featuring LeBron James, Carmelo Anthony, Dwyane Wade, and Chris Bosh rookies, plus veteran cards, including Michael Jordan.

The final licensed Topps and Upper Deck basketball products appeared in 2009 and 2010, and then Panini took over the licenses. Everything changed in 2012 with the introduction of Panini Prizm Basketball, a chromium stock product featuring refractors known as Prizms (and in subsequent years rebranded as Silvers). The gold parallels are some of the most sought-after basketball cards from the entire Panini era. Panini subsequently introduced Select Basketball (a product formerly produced by Pinnacle in the 1990s) and began producing Donruss Optic basketball in 2016.

Those three products — Prizm, Select, and Optic — are among Panini's flagship sets and some of the hobby's most popular releases. Some of the most notable inserts from the Panini era include Kaboom!, Downtown, Color Blast, Stained Glass, Blank Slate, Aurora, My House!, and Marvels.

While these products are great for those of us on a budget or in a middle tier, the real revolution by Panini arguably came in the form of the high-end market with products like National Treasures, Flawless, Immaculate, Impeccable, and Noir (to name a few).

Where many of Topps's high-end products have remained relatively constant in collectors' minds for baseball, Panini managed to massively elevate the prestige of its high-end products, first with basketball and, more recently, with football as well. In 2022, the LeBron James Flawless Triple Logoman sold for a whopping $2.4 million, while Luka Doncic's National Treasures 1/1 logoman autograph sold in a private sale in 2021 for $4.6 million.

Key baseball card sets

One of the most fascinating things about the vintage world is the option to go mainstream (with the most iconic sets) or super niche (with oddball sets that nobody else has heard of). A holistic treatment of all vintage would fill more pages than this book allows, so we're sticking to what's iconic and treading beyond what we've already covered.

At first glance, the naming conventions and letter designations for vintage baseball cards can seem a bit cryptic. Most products begin with a letter followed by some number. These letter designations are broken down like so:

» **N:** Nineteenth century

» **D:** Bakery sets

» **E:** Early gum and candy

» **M:** Magazine and newspaper inserts

» **T:** Tobacco

» **R:** Gum and candy of later decades

» **W:** Miscellaneous cards

The number designations, unfortunately, are not as clear and were often assigned by the companies producing them.

By now, you know the history of tobacco cards, especially T206. Let's jump back in time to 1886–1890 N172 Old Judge cards, considered by many to be the first major set. This set had a huge checklist of at least 250 to 350 different cards, notably featuring Cap Anson, King Kelly, and Harry Wright.

There were also Allen & Ginter and Gypsy Queen cards in the late 19th century, two products that still exist as Topps brands to this day.

TECHNICAL STUFF

Did you know that there is also a T205 set from 1911 featuring many of the same iconic players, all at a discount relative to the T206 prices?

American Caramel had a handful of sets from 1909 to 1910, including Joe Jackson's rookie card and many of the same cast from the T206 checklist. The 1914 Cracker Jack (see Figure 2-3 in Chapter 2) set, featuring a striking red background, is definitely an all-time great set.

Fleer began making baseball cards in the early 1920s, while 1933 Goudey, 1938 Goudey Heads Up, 1939 Play Ball, and 1941 Play Ball were all important pre-war sets.

Once we move into the post-war era of cards, it all starts with 1948 Leaf. Bowman products ran from 1948 to 1955 before being acquired and discontinued by Topps until being resurrected in 1989. Donruss also made its entrance in baseball cards in the 1980s.

One of baseball's most historic releases came with 1989 Upper Deck Baseball. Considered by many to be the first premium set, Upper Deck's card debut changed the hobby forever with a glossy finish, holograms, and even packs that felt premium.

Like basketball cards, baseball saw many innovations during the 1990s, involving many of the same insert sets like Essential Credentials, Precious Metal Gems, and Ultra Platinum Medallions.

REMEMBER

Derek Jeter's 1993 SP Foil rookie card is one of the most iconic cards of the decade and is rarely found in high grades because of various issues.

All of the Topps Finest sets of the '90s, starting in 1993, tend to be highly sought after by collectors. The same goes for Topps Chrome, which debuted in 1996. Flair Hot Gloves are also fan-favorite die-cut sets.

Some specifically sought-after inserts are from Fleer Ultra Thunder Clap, Home Run Kings, Diamond Producers, and Diamond Immortals.

In addition to a superabundance of relic cards, parallels, and autographs from Topps, Topps Chrome, and Bowman Chrome have all been go-to cards during the 2000s.

Since 2010, Topps has continued to run the baseball card market and has most notably increased its high-end product offerings with products like Topps Definitive, Dynasty, Sterling, Diamond Icons, Triple Threads, Gilded Collection, and more. These products all tend to feature well-designed, elegant relics and autograph cards with a unique flair.

The double-edged sword is that Topps has produced many relic and autograph cards across all tiers of products, leading some to argue that all the high-end products end up watering each other down. Since Fanatics purchased Topps to produce trading cards, there has been an attempt to make sure that every product has a clear identity and notable chase cards. As Fanatics begins to take over the licenses for basketball and football, it will be interesting to see how product lines evolve with those sports in the mix with baseball.

Topps has also had several flash-in-the-pan products and other gimmicky products in the last decade, but its flagship and iconic offerings remain strong. To the benefit of the everyday collector, Topps has managed to keep the prices of sealed products far more affordable than Panini has. While this may seem bad for corporate interests, prices should remain sustainable, with clearly delineated tiers for every financial class.

Prospecting and Minor League cards

Baseball, entirely in a league of its own, gives collectors and investors alike a unique opportunity to "get the jump" on a player's career well before they ever set foot on a Major League diamond. The most sought-after cards for modern players are the 1st Bowman cards — particularly its 1st Bowman autograph cards (see Figure 14-1 in Chapter 14). More than any rookie autographs, these prospect cards tend to be the must-have baseball rookie cards.

Technically, Topps began producing 1st Bowman cards in 1996 with the likes of Todd Helton. However, in 2003, these cards really became a staple in the hobby with players like Ryan Howard and Robinson Cano. Understanding Bowman products and prospecting can be a little bit tricky. At a high level, there are three key product releases each year:

>> **Bowman:** Bowman is released each spring and features players who were left off the checklists from the other two products, as well as veteran cards and rookie cards.

>> **Bowman Chrome:** Released in the summer and features veterans and prospects of international signings.

>> **Bowman Draft:** The final product release of the year is the most important — Bowman Draft, which drops in the winter and is filled with prospects drafted out of high school and college. This checklist comprises both 1st Bowman cards and non-1st prospect cards. To add to the confusion across these three products, both Bowman and Bowman Draft include Chrome cards in checklists, whereas Bowman Chrome comes only in a chrome format and does not include paper cards.

In recent years, Topps has also offered 1st Edition versions of these products as well as Sapphire versions. Learning the ins and outs of Bowman prospecting is somewhat complicated based on the product mix but also somewhat straightforward because following the MLB Pipeline Top 100 prospects list is a pretty handy cheat sheet.

TECHNICAL STUFF

If you are an investor, one of the most consistently predictable trends in all sports cards is that a player's card prices will spike when it is announced that they are called up to the Major Leagues. Unless you plan on holding a player long term, it's prudent to at least consider selling from the moment you get that push notification to your phone or see it in your social media feed.

Beyond just prospect cards, some products feature Minor League cards, such as Topps Heritage Minor League. These cards, much like non–1st prospect cards, aren't generally good investments unless the player has no other notable prospect or rookie cards (which is incredibly rare). Some collectors enjoy these cards if they live close to one of those Minor League affiliate teams, but generally, that audience is pretty limited. It's best to avoid those cards from an investment perspective.

Key football card sets

Though many collectors heavily associate vintage cards with baseball, football has a robust selection of early sets. The 1933 Goudey Multi-Sport set, for example, featured Jim Thorpe. The 1948 sets for Bowman and Leaf were the first major sets following the end of World War II. While 1948 Bowman featured black-and-white photos, 1948 Leaf delivered some color.

Major Topps sets through the '50s, '60s, and '70s were highlighted by rookies for stars like Jonny Unitas (1957), Joe Namath (1965), and Walter Payton (1976).

In the 1990s, many fan-favorite cards played big parts, like Precious Metal Gems, SkyBox Star Rubies, E-X Essential Credentials, Finest Embossed Refractors, Ultra Gold, and Platinum Medallions.

SP, SPx, and UD3 were offerings from Upper Deck that utilized holograms, die cuts, and foil to perfection. Collector's Edge, laden with flash and foil, Pacific with its Crown Collection and Prizms, Pinnacle with its Mirror Gold parallels, Score with Epix and Artist Proofs, and Select with Mirror Parallels were unique to football.

Topps continued to produce football cards until 2015 with a lineup of refractors, autographs, and relics. The 2000s in football really only stand up in time because of the *who* more than the *what*.

Once we get into the Panini era, as we mention in Chapter 5, one of the most iconic cards is the Contenders Rookie Ticket Autograph. Insert sets like Kaboom!, Color Blast, and Downtown are also extremely popular among football collectors.

TECHNICAL STUFF

Fanatics's entrance into the sports card hobby also brought with it a new focus on collegiate cards. Panini had made licensed cards of college football and basketball players for years, but 2022 Bowman Chrome University delivered an all-new product that shifted the market. Bowman had been the prospecting brand for baseball, and now it could serve the same purpose for football and basketball. While college cards may never be as popular as the professional leagues, they were happily welcomed by collectors with college interests.

Hockey cards

Wayne Gretzky may easily be the best hockey player ever, but key sets go back into the early 1900s with 1910 C56 Imperial Tobacco as an important starting point.

Best known for its hockey products and partnership with Topps, which we cover more in Chapter 2, O-Pee-Chee began making hockey cards in the 1930s.

The 1950s and 1960s saw the rise of the Parkhurst Hockey sets. Parkhurst debuted in 1951 with a series of smaller cards but went bigger in 1953 with a similar design but a larger card. The brand is still produced by Upper Deck today.

Topps competed with Parkhurst in the hockey market for years until Parkhurst's final set — at least in its current iteration — in 1963-1964. Topps and O-Pee-Chee largely maintained control over the hockey market until the early 1990s. Gretzky's rookie is found in the iconic 1979 Topps and O-Pee-Chee sets.

The 1990s ushered in a wave of innovation with the introduction of holograms in the 1990 Upper Deck set, while 1994 SP marked Upper Deck's inaugural stand-alone SP product (the product is called SP, not to be confused with the acronym SP for "short print"). The advent of jersey cards in the 1996 Upper Deck transformed the landscape with Game Jerseys, igniting a fervor that endures to this day. Sets like Black Diamond Run for the Cup, Metal Universe Ice Carvings, Lethal Weapons, Cool Steel, and Bowman's Best Atomic Refractors are some of the decade's most coveted cards. Critically important was the debut of SP Authentic in 1998, paving the way for the famed Future Watch Autos, the most popular rookie cards behind Young Guns today.

As hockey crossed into the new millennium, the hobby saw the introduction of groundbreaking editions like the 2000 Upper Deck Premier, the first notable high-end hockey product with autographed rookie cards. The 2002 Upper Deck Premier set was the first set to include Rookie Patch Autographs (RPAs) and the first $1,000 modern hockey rookie card of Rick Nash. Notably, Upper Deck gained exclusive licensing rights, leading to a sharp drop in the overall diversity of product offerings. The Cup was introduced in 2005 as one of the best products ever, showcasing the high-end rookie cards of Sidney Crosby and Alexander Ovechkin. Some notable subsets of The Cup are Emblems of Endorsement, Honorable Numbers, Limited Logos, and Signature Patches.

For a brief stint, from 2010 to 2013, Panini held a license from the NHL Players Association, allowing it to produce cards featuring players but not the team logos and NHL trademarks that Upper Deck had exclusive rights to. The most notable set produced by Panini during that time was Dominion, featuring RPAs of P.K. Subban, Taylor Hall, and others.

Then, in 2012, Upper Deck — having acquired Fleer licenses in 2005 following its bankruptcy — produced a genius product called Fleer Retro featuring several of the most iconic innovations of the aforementioned famous Arena Design, including Precious Metal Gems, Jambalaya, Essential Credentials, SkyBox Autographics, Electrifying, Golden Touch, Intimidation Nation, Noyz Boyz, Playmaker's Theatre, and a massive checklist of throwback card designs like Ultra and Metal.

This list could essentially be a copy and paste of the most important and sought-after inserts and parallels from basketball and football in the '90s, and the hockey community wasn't initially enthusiastic about it. A smaller number of hobbyists were thrilled, especially those who also collected other sports and had fond memories of those sets. In the last three to five years, Fleer Retro's popularity has exploded and garnered much more attention. In 2013, Panini produced National Treasures Hockey in its last year with the NHLPA licenses. The set included several popular subsets such as Buried Treasures, Numbers Patches, and Flawless, which include an embedded diamond.

O-Pee-Chee Platinum launched in 2014 and has since become a very popular release each year, known for its chromium finish and vibrant, colorful designs. O-Pee-Chee Platinum is the Upper Deck product that most closely resembles a Panini offering like Prizm or Donruss Optic. The most notable inserts from the set are the 1/1 Golden Treasures and the Seismic Golds numbered to just 50 copies.

In 2015, with the debut of Connor McDavid, Upper Deck introduced e-packs, allowing users to digitally open card packs. This allowed collectors to trade cards virtually or to have physical copies shipped to them through the mail, exclusively via Check Out My Cards (COMC). This innovation helped provide on-demand supplies of packs, especially for fans who may not be close to a local card shop or have easy access to sealed boxes. In 2020, SkyBox Metal Universe was released with Precious Metal Gems, Jambalayas, Platinum Portraits, Star Rubies, and other iconic throwback parallels and inserts. Most would agree that this product was not as well executed as 2012 Fleer Retro, and hobbyists weren't as enthusiastic about it this time around. Most recently, Upper Deck released new Young Guns parallels, including Outburst Silver, Outburst Red, and Outburst Gold, numbered to just 1.

Other notable sports and key sets

There are, of course, key sets, parallels, and products for some of the other notable sports outside of the Big Four. Largely produced by many of the same manufacturers, some of the most important products we cover earlier are important here, too. But there are a few extra twists.

Key soccer card sets

Within vintage soccer, as we say earlier, the number and diversity of sets are far too great to list. Using tools like COMC or grading company set registries can be a great way to do research. We can note that Panini entered the hobby in 1961 with stickers and has had a footprint in soccer products ever since. Many of the products from the '60s through the '80s were done as regional releases specific to certain countries.

Merlin Publishing began making cards in 1994 before being acquired by Topps in 2008. Futera was established in 1989 and is known for incredibly stunning, simple, and elegant designs with foil trim, relics, and autographs. Futera has specific licensing agreements with clubs like FC Barcelona, Paris Saint-Germain, Liverpool, Arsenal, and others. Panini World Cup has been an exceptionally popular product since 1994, starting with stickers but evolving over time into separate sticker and trading card products with every four-year cycle.

Topps produced MLS sets in the early 2010s before the first real breakthrough product with 2017 Topps Chrome Champions League. Since then, Panini Prizm World Cup and Topps Chrome Champions League have stood out above the rest as the most notable modern soccer products.

Panini has produced other sets like Prizm English Premier League, Mosaic La Liga, and Series A, and Topps has offered Topps Chrome Bundesliga and MLS. None of those products are as popular as Prizm World Cup and Topps Chrome Champions League. Topps Museum Collection, Topps Finest, Topps Stadium Club, and the aforementioned Topps Merlin are other popular soccer products over the past few years. Panini has continued with its line from other sports, including Donruss (which includes chrome

Optic cards within the paper product), Revolution, and Select. The 2022 Eminence World Cup set was an incredibly high-end product produced by Panini.

Key boxing and MMA card sets

We already covered many of the key boxers and fighters, so here's a quick overview of some of the important sets for combat sports:

» 1960 Hemmets Journal was a multi-sport card set in the popular Swedish magazine of the same name. Collectors would hand cut the cards out, including the famous Cassius Clay/Muhammad Ali rookie card.

» 1979 Venorlandus Limited's "Our Heroes World of Sport" is a popular multi-sport set that featured a playful Muhammad Ali caricature dancing with a bee.

» 1985's Fight of the Century features smaller cards with cartoons of many key fighters over the years.

» 1991 Kayo features colorful action shots with a blue border and holograms, most notably the timeless image of Muhammad Ali standing over a fallen Joe Frazier.

» 1996 Ringside was a visually stunning set with colorful rainbow foil finishes, including a card of Roy Jones Jr. with his championship belt over his shoulder. Collectors love to pursue copies of this card with authenticated in-person autographs.

» 2011 ushered in the first Topps Finest UFC product as well as Topps Moment of Truth and Topps Title Shot.

» 2012 and 2013 Topps UFC Bloodlines have a number of the first notable cards from many of the stars we have known from the last decade, and Topps continued to produce various UFC sets throughout the 2010s.

» The first Topps Chrome UFC came in 2017 and continued through 2019, which was the last set produced.

» In 2021, Panini obtained the exclusive rights for UFC and successfully debuted Prizm UFC.

Panini has produced Prizm UFC in each of the subsequent two years and has really leaned into that partnership with additional sets like Chronicles, Donruss Optic, and Select, as well as high-end Immaculate UFC.

Key golf and tennis sets

As it relates to golf cards, there have been a number of vintage manufacturers over the years. Donruss had sets in 1981 and 1982. Pro Set had sets from 1990–1992. Since then, it's all about Upper Deck and SP Authentic. There aren't a ton of golf products out there, but 2001 Upper Deck is the most iconic and notable because Tiger Woods had multiple rookie cards in the set. There were subsequent sets in 2002–2004 and a 2014 Upper Deck Exquisite set. The 2021 SP Authentic set was the most recent golf product to hit the market.

Tennis cards have existed for decades and, like many vintage cards, started out in a hodgepodge of manufacturers' sets. Starting in the 1980s, NetPro began producing cards sporadically and continued producing them into the 2000s up to today. Most recently, we have also seen tennis cards from both Topps and Upper Deck.

The previously mentioned 1979 Venorlandus also featured fun golf and tennis cards.

Key racing card sets

From a vintage NASCAR perspective, 1988 Maxx is the first majorly produced racing set. The set was produced in two locations, Myrtle Beach and Charlotte. The first location, Myrtle Beach, was much more limited than Charlotte's (some sources indicate a fire may have destroyed the Myrtle Beach factory). Dale Earnhardt Sr. was not in the set as he and Maxx couldn't come to an agreement. Later, Earnhardt Sr.'s card was an insert redemption in 1994.

For modern NASCAR cards, Press Pass was the key manufacturer of racing cards from the early '90s up until 2015. Once 2016 came, Panini acquired the license and created four products for that year, including National Treasures and Prizm. Prizm has key rookies for Chase Elliott and Ryan Blaney. What makes Prizm racing unique, as opposed to the other sports, are the rainbow prizms — paying homage to Jeff Gordon — as well as the white flag and checkered flag parallels.

Chapter **7**

The Importance of Card Condition — From Printing to Grading

The life of a sports card is a dangerous one. To a collector, a card can be the intersection of powerful photography, meticulous design, and sports history, resulting in timeless art worth cherishing. To the uninitiated, it's a delicate piece of cardboard with edges ripe for tearing, corners prone to bending, and surfaces vulnerable to scratching.

In a perfect world, cards would be printed without errors, packed carefully, and transported safely from manufacturer to collector. In the real world, cards often leave the printing press with various defects long before exposure to bigger threats like earth, wind, and fire.

These seemingly endless obstacles make finding a card in pristine condition a minor miracle, so it's essential that you know it when you see it. Nuances across eras, from vintage cards to ultra-modern sets, also make simply labeling a card's condition "poor" or "good" extremely subjective and more difficult than it seems.

In this chapter, we teach you how to determine the condition of your cards, explain when and why you should consider grading, and then give you the same tips and tricks the grading companies use to evaluate them.

Physical Aspects of Cards

A card's physical condition is important for a variety of reasons. For collectors, cards are often meant to be displayed. Like fine art, a card can be the centerpiece of a home office or a conversation starter with friends and family. But is a heavily damaged card worthy of display? In most cases, probably not. Condition is, of course, incredibly important for those looking to sell cards, too. Broken TVs aren't worth much, so your damaged cards probably aren't either unless they are very rare or very old. The margin for error is also much smaller when buying and selling cards hoping to make a profit. Accidentally buying a damaged card for your personal collection stings. Buying a damaged card that you wanted to sell for money *hurts*.

Diving into the sports card hobby can be overwhelming for beginners. From historical nuances to a constantly changing secondary market, there's a lot to learn. Some skills are more important than others, though, and some topics shouldn't be skipped under any circumstances. Understanding card conditions is one you shouldn't skip.

Surface condition, centering, corners, and edges

A card's condition has four main aspects: centering, corners, edges, and surface. Grading companies harshly scrutinize each, and while each aspect's name is largely straightforward and self-explanatory, the details within each are anything but. The following sections explain the main aspects and what you need to know about each:

Centering

Often, but not always, trading cards are designed with a defined border that runs along all four sides of the card. The quality of centering is determined by the space of that border along all four sides, with perfect centering featuring a completely symmetrical border throughout. Centering is commonly broken down into two additional categories during grading: top to bottom (T/B) and left to right (L/R). Borders can be too heavy or thin along each side (see Figure 7-1), and the severity of each is factored into a card's overall grade.

Courtesy of Goldin Auctions

FIGURE 7-1: 1948 Bowman George Mikan, PSA 8 (off-center)

The centering of the back of the card matters, too, though to a lesser extent. While some graders require no worse than a 60/40 ratio on the front to be considered for the highest grade, a card may only need a 75/25 ratio on the reverse to qualify.

TECHNICAL STUFF

Cards that are perfectly centered, with all four borders completely identical in size, will have a ratio of 50/50 left to right and top to bottom. A card with a "60/40 ratio left to right" means that the card is slightly off-centered, with a larger border on the left that pushes the card too far to the right.

While borders are a great design feature for many cards, they also clearly show off a card's centering (good or bad). But what happens when a card doesn't have a border at all? Some sets, like Topps Stadium Club or Panini Luminance, feature full-bleed designs, where the photo stretches completely to the card's edges, making identifying centering more difficult without a guide.

TIP

However, there are other ways to judge centering without borders, and you'll use the same tricks grading companies do. Without a clear border, you'll have to rely on other identifying factors across the card's surface. Manufacturer logos, rookie card designations, and even player names can all provide hints about a card's centering. Examine the space between a logo and the edges of the card on one side and the space between a player's name and the edges on the other side. Do they match? If not, your card is likely off-centered.

WARNING

Rules are made to be broken, of course, and the sports card hobby loves doing exactly that. The tricks above for rectangular cards might be worthless when handling a die-cut card with an irregular shape or something other than four sides and four corners. Those unique properties make die-cut cards especially difficult to evaluate, so submit them for grading at your own risk.

Corners

Not unlike centering, the corners category is mostly straightforward during evaluation. Do the corners appear razor-sharp? If yes, those are high-quality corners. Anything resembling a dent, ding, or bend, as shown in the Mickey Mantle example in Figure 7-2, is a major indicator that your card had a bump along the way and is considered a "soft" corner.

TIP

Spotting impacted areas may not always be easy. Always use proper lighting and a tool with high magnification to examine corners because even the smallest imperfection can push your card in the wrong direction on the grading scale.

Thicker cards are especially prone to damaged corners due to more surface area, but thin cards also pose challenges. Cards in the 35-point and 55-point range can feature small bends or tears in the paper along the corners. It's hard to spot with the naked eye but can be detected under magnification or with a blacklight — a tool we cover in the later "Spotting print defects, damage, and other issues" section. Cards with dark borders tend to have more visible corner and edge issues, which make them less likely to receive higher grades.

Soft corner

1952 TOPPS #311
MICKEY MANTLE FR
1.5
64546810

Crease

Staining

Courtesy of PSA

FIGURE 7-2: 1952 Topps Mickey Mantle, PSA 1.5

TECHNICAL STUFF

For reference, most cards made with paper cardstock are in the 35-point thickness range. The typical Topps baseball or the Donruss basketball cards are generally 35-point cardstock. If you're unsure, do a quick online search for the "BCW Card Thickness Point Gauge." You can purchase this handy reference or print one to compare to your cards before you start stuffing them into Toploaders.

Regarding card thickness, it's important to remember that not all cardstock is created equal. A 35-point card might not have a lot of surface area to damage, but paper stock is extremely prone to bends and dents because of its softness. A 35-point card with chromium stock is much sturdier, so popular chrome sets like Topps Chrome and Panini Prizm hold up better than paper cards like Panini Donruss and Topps Heritage. Details about card thickness and the different cardstocks are found in Chapter 3.

Edges

Unlike the centering and corners categories, the edges of a card can be a little more difficult to evaluate for condition, depending on the thickness of the card. Like with corners, a thicker card's edges are much more prone to damage simply because of the surface area. Dents are common, and fraying can occur on thinner cards and those made with chromium stock. In Figure 7-2, clear staining along the right edge of the card will greatly impact the card's grade.

Surface

The surface category is likely the hardest and most confusing for collectors and graders to properly evaluate. Along with centering, this is where manufacturer defects are most likely to come into play. Print lines, the imperfections laid into the card during the printing process, can be extremely difficult to spot by the naked eye.

The hobby's obsession with refractors and parallels during the Ultra-Modern Era has only complicated this issue. Popular prismatic effects like Cracked Ice or Wave Refractors are some of the most eye-catching for collectors. However, the printing process to create those designs can leave unintended lines across the card's surface that graders often count as a major flaw.

REMEMBER

Grading standards across the different companies vary. The subjectivity in grading by humans is difficult to quantify, so one company may be more lenient on a print line than another. It's also not unheard of for some graders to ignore certain flaws if a card is widely known to have that specific issue across its entire print run. Some companies are believed to be harsher when grading things like centering, but others demand only the sharpest corners.

Along with print lines, things like dimples, scratches, dents, creases, and even bubbles (see Figure 7-3) can occur during printing. Issues like dents and bubbles often show themselves when cards are made of metal or acetate. Metal cards sometimes even come with a peelable plastic cover to help negate scratches and dents, although the printing process for acetate cards often leaves them with pockets of air inside.

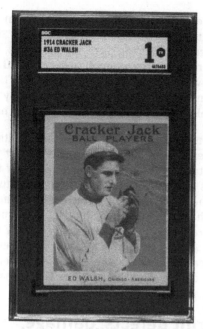

Courtesy of Heritage Auctions

FIGURE 7-3: 1914 Cracker Jack Ed Walsh, SGC 1

In case you were wondering: Yes, graders take these issues into consideration. And no, they won't show you mercy.

The surface and edges of a card can also tear or peel when being pulled out of a pack. This is commonly found in older cards that have been sealed for years or even decades. These cards can be susceptible to bricking, which is where the cards begin to stick to one another from sitting for so long, forming a solid brick-like shape. You need to take care when separating these cards from each other to avoid edging damage or even parts of the surface sticking and tearing away from the card above or below.

The quality of a card's image also impacts the surface condition. Photos and other designs can print foggy or out of focus completely.

Before moving on, it's important to cover some nuances between the different card eras found in Chapter 2. We won't spend too much time here, but you'll find that cards from different periods have their own unique issues based on the printing technology of the time. Some of the earliest vintage cards from the early 1900s were miscut or printed with major color issues. Significant miscuts are less common among ultra-modern cards, but these sets can feature print lines from complicated designs that simply weren't possible with older printing technology. New technology has mostly eliminated certain issues from the hobby's earliest releases, but it's also introduced others that collectors now battle.

REMEMBER

Even if a card is properly protected over the course of its life from bumps and bruises, general aging can greatly impact the quality of a card. Vintage cards see their colors fade over the years, making early sets especially desirable if they still feature bright, vibrant colors. The introduction of refractors in the modern era also brought with it "greening" or "hulking." As time passes, some cards with refractor finishes turn green, greatly impacting their eye appeal. Aging can impact a card's overall eye appeal, which can significantly impact card prices. Unfortunately, when it comes to aging, fading, and greening, Father Time remains undefeated, and your card collection is no exception.

Spotting print defects, damage, and other issues

After you know the basics of card condition (see the preceding section), the next step is to put that knowledge to work. Evaluating a card requires much more than a quick pass with the eyes but is often worth it in the end. It takes time and effort, and anything less can result in emotional and financial frustration.

The good news is that you have plenty of tools and tricks at your disposal to make the evaluation process smooth and simple. In fact, you can put together a toolbox of items that isn't that different than what professional graders will use during the submission process. Below are tools to upgrade your evaluation process:

>> **Microfiber cloth:** Newton's Fourth Law of Motion states that any dust, hair, or other loose matter can and will find its way to the surface of your trading cards. Even the seconds from the sealed pack to a protective sleeve is more than enough time for dust to completely take over your card. You'll want to get rid of that.

TIP

The first step of any card evaluation should be a quick pass with a microfiber cloth to remove anything that has made its way to the card's surface. You're not polishing the card or using any cleaning products or water here. You're simply removing dust, dirt, fingerprints, and other elements from the surface. The approach is essentially the same as cleaning a pair of glasses. Start with a gentle huff of warm breath. Be firm but careful when applying the cloth. Once cleaned, you may find that the dimple or dent dropping your card's grade from a 10 to an 8 was simply a piece of dust.

>> **Jeweler loupe:** If you've ever been to a jewelry store, you probably noticed a small magnifier to examine stones, rings, and other items. You'll use it for the same purpose here. A loupe with even just 10x magnification will instantly improve your ability to evaluate card condition properly. Widely considered the most important tool when examining cards, a quality loupe is a must-own for this process. And they aren't very expensive either.

A simple search online for a jeweler loupe will yield plenty of adequate results; many even come with additional lighting built in. Proper evaluation requires good lighting and strong magnification, and the jeweler loupe provides both. Some card collectors never leave home without it.

TIP

When using the loupe, hold it close to the card and focus on small, specific areas. Focus on all four corners individually and always make a pass along all four edges. You'll also want to closely examine the surface; a good trick is to focus on a single spot while tilting the card to different angles. A print line may be invisible at one angle but clear as day in another. Remember, submitting a card for grading isn't cheap, so a few extra seconds with your loupe is worth it.

>> **Blacklight:** A blacklight isn't generally considered a must-have for many collectors, but it can make spotting certain issues much easier, especially for beginners. A quick pass with a small handheld blacklight can make elusive print lines pop visually, while a corner with a small ding will shine. Blacklights are especially helpful in spotting damage along the edges of a card. Remember those cards that don't have clear borders? A blacklight will make spotting any chipping along the edges easier. The backs of your cards shouldn't be ignored either, as small chips or dents, even in one of the back bottom corners, can be a fatal flaw.

Cleaning or altering?

Regarding card evaluation, few topics are more controversial than the debate between cleaning and altering a card. One is acceptable, but the other is one of the most unethical and immoral decisions a hobbyist can make. But what's the difference, exactly? That's where things get complicated.

Generally, most collectors consider cleaning a card to be acceptable, with the term cleaning meaning that you are simply removing any dirt, dust, or other materials that landed on the surface after production. Beyond that, many collectors consider a card to be altered when using any additional substance to enchance the card. Below, you'll find examples of alterations:

>> **Polishing:** Cards can sometimes arrive with scrapes, smudges, and other blemishes from production that aren't easily removed with a microfiber cloth. The use of cleaning materials to polish or buff out these imperfections is often considered altering a card. Fit for your car, but not your card. Supporters of the practice argue that collectors have a right to remove production-related issues. They may also believe it's their right to do whatever they wish with a card they own. In some cases, collectors may attempt to clean or polish a card so that it accepts an autograph better. Detractors typically consider the use of cleaning products to be *adding* an element to a card, which is harshly rejected by some.

>> **Re-coloring:** Re-coloring is one of the most common practices when adding an element to a card. Re-coloring is popular because the value of vintage cards relies heavily on the brightness and vibrance of the colors as they age through the years. It's not uncommon for cards of similar physical condition to sell for extremely different prices based on the overall color quality and eye appeal.

Re-coloring involves adding color to a card's image, either to make faded areas more vibrant or to fill in areas that have been damaged or no longer contain any color at all. This is considered extremely unethical. Cards with white or black borders are easier candidates to adjust, although brighter colors require more precision. Specialty paints, pens, and pencils are generally the go-to tools.

>> **Trimming:** The subject of countless scandals throughout the sports card hobby's long history, trimming is likely considered the worst alteration you can make to a card. The process is simple, with a cutting tool used to alter the card corners and edges. Trimming can turn a soft corner into a sharp one, be used to improve the centering of a card, peel off edge damage or wear, and even fix a factory-produced miscut if needed.

Trimming has evolved through the years as well, and today's trimmers are known to use tools meant for surgery to make alterations. In fact, trimmed cards are sometimes discovered because the cuts are clean beyond what the manufacturer can produce.

Trimming, re-coloring, and making other alterations aren't explicitly illegal. You won't go to jail for trimming a card in your home and putting it on your shelf. Selling an altered item without disclosing it is a different story, however, and you can face serious consequences for doing so. Illegal or not, the practice is severely frowned upon, and you may lose friends and credibility in the community. Grading services may even decline to grade your card if alterations are found. The card may also be encapsulated in plastic, labeled as Authentic but Altered (see Figure 7-4), and won't receive a numerical grade on the grading scale. Some known card trimmers have even been banned from submitting by the grading companies.

It's worth noting that some of these alterations aren't unique to sports and trading cards. It's not uncommon for high-end pieces of art to be restored and then sold for millions. It's also acceptable for a professional to press items like comics or magazines before being sent in for grading. What's considered acceptable or not completely depends on the feelings of that specific collectible community, and it is highly recommended that you don't pursue these techniques with your sports cards, as this community is not accepting of these practices.

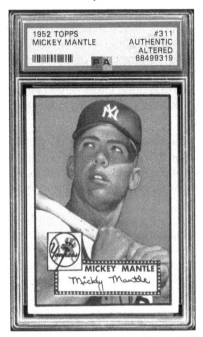

1952 TOPPS   #311
MICKEY MANTLE   AUTHENTIC
                 ALTERED
        PSA   68499319

Courtesy of PSA

FIGURE 7-4: Altered 1952 Topps Mickey Mantle

Card Grading

Outside of the card manufacturers, an argument could be made that third-party grading services are the most important companies in the hobby. The manufacturers deliver the cards, but grading services provide various other benefits that keep the hobby healthy and safe.

The hobby's recent focus largely targets grading scales and their numerical values, but card grading originated as a way for an independent party of industry experts to authenticate the legitimacy of cards. Once authenticated, cards are encapsulated in a plastic holder, called a "slab" for short, then labeled and shipped back to the customer. Your cards are authenticated and given serious protection in a single swoop.

Most of the cards pictured in this book have been encapsulated or" "slabbed."

TIP

REMEMBER

Authentication is necessary because, along with being altered, cards are sometimes faked completely. Iconic cards are especially prone to having fake copies created, and collectors should have their card's authenticity guaranteed when investing their hard-earned money into a collectible. You wouldn't be happy with a fake watch, so you shouldn't be happy with a fake card, either.

The actual grading process is straightforward and not dissimilar from what you've hopefully been doing with your cards. After a grading company receives your submission, your cards are delivered to a series of experts who authenticate and evaluate them for imperfections and eventually send them off for encapsulation with an assigned numerical grade. Ideally, you'll have caught any issues before sending in your cards, but no one is perfect, and these graders are, despite what you might read on social media, often very good at their jobs. Once the cards are encapsulated, sealed, and labeled, they'll be mailed back to you for what is hopefully a wonderful mail day.

Benefits of grading, from authentication to market value

You've likely put together some reasons why you should consider grading your cards already, but it's always good to cover them specifically. Here are the major reasons you should consider grading your cards:

>> **Authentication:** Submitting your cards and having them authenticated is by far the most important reason that you should consider this process. Fake cards are worthless, and any alterations must also be called out, especially for vintage cards. Even if you don't intend to sell your cards to make money, you deserve an authentic collection to be proud of.

WARNING

It should be noted that on rare occasions, grading services don't always catch alterations or fake cards. Mistakes happen, and grading companies are generally willing to fix their mistakes when presented with the evidence. When a grading company becomes aware of a mistake made when authenticating an item, they will deactivate the certification number in their database. If you're about to purchase an expensive graded card, it's always good to look up the certification number to ensure that it's still active and legitimate.

- **Encapsulation:** Outside of authentication, the encapsulation process that protects the card is probably the second most important part of grading. Penny sleeves, top loaders, and one-touch holders are great, sure, but there is no better protection for a card than the encapsulation process grading services provide. These holders are sturdy and tamper-proof, helping your cards maintain their condition for years to come.

- **Market Value:** The reality is that authentication and encapsulation increase the market value for many cards. Buying cards raw can be tricky, and it can also be hard to spot damage in photos online or even in person. The grading process helps cut through that noise. In general, you can expect that your card is truly authentic. Although not every SGC 9 is in the exact same condition as another SGC 9, these grading values give you a strong baseline for the condition.

REMEMBER

This is a friendly reminder to collect what and how you want to. Identifying conditions and grading cards is an important part of the hobby, but it doesn't have to matter to you. Some collectors only own graded cards, and some don't own any. Some hobbyists only buy cards in pristine condition, but others don't care at all. The choice is yours to make.

Trusted grading companies

From here, you need to know the major grading companies and key details about each. These services are not created equal, and the trading card boom in 2020 has brought with it a rise in new companies. While some companies employ hundreds, if not thousands, of people, others can simply be a collector with a label maker and some plastic holders in their garage.

REMEMBER

If you take away only a few tips from this book, one of them should be that the grading companies you choose to do business with — either by purchasing a graded card or by sending in cards yourself — is one of the most important decisions you'll ever make as a collector. Below, you find the industry's most trusted grading services and key information for each:

- **PSA (Professional Sports Authenticator):** Founded in 1991, PSA is, by far, the most popular grading service in the sports card hobby. There is always debate about the quality of the grading services, but today, there is no debate in terms of volume. For perspective, GemRate, a third-party website that tracks graded items across the major services, found that PSA graded about 11.2 million items (not just cards) in 2022. The runner-up finished with 1.4 million.

PSA grades everything from cards to tickets and even Funko Pops. Generally considered the go-to service for modern and ultra-modern sports categories, cards graded by PSA often carry a price premium on the secondary market. Cards graded by PSA are easily identifiable by a thin, clear holder and a label with a red border. The simplicity of the label and the holder are a major selling point for the company.

>> **SGC (Sportscard Guaranty):** Founded in 1998, submission returns are called "Tuxedo Time," a callout to SGC's iconic black matting and white label. Collectors often associate SGC with expertise in grading vintage cards. While PSA-graded cards can carry a secondary-market premium for many other categories, many collectors apply that same value to SGC and vintage cards. This isn't a blanket rule, though many collectors will *only* grade with SGC, and a good number of those have large vintage collections.

>> **BGS (Beckett Grading Services):** Founded in 1999, BGS is an extension of the Beckett brand of magazines and price guides started in the 1980s. If you collected sports cards in the 1980s and 1990s, there's an extremely high chance you opened a *Beckett Price Guide* at some point and skimmed for a card price.

Known for thicker slabs that are also great for holding memorabilia cards, BGS has long been a favorite of detail-oriented collectors because it provides something PSA and SGC don't: subgrades. Labels for PSA and SGC provide identifying information for the card, the final grade, and an ID number, but nothing else. Beckett takes it a step further and provides grading transparency with subgrades. If requested during your submission process, Beckett will provide you with the individual grades for centering, corners, edges, and surface that make up your final grade. This aspect has made BGS the *only* option for many collectors despite PSA and SGC taking on a much larger market share since 2020.

>> **CGC (Certified Sports Guaranty):** Although PSA, SGC, and BGS have spent decades building trust with the community, newer companies can also be trusted with your business. One example is CGC. Already a leading source for graded comics, the CGC brand has carved out a following in categories like Pokémon, Marvel, and sports cards. CGC Cards was formed when CGC Trading Cards and CSG (Certified Sports Guaranty) merged in 2023.

Beyond these four major services (see Figures 7-5 through 7-8), finding companies with an established track record in authentication and grading can be difficult. Companies like TAG (Technical Authentication Grading) have gained traction in the hobby due to their use of computer and machine vision and transparent grading reports. However, it still trails behind the other four services in popularity.

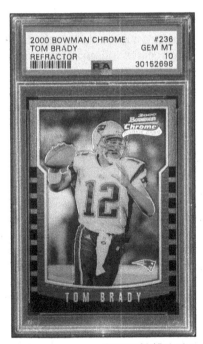

Courtesy of Goldin Auctions

FIGURE 7-5: 2000 Bowman Chrome Refractor Tom Brady, PSA 10

Courtesy of Goldin Auctions

FIGURE 7-6: 2000 Bowman Chrome Refractor Tom Brady, BGS 9.5

Courtesy of Goldin Auctions

FIGURE 7-7: 2000 Bowman Chrome Refractor Tom Brady, SGC 10

Courtesy of Goldin Auctions

FIGURE 7-8: 2000 Bowman Chrome Tom Brady, CSG 8

REMEMBER

Choosing the right grader is one of the most important decisions you can make for your collection. A cool label and a great price don't always mean a grader is right for you. In fact, many graders outside the above list don't authenticate cards at all. Your card will be assigned a numerical score for the condition, but that doesn't mean the card is real or hasn't been altered. The hobby's most trusted companies also have higher-quality slabs that are studier and harder to tamper with. When it comes to choosing the right grading service, it's important to do your own research and find the right fit. But there's also a reason you don't see many of these smaller companies at card shows or in online marketplaces often. Don't turn an easy decision into a hard one.

Grading scales and numerical values

As the preceding section reveals, there are plenty of differences between the major grading services — different slabs, labels, and areas of expertise. Here's the best part: They all have different grading scales, too. Did you think a PSA 10 would have the same meaning as a BGS 10? That's wrong. What about a BGS 9.5 and a PSA 9.5? A PSA 9.5 doesn't even exist.

The convenient part of grading services is that they evaluate a series of variables on your card and turn it into a single number on a scale of 1 to 10. The frustrating part is that those numbers from 1 to 10 don't mean the same thing across each company, and it can be a mess to sort out. It's best to visit each company's website directly to confirm the numerical scale before submitting your cards. These scales can be fluid and may change to better fit the needs of the hobby at the time.

However, similar terms are used across the various companies, and they often align in spirit if not in exact value. Terms like Good, Excellent, Near Mint, and Mint often fall in similar numerical values across the companies, and Gem Mint is typically considered the top condition that can be regularly achieved. For example, a card in Gem Mint condition receives a 10 from PSA, SGC, and CGC but a 9.5 from BGS. It's important to know that Gem Mint doesn't mean perfect, as there's always some wiggle room with subjective evaluation. Graders like BGS, SGC, and CSG also have terms like Perfect or Pristine that fall on the scale as a 10 but describe the card as nearly — if not completely — flawless.

The grading process

If you've already evaluated your cards for condition and set aside only the best of the best to be graded, the next step is deciding why you want to submit them. If you only want cards for your personal collection, consider submitting whatever you want — it's your collection, and you should collect what you like and how you like. If the goal is to make money by selling cards from this submission, you'll want to research how much your cards could be worth after grading and consider the cost of the process itself. Is there enough room for profit? That's up to you to decide. Valuing your cards and selling them is covered more in Chapters 15 and 16.

Now is also the time to pick a grading company if you haven't already. Refer to the previous sections on the grading services and their scales. Pick the company that best fits your cards, budget, and personal preference, and ensure that you're happy with the grading scale you'll receive.

Once your cards are selected and evaluated, you'll need to prepare them to be shipped. This process is extremely important, as you don't want any damage to occur during shipping. You'll want to visit the grading service's website to see the exact requirements, but below, we include a general step-by-step guide.

1. Protect the cards.

While some companies don't have strict requirements for protecting your cards during shipping, the widely accepted practice is to place each card inside a semi-rigid holder. These are often called Card Savers, the name of a popular brand of semi-rigid holders.

Semi-rigid holders come in various sizes and are preferred over Toploaders and One-Touch holders because they allow very little movement when being shipped but allow the cards to be removed easily without damaging them. More information about protecting and displaying your cards is found in Chapter 9.

2. Fill out the form.

Each grading service will require you to fill out a form for your order. This form will identify the type of service you've requested and details about the items you sent. This is where you'll select whether you'd like your items to have a numerical grade or just be authenticated and encapsulated. If your cards feature autographs, this is where you can request to have the signature authenticated and graded. Find each form on the grader's official website and take care filling it out, as mistakes here can slow down the entire process and delay when you get your items back. Submissions with different types of items (cards, tickets, Funko Pops) require different forms.

This form is also where you'll choose your service level. A service level refers to how quickly you want your cards to return. The faster the return, the more it typically costs. It's also important to know that cards of certain values are only eligible for specific service levels. As an example, PSA's Value Service may cost $25 per card to submit, but cards at that level must have a declared value of $499 or less. Declared value is the estimated value of the card after grading. The tier above Value, called Regular, allows cards to have a declared value of up to $1,499 but costs $75 per card. If you have a card with a declared value of $1,000, it would be eligible for Regular but not Value. Choosing the right declared value is important, as some companies will upcharge after grading. This practice is controversial, as the value chosen by the grading company may differ from what the card is worth on the open market.

TIP

Watch for grading specials across the different companies. Like your local chain store, grading companies will run sales, often targeting specific categories of cards (Baseball, Football, *Star Wars*) or eras (Vintage, Modern, Ultra-Modern).

REMEMBER

You must also list your items on the form in the order they are packaged inside the box. If you place a stack of 20 cards together, the form needs to reflect that same sequence.

Once completed, you'll print multiple copies of this form, keeping one for yourself while placing the other copies inside the box.

3. **Pack the box.**

With your forms inside the box, carefully place your cards inside with little room for movement. Collectors will often fill the inside of the box with bubble wrap and package cards into stacks. If you're shipping 40 cards, consider splitting that into two 20-card stacks and wrapping each in bubble wrap. You could even place five cards with their semi-rigid holders into a team bag to keep them secured together.

TIP

A team bag is a plastic bag sized for the item(s) in question. Made to hold either small stacks of loose cards or cards packed in semi-rigid holders, Toploaders, or one-touches, these bags feature re-sealable closures that allow the top of the bag to be temporarily closed and reopened several times before the seal loses its stickiness. Team bags can be purchased in packs of 25 or more and add an extra layer of protection for your cards.

4. **Ship the box.**

Once your box has been packed and sealed, you'll need to mail it to the proper address. For a company like PSA, there are various addresses to send to depending on the type of collectible you're submitting. Visit your grader's official website for the exact addresses and confirm the accepted mailing services, as the one you've chosen may accept FedEx but not UPS.

TIP

Consider purchasing additional insurance for your package. These are valuable collectibles that you don't want lost in the mail. Some collectors have also been known to ship with extreme caution, splitting a large, valuable submission into two smaller ones to mitigate risk. Once your items are graded, they'll be shipped back to you. Don't expect the grader to pay return shipping.

While intimidating at first, submission processes are quite straightforward. You'll get the hang of it. You'll also be able to follow along with the process at each step. Once your grading service has received your submission, you'll generally be able to follow the process in a tracker. From authentication to grading, labeling, and quality control, you'll always know where your cards are.

TIP

If this process still seems overwhelming to you, you're not alone. Consider finding a "group submitter" who will do this process for you for a fee. Verified group submission dealers can be found on your grading company's website and can handle much of this process for you. In addition to handling the forms and shipping, group submission dealers can package multiple orders into one to get better pricing and faster turnaround times. Many also offer exclusive grading discounts or pre-screening services to give your cards a second evaluation for condition before being submitted. Consider checking with your local card shop, as many offer group submission services.

TIP

Once your cards are returned, consider recording yourself unboxing your cards. In addition to having a record of any issues that could pop up, grading return videos are a great source of entertainment in the sports card hobby. Your friends will love it, and the community will enjoy it, too. If you're an aspiring hobby content creator, consider starting with a grading return.

3

The Basics of Buying and Collecting

1909 T206 Honus Wagner

1933 Goudey Babe Ruth

1948 Leaf Jackie Robinson

1952 Topps Mickey Mantle

1979 O-Pee-Chee Wayne Gretzky

1980 Topps Scoring Leader Larry Bird, Julius Erving, and Magic Johnson

1986 Fleer Michael Jordan

1989 Upper Deck Ken Griffey Jr.

2000 Playoff Contenders Championship Ticket Autograph Tom Brady

2003-04 Exquisite Collection Rookie Patch Autograph LeBron James

2009 Bowman Chrome Draft Prospects Refractors Autograph Mike Trout

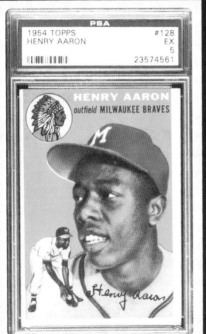

1954 Topps Hank (Henry) Aaron

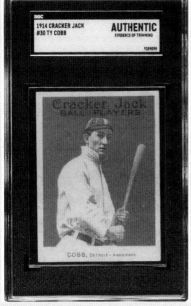

1914 Cracker Jack Ty Cobb

1887 Allen & Ginter Cap Anson

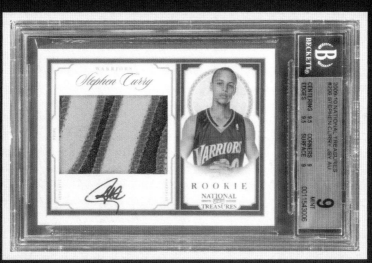

**2009-10 National Treasures Stephen Curry Rookie
Patch Autograph**

**2019-20 Panini Chronicles
Luminance Bronze Ja Morant**

1952 Topps Willie Mays

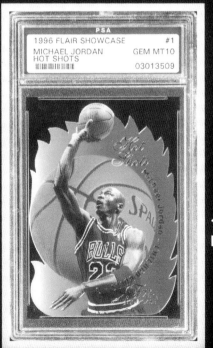

**1996 Flair Showcase Hot Shots
Michael Jordan**

**2019 Panini Kaboom!
Gold Patrick Mahomes**

1965 Topps Joe Namath

1948 Leaf Stan Musial

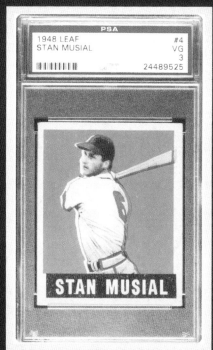

**2020 Bowman Chrome Refractor
Tom Brady**

**2004-05 Panini Megacracks
Lionel Messi**

1951 Bowman Mickey Mantle

Chapter **8**

Deciding What Kind of Collector You Will Be

t's good to have a plan, and collecting sports cards is no exception. We cover the basics of buying cards to build your collection in the next chapter, but it's good for you to be focused before dedicating any significant amount of your budget to collecting.

You can collect how you want, of course, so don't feel too much pressure to have a ten-step plan when first diving in.

In this chapter, we help you keep your collecting journey on target by building goals while maximizing your budget to meet them.

Setting Your Collecting Goals

Before you buy another card, ask yourself this: What is my objective with collecting? Are you looking to have fun, or are you looking to flip cards for a profit? Do you want to impress your friends and family with a rare and impressive collection, or do you want to feel closer to your favorite players and teams with their key cards?

There is no *right* answer here, but setting goals early is important for maximizing your budget.

Setting realistic expectations

When it comes to setting your collecting goals, it's important that you first consider what is achievable. Most collectors would love to own a museum-worthy lineup that impresses all, but this just isn't realistic budget-wise for most collectors.

Setting goals based on what your budget allows, how much space you can spare to store your collection, and the amount of time you can dedicate to collecting overall is critical. This is meant to be a hobby — first and foremost — and it's not worth damaging your personal financial obligations to participate.

If your budget is $50 a month, stick to that. If there's a card out there for $100 that you want, it means you may need to take a month off and roll your budget over. You can also consider selling cards to fund the purchase of others. If you're operating on a tight budget, consider regular collection audits. If a card is no longer super exciting to you, consider selling it to fund the purchase of something that is. There's nothing wrong with regularly selling parts of your collection to make it better.

You can also consider "trading up" to get items that may be out of your current budget. If a key card for your collection is a little too expensive in a PSA 10, consider purchasing a PSA 9 and then combining that card with your budget later to get the 10. Many collectors also use other grading companies like SGC, BGS, and CGC, and cards of the same or similar condition can often be had for a discount relative to PSA 10 prices. Buying a card in a slightly lower grade is a common compromise for many collectors to get a key card now without breaking their budget.

REMEMBER

Along with your budget, two other key components of collecting are time and patience. Your collecting goals don't need to be completed immediately. In fact, part of the fun of collecting is slowly building up to completing goals. Even if your budget allows you to complete a goal quickly, consider taking your time or increasing your number of goals. Collecting cards is a lifelong journey for many, so feel free to take your time and enjoy the ride.

Quality versus quantity

The physical space you can commit to collecting is also extremely important. How to properly store and protect your cards is covered more in Chapter 9, but the key concept to know now is that you need space for your collection. A small apartment can mean that your collection needs to be more curated, while a home with plenty of storage can allow you to buy with volume. In short, don't try to buy one million Chicago Cubs cards if you have no place to put them — even if you have the budget for it.

Start off with a small, curated collection and grow your collection size as budget and space allows. It's much easier to start small and go bigger than it is to trim your collection down and offload cards you no longer want or can afford to keep.

Tips for staying on track

Setting a collecting goal is easy. Staying on track is easier said than done. Collecting sports cards is an especially tricky hobby because you'll constantly be tempted by a nearly endless number of cards *perfect* for your collection.

Stay strong, friends. Below, you'll find some tips to keep you on the path.

Setting buying priorities

We'll cover the different types of collectors shortly, but it's a good idea to keep your purchasing priorities updated when you do know what you're looking for. You don't need to buy the cards you want as soon as you see them, and it's a much better idea to shop around and take your time.

Consider creating a ranking of the players you plan to collect in order of priority and take it into account when buying. You'll likely be faced with scenarios where you could snag three cards of your number two-ranked player instead of one card of your number one-ranked player. These things matter to your budget, and it's better to be prepared than not.

Taking this a step further, it's important to understand how much certain players cost when you develop your priorities. Buying a current star QB will be much more expensive than a top-tier tight end, so how far your budget will go is something to always be aware of.

Avoiding FOMO

The Fear of Missing Out is a card collector's number one enemy. You will be tempted to purchase for a variety of reasons. Don't give into hype, story lines, and what you think other hobbyists are doing at the time. Collectors often flock to buy cards of players doing incredible things in the moment, so this can often result in the highest prices and might be the worst time to buy.

TIP

Remember that prices going up after a big moment isn't guaranteed. In fact, it's not uncommon for players to have high prices because collectors believe they will *eventually* achieve something — think an MVP or championship. This can sometimes result in prices for a player going down after a title win because the season is over, and interest in the sport will fade for some time.

Buying players when they are most relevant is certainly fun, but be careful to purchase at the right price. Prices will almost definitely go down in the offseason, and you can buy at a discount. You can even sell the most hyped players to make a profit before buying back into them when their prices have regressed.

If you're unsure of a purchase, feel free to walk away. Outside of a few exceptions, that card will almost *always* pop up again and might be in your price range.

Collection tracking and online cataloging

There are few better ways to stay on target than by tracking your collection. This doesn't have to be complicated; many hobbyists simply use a plain accounting-style document to keep things organized. A simple Excel document or a Google Sheets page is a great start.

For something with more depth and pricing data, consider the (shameless plug incoming) My Collection feature from Market Movers. In addition to basic cataloging, My Collection allows you to track prices for individual cards as well as the value of your entire collection.

Depending on your tracking needs, other tools like the crowdsourced Trading Card Database (www.tcdb.com) are also worth using.

TIP

In addition to tracking apps and sites, consider sharing your collection on social media to catalog your card-collecting journey. Platforms like Instagram, X, Discord, and Facebook have extremely robust communities, and finding a group with similar interests won't take long.

Picking Your Personal Collection Themes

At this point, you should understand how many cards you want to collect and how much you can afford to spend. If you don't, we recommend skimming through the previous section to get you prepared. With a budget and achievable goals in mind, you can start conceptualizing the types of cards you will buy.

As we cover in the previous section, most collectors focus on a handful of themes for their collection. Along with the number and value of cards, themes include players, teams, sets, and beyond. Focusing on a theme is often particularly beneficial to newer collectors because they can learn and master specific types of cards instead of stretching themselves too thin across the entire universe of cards.

What kind of collector are you?

There are almost unlimited themes for you to pursue in the sports card hobby, and while we recommend starting with just a few at most, the scope of your collection is completely up to you. It's perfectly acceptable to buy only Mike Trout cards if you want. You can also collect any card that you find cool at the moment if you'd like. There's no right number of themes for your collection, but we have some popular ones below to get you started.

Player and team collectors

Undoubtedly the most common type of collector, many hobbyists largely focus on specific teams and players. This is a simple concept and involves focusing on a few specific teams and often favorite players from those teams. For example, a collector from Atlanta may focus their energy on a mix of the Braves, Falcons, and Hawks with a priority on Ronald Acuna Jr., Matt Ryan, and Trae Young.

While pro franchises are the most popular teams by far, some hobbyists focus on their favorite colleges or alma maters, too. Along with buying collegiate products, these collectors may target players who attended those schools regardless of their pro teams.

Set collectors

Though less popular in the Ultra-Modern Era, many hobbyists consider themselves set collectors. These collectors will focus on completing an entire set of specific products — a common goal is the complete set of Topps Series 1 Baseball and Series 2 Baseball every year. Beyond collecting the Base set, some collectors will also add in the insert or autograph sets. Set collecting is especially popular in vintage sports card circles.

Many collectors will also combine the concepts of collecting teams or players with set collecting. These hobbyists may strictly focus on collecting all cards of a specific team within a set. Rather than completing all Base cards from Topps Series 1, they may focus on just the Atlanta Braves from year to year.

Autograph and memorabilia collectors

Some of the most desirable cards in the hobby have autographs or pieces of memorabilia, so you can imagine that these cards also end up being some of the most collected. Some hobbyists even attempt to finish complete sets with an autograph on every card.

Hobbyists will not only chase autographs and memorabilia of their favorite players through packs but also travel to card shows and other events to have their own items signed. A strong lineup of signers can make a good show a great one, and the autograph pavilion at the National Convention is one of its biggest draws every year.

In addition to securing autographs in person, many hobbyists collect Through the Mail (TTM). This process includes sending items to an athlete's home or business with the hope that they be returned with an autograph. An extremely passionate and organized community of hobbyists dedicates much of their time to securing autographs this way. For a small annual fee, SportsCollectors.net (www.sportscollectors.net) — usually referred to as SCN — is considered the go-to resource for TTM autograph collecting. There, you can find addresses, fee information, and much more. You can even track your requests and share your successes with other collectors. Sports Card Forum (www.sportscardforum.com) is a free resource that includes some of the same features found on SCN.

Another way to obtain autographs is through "private signings," where a promoter gathers items from collectors and gets them signed by an athlete in a private setting for a fee. The promoter then returns the signed items to the collectors who paid to have them signed. Several Facebook groups are devoted to private signings and are a great resource.

TIP

Many sports memorabilia shows around the country feature appearances from some of the biggest names in sports who are there to sign for fans (usually for a fee). This is a great way to meet your heroes and get your items signed. However, if you cannot attend a show in person, check with the show promoters to see if they accept mail-in autograph requests. Many shows allow collectors to prepay and mail in their items for signature. After the show is over, they'll mail your signed items back to you.

Era collectors

Some hobbyists are passionate about a specific era of cards and focus heavily on collections from certain years rather than teams and players. This can be for a variety of reasons, though some common ones are design, rarity, and value.

While not always exceptionally rare, tobacco cards from the pre-war era are common targets for some collectors due to their design as well as the wide variety of sports and non-sports sets available to collect. You'll also find that '90s collectors are among the most passionate (and sometimes most opinionated).

Sport and brand collectors

Often pairing it with set collecting, some hobbyists strictly follow a single sport and, thus, heavily focus on those cards. It's not uncommon for some collectors to be exclusively focused on football, baseball, basketball, or other single sports.

Because of how exclusive licensing rights work with trading cards, which we cover more in Chapter 6, some collectors may focus heavily on brands like Topps Chrome Baseball, Upper Deck Hockey, or Panini Prizm Basketball.

Other unique collecting styles

Although basic concepts are often the most common, don't be shocked to find collectors that get extremely specific in what they target. Collecting styles can include specific parallels beyond the themes we cover earlier — basic refractors or color parallels matching the team's jersey are common.

Some collectors may strictly target short-printed image variations or even serial-numbered cards matching the player's number (think cards numbered 15/99 for Patrick Mahomes's No. 15 jersey).

The rise of parallels during the Ultra-Modern Era has also introduced the concept of "rainbow" collecting, where every parallel (see Figure 8-1) for a specific player within a set is acquired. These rainbows can feature any number of cards, from just a handful to two dozen or more.

Courtesy of Goldin Auctions

FIGURE 8-1: 2014 Joel Embiid Prizm Rainbow Lot

Some themes are certainly more difficult than others, but at this point, if you can think of it, some collector out there is likely trying to do it.

Chapter 9

Buying Basics and Building Your Collection

C hances are, if you're reading this book, you've either already purchased cards or plans to do so soon. For many, the acquisition of cards is the highlight of their collecting journey. You can buy through online retailers and marketplaces, or you can get social at local card shops and shows.

However, there will be challenges ahead wherever you choose to do business. Marketplaces come in all shapes and sizes, and they aren't created equal. In fact, the different places to purchase cards all present various advantages and disadvantages. While online marketplaces often provide the largest selection, they also require shipping and handling before getting your cards. Local card shops and shows have a more personal touch but will offer less inventory to choose from.

In this chapter, we help you buy cards to build your collection while scoring great deals from the most trusted marketplaces in the hobby.

Buyer's Market

Before you start buying any cards — if you haven't before— it's important to know what you're getting when you purchase. Generally, you can make several types of purchases — all covered in this chapter.

Sealed products

Many new hobbyists start their collecting experience by opening packs and boxes known as "sealed products." Because they were once made from wax material, packs are often called "sealed wax" or "wax packs," even when they are made from other materials, such as foil.

At the most basic level, sealed products are easy to understand. Each box contains a set number of packs, and each pack contains a set number of cards.

REMEMBER

Cards come in a variety of formats. Sometimes, you can purchase individual packs from an open box, but sometimes the boxes are sealed, so you must purchase the entire box.

There are also a variety of configurations of sealed products, though they are typically broken into two formats: retail and hobby. Hobby configurations are generally only found in hobby stores, directly through the manufacturer, and online through major trading card retailers. These are more expensive but generally offer better odds at pulling the best cards. Retail configurations are found in stores like Target, Walmart, pharmacies, and grocery stores. These formats are cheaper and typically offer a smaller chance at the best cards.

TIP

Don't forget to check the types of cards included in each format before you consider buying. To promote the purchase of each format, manufacturers will often make certain cards available only in specific configurations. This may mean that a certain parallel is only found in blaster boxes, but a specific insert set is only found in hobby boxes.

TIP

A deeper dive into checklists and product configurations can be found in Chapter 4.

It should be noted that while opening sealed products may be an easy way to acquire a high volume of cards, it's not the most cost-effective way to secure the best cards. Remember, most cards in a sealed box or pack likely won't be the major chase cards — unless you're lucky enough to score a hot pack. Considered extremely rare, hot packs are individual packs almost exclusively filled with major chase cards. The manufacturer purposefully creates these to deliver a pleasant surprise to the buyer.

Some set collectors build a set through sealed products because they need many cards to complete the set. Other collectors also only purchase sealed products, as the thrill and experience of opening packs are just as important as owning the card at all. You can learn more about the different types of collectors in Chapter 8.

REMEMBER

Opening sealed product is some of the most fun you can have in the hobby, but buying the exact cards you want is the most cost-effective way to build your collection. Of course, if you have a large budget for collecting and only want to open sealed products, go right ahead — this is your hobby, and you should enjoy it how you want. Most hobbyists can't collect this way, however, so more budget-friendly options are needed.

Box breaks

Buying into box breaks can sometimes be considered a more budget-friendly option when dealing with sealed products. Rather than buying an entire box, breaks allow collectors to purchase a *piece* of the sealed product, often opened live on a streaming platform. Box breaks work by allowing collectors to purchase the rights to potential cards in the box before it's opened. This may be a specific team or a specific player. For example, you could purchase the rights to the Atlanta Braves for a lower price than what the entire box costs. You'll then win any Atlanta Braves cards that come out of the box — if any do.

Unfortunately, the value proposition for box breaks is that while you pay less than what an entire box costs, you also risk coming away with nothing if the category you selected comes up empty. In some cases, you can purchase the rights to a specific card within a pack. In this example, you would be awarded the first card in the pack or the fifth card in the pack. This guarantees you come away with *something*.

Slots for box breaks are also priced accordingly. The teams with the best chances at top cards are more expensive, and teams with fewer great cards are typically cheaper. You can also choose a random break, which has every participant pay the same price, but the categories are randomly assigned before the break starts. There are dozens of ways for breaks to operate, depending on your personal preference.

TIP

Countless individuals and companies offer box breaks, and you should consider shopping around for the best value if you choose to participate. Check prices for the category you're looking to buy into before selecting a breaker, as prices can be drastically different. Also, consider buying into breaks with people you enjoy watching and engaging with. In addition to strong pricing, many breakers provide additional value because the overall experience is entertaining. Consider what matters to you and find the right breaker based on your preferences.

REMEMBER

Although buying into box breaks can be a slightly better value proposition for some collectors, there's still much risk involved. Buying the exact card you want will almost always be the most cost-effective collection method. Spend your money how you like, but consider whether the entertainment aspect of breaks or sealed products is worth the risk.

Singles

Buying singles is exactly what it sounds like. You buy single copies of the exact cards you're searching for. No more hoping for the best when opening a pack or box. In most cases, this is *the* most cost-effective way to collect for those on a budget.

Although desirable cards will often be more expensive than an entire box, it's important to remember that the chances of you pulling that card are extremely low. Even if a card is more expensive than an entire box, you will almost always spend more money searching through packs than just buying exactly what you're looking for. Sure, you could get lucky. But the odds are not in your favor.

Lots

Lots might be for you if you want to split the difference between singles and sealed products. A lot is a larger group of cards purchased all at once. For example, you could buy a "lot" of 50 Chipper Jones cards. You'll get a good volume of single cards without opening sealed products in hopes of finding them.

Searching for lots is a great way to build out your collection if you're just starting to collect a team or player. You likely won't find many hidden gems, but it's a great way to add volume at an affordable price.

TECHNICAL STUFF

This term shouldn't be confused with *auction lots*. Auction houses refer to individual auctions as lots, but a lot isn't always for a group of cards. For example, an auction house might refer to a single card as a lot because doing so is easier for them and bidders to track. Let's say there are three separate auctions for 1954 Topps Hank Aaron rookie cards. Rather than referring to each in a complex way to separate one auction from another, the auction house might refer to them as Lots 404, 405, and 406.

Online Marketplaces and Retailers

Now that you know the different ways of buying cards, it's important to know *where* you can safely purchase cards. Again, not all marketplaces are created equal. Some offer many low-dollar cards, but others focus on high-end pieces.

A combination of marketplaces and retailers will likely be best for your collecting journey. There is certainly an amount of brand loyalty in card collecting, but most hobbyists use multiple marketplaces to find what they need.

When it comes to overall volume, online marketplaces and retailers are the best options. More options can also mean better prices, but you'll need to shop around. Below is a list of trusted retailers and online marketplaces and a brief description of what you can expect from each. This list is not exhaustive but does cover many of the shopping essentials.

eBay

When it comes to buying cards online, the discussion must start with eBay. Founded in 1995, eBay has become a marketplace for countless types of items and the go-to for sports and trading cards of all kinds.

Millions of cards are sold on eBay each year, and it's hard to argue against the selection offered here. Although some high-end cards are sold on eBay, the platform is typically used for less-expensive cards.

The platform also offers multiple ways to buy cards, including auctions, fixed price "Buy It Now," and "Best Offer" listings.

REMEMBER

Though eBay is a great place to find deals, shipping costs aren't standardized across the platform. Some sellers may look to make a few extra bucks by charging more for shipping when they don't need to. Shipping methods vary by seller, so make sure that the $4.99 shipping option is a bubble mailer, not a plain envelope. This is especially important when purchasing high-value cards. A bubble mailer is great for most cards, but your $500 Ted Williams deserves to be shipped in something sturdy with insurance.

COMC

Short for Check Out My Cards, COMC is a massive marketplace of mostly low-dollar cards. Shipping and handling can be a massive added cost when buying online, and COMC helps curb that by allowing you to store your cards with them before shipping a bulk lot at once. A great option for shipping multiple cards, COMC might not always be the best option for buying and shipping a single card at a time. COMC's site is also set up as a structured database of complete checklists of products. As such, it's a great way to explore which cards exist for different players and in different products.

Although COMC sells various high-end and graded cards, the collecting community mostly associates COMC with low-dollar raw cards. Many of COMC's items are also cross-listed on a platform like eBay.

MySlabs

Founded in 2019, MySlabs launched with a priority on protecting buyers and sellers from bad actors. Transacting online can sometimes result in buyers or sellers backing out of sales or refusing to pay, and MySlabs focuses on limiting those poor interactions while also offering low buying and selling fees.

Originally featuring only graded cards, MySlabs has since expanded to also offer raw cards and sealed products.

Alt

Another relatively new platform, Alt combines a variety of features into one. Alt focuses on graded cards, and along with a fixed-price marketplace and regular high-end auctions, buyers and sellers can store their cards in the vaulting service. Like COMC, buyers can keep their purchases with Alt for easy selling or save them for shipping all at once. Many of the cards listed on Alt are also listed on eBay.

Blowout Cards

Founded in 1999, Blowout Cards is one of the largest online card retailers in the world. Blowout Cards is best known for selling sealed products and offers single cards and box breaks.

Dave and Adam's Card World

Dave and Adam's, or DACW for short, is another trusted major online retailer that focuses on delivering sealed products. In addition to sealed wax, DACW also carries a selection of singles and offers box breaks.

Others worth considering

Though less popular than some previously listed marketplaces, Sportlots has an extremely robust selection of sports and non-sports cards. The platform Mercari is also sometimes used as an alternative to eBay.

Even though they are not exclusively trading card sellers, big-box stores like Target and Walmart often carry a selection of cards. In fact, this is where you'll find retail products for the intended retail price. Although marketplaces like those listed above may have a larger selection, prices on these items will be higher, as they are considered the secondary market.

Buying directly from retailers like Target and Walmart and even pharmacies like Walgreens or CVS can net you the best retail prices on sealed products, but selection and availability are always challenging. It's also critical to know that these online and in-person locations carry only retail configurations and won't include hobby boxes.

Take It to the (Auction) House

When it comes to buying or selling cards, online marketplaces are great for what most collectors consider to be low- or mid-end cards. When buying or selling high-end cards —generally in the thousands at the lowest — auction houses may offer a better experience.

Buying or selling through auction houses often includes additional fees not found with other marketplaces, but they offer other services that make the additional costs worth it. In general, auction houses offer a more premium experience.

When buying, you can expect additional protections, like a guarantee that the items are authentic. Mistakes can happen, of course, but working with an auction house can make you whole if something goes wrong. When selling, you can sometimes receive additional promotions for key items, ensuring that your item is put in front of the *right* collectors, not just the most collectors.

It should be noted that many auction houses now also include more traditional fixed-price marketplaces that aren't much different than a platform like eBay. However, the platforms listed below are most associated with weekly or monthly auctions that feature high-end pieces.

Goldin Auctions

Founded by Ken Goldin, Goldin Auctions regularly features some of the most desired cards and collectibles and has sold some of the most expensive cards ever. The company is featured in the Netflix show *King of Collectibles: The Goldin Touch*. Goldin Auctions also offers a vaulting service through its parent company, Collectors Holding Company, which also owns PSA grading.

PWCC

Founded in 1998, PWCC has been a major seller of cards and collectibles in the hobby for decades. PWCC also offers a vaulting service for hobbyists. Fanatics Collectibles acquired the Oregon-based company in May 2023

Heritage Auctions

A major auction house featuring cards, comics, art, and other collectibles, Heritage has been a trusted seller since 1976. Heritage has been a seller of some of the hobby's most expensive cards, including a 1952 Topps Mickey Mantle SGC 9.5 that sold for $12.6 million in 2022.

Others worth considering

Collectors can also trust a variety of other auction houses, including Lelands, Memory Lane, Mile High, Pristine, Robert Edwards Auctions, and SCP Auctions.

It's Always Personal

Shopping online is great, but sometimes you need to stretch your legs. When the occasion arises, try to get out and about by visiting local card shops, shows, and trade nights. These are great places to browse, learn, and even make friends. You might find a better variety online, but chatting with people in person is also nice.

Local card shops

A good local card shop (LCS) should be your first stop if you aren't buying online. No two are identical, and although some offer great prices and build relationships with their patrons, others sell at high prices. High-quality shops offer a service; you should consider giving them your business if possible.

Local card shops are especially good resources for information and news about the hobby and are a great place to make new friends.

If you're a fan of a local team or player, card shops should be your first stop in your card search. They'll likely carry a larger inventory of local teams and stars, so you can ideally scoop them up at a discount.

Much like card shows, card shops allow you to negotiate in person, and it can be easier to come to a deal this way. Building a great relationship with your local card shop is a great chance to become a bigger part of your collecting community and score some good deals down the line.

Card shows

Along with your local card shop, card shows are great places to buy in person. Honestly, it's just really fun to window-shop as you walk down the rows of dealers. This is also a great chance to see some cards you probably didn't even know existed before. Work through the showcases with a purpose, and you should be able to find some great cards worth adding to your collection.

Card shows are also a great place to meet new friends. Card show dealers can serve as great resources for learning about cards, and it turns out they are easy to befriend — your love of cards already gives you something to talk about. You can learn more about navigating a card show in Chapter 10.

Trade nights

If you want to take things a step further, local trade nights are great places to pick up cards. Mostly meant for trading, you can still buy and sell at these events. Local card shops are often the location for trade nights, so check to see if your favorite spot is hosting one soon.

If not at a local shop, trade nights are also commonly held after major card shows. If the show doesn't host an official trade night, you might find one (or two) unofficially in a hotel lobby close by with those who traveled into town.

Let's get social

Social media is a tricky place to make deals, but it's where many collectors go to cut out the various fees from online marketplaces. Facebook Marketplace can offer a wide variety of cards and collectibles to snag, and other platforms like Instagram and Discord have massive card-collecting communities perfect for transacting.

Although it's not hard to find buy, sell, or trade posts on these platforms, you must tread carefully. Platforms like Instagram and Discord aren't built for this type of commerce, so you'll need to be careful when doing business. Generally, someone may post a card for sale, and you'd agree to pay for it by posting something like "claim" under it. The payment is where things can get tricky.

In most instances, you'll be asked to pay using digital services like PayPal, Venmo, or Cash App, and you must use these apps' business features. Although using something like a "Friends and Family" transaction to avoid paying extra fees and taxes may seem nice, losing the business protections offered is seldom worth it unless you know and trust the seller. Consider paying while marking the transaction for "Goods and Services" to make sure you can access returns and other support if something goes wrong.

WARNING

The card-collecting community wants to give people the benefit of the doubt most of the time, but the reality is that scammers and other people are attempting to make a buck off you in any way they can. Be smart and protect yourself. It's better to be out a few dollars in fees than out an entire card and the cash you paid because the card was never shipped or was "lost" in the mail.

Great Deals (Aren't) Hard to Find

It's time to find some deals. Don't worry, it's easier than you think. When imagining getting a deal, you probably start by thinking about a negotiation ending closer to your original price than the seller's. Some of the best deals out there don't even require you to make an offer. In fact, some of the best deals exist because someone messed up and didn't notice. Here are some tips to navigate the negotiation and spot mistakes that could save you a few bucks (or more).

An honest mistake

We all make mistakes. We're humans, after all. Moving forward, we're not encouraging you to take advantage of a mistake in a way you might consider to be diabolical. A lack of attention to detail can help you score, though, and we consider that fair game.

Misspelled or mislabeled

Look, everyone makes a typo here or there. Or they spelled the name Trea Young instead of Trae Young. It happens. You'll probably do it plenty of times when searching for a player's cards. Next time you make a typo, though, peek at which cards pop up — the seller may have done the same thing, and fewer eyes are on that auction because of it.

Cards are often mislabeled, too, and you can use that to your advantage. Maybe a card is labeled Aqua instead of Blue, and that Blue variation might be numbered /99 instead of /199. Simple things like this pop up all the time. Your attention to detail — and the seller's lack of attention — could score you a nice deal.

Right place, right time

There is a right time and wrong time to end an online auction. Early morning on a Thursday? That's not great. Prime time on a Sunday? There could be lots of collectors settling in for a football game while scrolling for cards. Keep this in mind, and the next time you decide which cards to battle for, consider whether it has an odd ending window that you can be prepared for.

Chances are, if you're willing to put in extra effort, you could be bidding against yourself for a key card if you wake up early on a Saturday or stay up late on a weekday.

The great negotiator

Negotiating is an art form, but you don't need to be Picasso to get by in the hobby.

A major negotiating key is understanding that you and the seller have goals. You want a good deal, and they want to make money. In an ideal scenario, you'll offer below their initial price, they'll counter with something closer to it, and you'll both meet in the middle. This can be done both online and in person. Either way, do your research on recent pricing data, if applicable, and know for sure where a good deal sits. Negotiating at a card show is covered more in Chapter 10.

TIP

If using something like eBay's Make an Offer feature, you get a few shots at coming to a deal. Sellers can set a threshold where offers are automatically declined or accepted, and you can use that to your advantage. It's less likely that you'll offend a seller online with a low offer, so consider a significant discount this way. If it's automatically declined, you have some work to do. If not, you might be able to snag yourself a significant discount. You may also be able to leave notes with your offer, so consider politely making a case for it. The best sellers are open to this, and you might be able to sway them.

TIP

Even if an item is priced way above your budget, consider adding it to your eBay Watchlist anyway. Sometimes, sellers will make private offers to buyers watching their items. This is a great way to score a big deal if they are ready to move on.

If negotiating in person, avoid making an offensive low-ball offer. You'll have to look them in the eyes after. We cover negotiating and card shows more in Chapter 10, but most deals can be closed within a few offers from each side. If you're struggling, feel free to walk away and re-engage later.

REMEMBER

Stick to your budget, and don't make a deal you aren't comfortable with. The card you're negotiating over will almost always pop up again.

R-E-S-P-E-C-T

Don't be a jerk. It really is that simple. You're negotiating with a human, and being disrespectful with an extremely low offer does no one any good. A little research on recent sales should give you more than enough data to work with, and knowing that price range should also allow you to know if the seller is willing to get a deal done. It's possible to be direct, too, without being offensive. Try something like, "This card is listed for $200 but recently sold for around $175 several times. Could you do $170?" A brief explanation like this is more than enough, and any seller who is frustrated by that or isn't willing to come down doesn't need your business.

Be reasonable with sellers at card shops and card shows, and you might be surprised how one deal could turn into more down the line. Sellers can be willing to give you even better deals if they know you're easy to work with and will have your business down the line.

Displaying and Storing Your Collection

You need somewhere to put all the cards you're buying, right? Well, there's a right and a wrong way to protect, store, and display your collection.

If possible, you should decide early on where and how you'll store and display your collection. Deciding what kind of collector you are is covered in Chapter 8, and those collecting goals must align with the space you have. If you have lots of free storage space, buying in volume could be an option for you. A small and curated collection could be best if you have a small apartment or share space with others.

Before we get into specific types of holders and sleeves, we must cover some basic concepts. It's probably obvious, but cards don't mix well with things like water, sunlight, extreme temperatures, and basically anything that could leave some type of residue on them. (Sorry, no snacking.)

A good rule to follow is that a card should be stored in a covered box or bin and away from light or moisture unless on display with the proper protections. Things like sunlight can slowly destroy colors and autographs, so it is necessary to store your collection properly.

Penny sleeves, Toploaders, and other holders

The value of a card will greatly determine how much protection is given it, but every card deserves *some*. Even the cheapest cards in your collection deserve to be stored, at a minimum, in a covered box or bin — you don't know, after all, who might be a backup now and a star later. Even if some cards aren't extremely valuable, keeping them organized and out of the way is best. At worst, they are out of sight, out of mind. At best, they are organized well enough for you to easily retrieve something later. Beyond that, most collectors use card value as a gauge for a card's protection.

Clear sleeves

The clear sleeve is the most basic form of protection for an individual card. These soft and thin sleeves are often called *penny sleeves* and will protect cards from scratches, but not much more. Cards worth between $1 and $5 deserve a penny sleeve. It should be noted that penny sleeves need to be included when storing cards in hard sleeves like Toploaders, which we cover next.

Toploaders and semi-rigid holders

The next step up from clear sleeves is a tier with Toploaders and semi-rigid holders such as Card Savers. Toploaders are more rigid than penny sleeves and offer significantly more protection. Semi-rigid holders such as Card Savers are similar to Toploaders but are thinner and take up less space. They are also often the requested form of protection when submitting cards for grading because they protect while allowing cards to be easily removed.

TECHNICAL
STUFF

Clear sleeves *must* be included when using Toploaders to prevent the card from being scratched during insertion and removal. There is some debate about using sleeves with semi-rigid holders, but we recommend using them when in doubt or sending the card to someone else.

TIP

Consider using painter's tape to help secure the opening on Toploaders if the card inside could shift at all. This tape is recommended over others as it's easier to remove and doesn't leave a residue behind.

Magnetic holders

Sometimes called One-Touch holders, magnetic holders are solid cases held together by a magnet that secures two plastic pieces together. These holders offer protection but are often more associated with display. Cards can be shipped in magnetic holders, but many collectors prefer sleeves and Toploaders instead. When it comes to displaying cards for eye appeal, magnetic holders are a popular choice for raw cards due to their simple and clear design. Magnetic holders replaced older, popular screw-down holders in the '80s and '90s. These holders could damage the cards by being over-tightened.

Team bags

Typically meant for storing stacks of raw cards together, team bags have grown in popularity to cover graded cards, Toploaders, and magnetic holders. These clear plastic bags are typically resealable and really only prevent scratches. Honestly, they are sort of a way to protect the protection. Some of the holders we cover above are susceptible to scratches, and it's much cheaper to replace a plastic team bag than a graded card or magnetic holder.

Boxes and bins

As we mention above, all cards deserve a little protection, and boxes and bins are the most basic option for groups of cards. The most popular set of boxes are called "shoe" boxes and are typically plain cardboard with a varying number of rows for organization. These boxes can hold from 50 cards to numbers in the thousands.

For something sturdier, some companies offer card bins, just plastic versions of cardboard shoe boxes. Boxes and bins are ideal for storing large groups of cards because they provide adequate protection and organization and can also be stacked on each other.

TIP

Before we leave this section, it's important to note that the various types of protection come in different sizes based on the card stock. Clear sleeves, Toploaders, and magnetic holders come in different sizes, and your card needs to fit properly. More details about card stock and card thickness can be found in Chapter 7.

Fit for a museum

Assuming that your cards are properly protected, we can also explore displaying them for you to admire. There are some supplies to improve your card's overall presentation, whether on your work desk or a bookshelf.

Card stands

The most common display is a generic card stand, found online with a quick search for "trading card stands." These don't have to be complicated and can just be black, white, or clear, if you want. Beyond that, some companies such as Stand Up Displays offer custom stands that can feature everything from your own custom branding to team- and player-specific numbers and colors to match the card.

Graded card bumpers are also available to protect and display your slabbed cards — these often come in various colors, and many collectors will match the bumper to the card for extra eye appeal. These also shield the slab if dropped.

Beyond individual card stands or card bumpers, there's also a variety of small shelves meant to hold multiple cards in a row.

Wall displays

Want your card to display like a painting or a photo? There are plenty of options out there for you. An online search for a "trading card frame" will get you what you need and allow you to mount your cards on the wall.

Try to avoid direct sunlight, especially with wall displays. You may find a great location, but if it's regularly hit by direct sunlight, your card will slowly decay and won't be worth displaying.

Overall, displaying your cards is a great way to find joy in the hobby, but do not sacrifice protecting them for displaying them.

Chapter **10**

Navigating a Card Show Like a Pro

While online marketplaces and social media communities have made buying and selling easier than ever, attending card shows remains a core element of the sports card hobby.

From meetups with friends to in-person negotiating and the trade nights that often follow major shows, these events offer a social element that just can't be replicated online. And for some collectors, those elements are non-negotiable — card shows are the *only* way to do business.

In this chapter, you learn how to maximize your card show experience with etiquette, navigation, and negotiation tips.

Don't Forget the Essentials

Before we dive into topics like negotiating deals, it's important to cover a few tips that will benefit any card show attendee regardless of their objectives at the show. Whether you're buying, selling, or just window shopping, there are things you can do to improve your experience before you ever step onto the show floor.

Straight cash, Homie

Most serious card show dealers will accept digital payment services like PayPal, Venmo, and Cash App. But in truth, they just want your cash. In fact, many dealers prefer cash so much that they may even be willing to give you a discount.

Cash is preferred for a variety of reasons. Credit cards, debit cards, and digital payment services certainly provide convenience for the buyer but also bring additional fees for the seller. Though not common, sellers may also have to deal with payment disputes for charges after the show, which can be messy to clean up. Cash is an instant, guaranteed payment.

Some sellers may also prefer cash for tax reporting purposes. They may find it easier to track transactions with cash rather than digging through bank statements and digital payment transaction logs.

These shoes are made for walking

It may seem like a no-brainer, but you really do need to wear a nice pair of walking shoes to card shows. Depending on the show, you may be on your feet for hours with few to no places to sit and rest. This can be especially important for multi-day shows like the National Sports Collectors Convention. The impact of all-day walking may not be felt on day 1, but you'll certainly feel it by day 3. Do yourself a favor and come prepared with the proper footwear. Your feet, knees, and back will thank you.

Baggage claim

Whether you're at the show to buy or sell, you'll want something to keep your valuable cards safe and secure. Consider a carrying case meant for trading cards for your next show if you don't already own one.

Backpacks and other bags will certainly do the job, though those likely aren't meant for cards. A quick online search for a "trading card case" or "trading card bag" will return the proper results.

Considered by most as a luxury item for your collecting travels, these specialized cases are meant for cards and will often come with organized slots or adjustable foam that can fit your needs. Carrying cases and bags like these will help keep your cards secure and are designed to avoid scratching the holders on your graded cards.

REMEMBER

Whether upgrading to one of these cases or simply sporting your go-to backpack, remember to avoid leaving it unattended at any time.

Navigating the Chaos and Making a Deal

Card shows are one of the best experiences in the hobby for many collectors, but it's important to remember that they present their own types of challenges. We wish we could tell you that card shows are always organized effectively and are easy to navigate — but we'd be lying if we did. We also wish we could promise that dealers will always negotiate with good intentions, hoping to make a deal. Again, that's just not the case.

Fear not, collector. We have advice for the road ahead.

Needle in a haystack

Even if you've never been to a card show before, you've probably rightly assumed that even the smallest shows will have *tons* of cards. Even 50-table events will likely have tens of thousands of cards to sort through. So, how do you find what you're looking for?

As we mention earlier, card shows can be quite chaotic. Most shows lack organization or any intuitive layout of the floor plan. For example, rarely, if ever, will you find a show with a dedicated vintage section separate from ultra-modern cards. While some dealers buy and sell everything, many specialize in specific sports or eras, and it would benefit show attendees to be able to home in on these dealers. Because of a lack of organization, you'll have to cover a lot of ground going from table to table to check out what each dealer offers. It's not ideal, but it's reality.

It's best to come prepared with a list of priorities to maximize the amount of ground you can cover. You can certainly window-shop as you please, but you may not have enough time to do this comfortably at the largest shows with 1,000-plus tables. If you arrive with a list of priorities, you can cut through the noise some.

While shows struggle to organize dealers into major sections, the best dealers organize their tables into different categories. Use this to save yourself valuable time. If you're looking for an ultra-modern card, take a quick glance at the dealer's showcase — if you see mostly vintage, skip that table. Instead of looking for specific cards, try to spot larger themes when first approaching a table. You realistically won't find many Michael Jordan cards at a dealer if the first 50 you see are vintage baseball.

This concept isn't perfect, of course. Some dealers carry a mixture of sports and eras, but you may not always have the time to dissect each table. It's also important to remember that taking a quick glance and moving on is perfectly acceptable. This isn't rude or inappropriate. Making a quick decision respects the time of both you and the seller, and moving on quickly frees up that space for someone who might be more interested in browsing.

Deal or no deal

So, you've navigated some tables and found the card you're looking for. Now comes the fun part: the negotiation. A major advantage that card shows have over online marketplaces is the ability to negotiate prices. Many online listings may accept offers, but talking to the seller in person can make a major difference.

Dealers will also vary drastically in terms of how they price their cards. Some display prices, and some don't. Some update prices based on recent prices, while others don't. Some will be willing to negotiate, and some will take offense at the most reasonable offers. Going in with this expectation will help you easily identify the sellers who will be the best to work with. Dealers expect etiquette from buyers, and buyers have the right to expect the same in return.

Negotiating doesn't have to be difficult. In fact, it doesn't even have to happen at all. If you've researched a card and its price and feel comfortable, there's nothing wrong with purchasing it for the listed amount without further discussion. If you think there's room for improvement, then you can start the negotiation.

Before asking for pricing adjustments, it's extremely important to know the current market value of the card. You can read more about card valuation and data tools in Chapter 16. If the last five sales of a card online are all between $150 and $170, it's not acceptable to offer $100. If the card is listed for $200, you should have some wiggle room.

A common question buyers have for sellers is, "Do you have any room?" Phrasing it like this is a polite way of asking how much lower in price the seller can comfortably go. Even if that card sells for about $160, the seller may have gotten "into" the card for $180 and be reluctant to sell for a loss. (When to sell, even for a loss, is covered in more detail in Chapter 16.)

In an ideal scenario for both parties, a price that lands somewhere between the original sticker price and the buyer's offer is agreed upon.

You should also consider the cost of doing business when making an offer. It costs money to purchase the table space, and travel expenses can also add up. Consider this and remember that buying in person also cuts out shipping costs and possibly other fees and taxes.

This isn't an excuse for sellers to charge outrageous prices, but it's something to consider when making a deal. The best card show dealers provide a service and deserve your support when possible.

If you're searching for even better deals, consider buying or selling in bulk. Sellers will often offer a larger discount on a series of cards rather than just one. Some might consider giving a 10 percent deal on a single card, but 20 or 30 percent is preferable if the deal involves multiple cards.

For the best deals, the final day of a card show is the place to be. Sellers often look to liquidate inventory on the final day of a show and are more willing to make deals — selling aggressively on these days means there's less to take back home, while the cash can go into an inventory refresh for the next event.

One important note: if you want to avoid upsetting dealers, avoid asking, "What's the lowest you'll go?" It's an absurd question, no different from a dealer asking, "What's the most you'll pay?" Asking open-ended questions can indirectly get you the same punchline, but explicitly asking for a dealer's "lowest" is condescending and ineffective.

TIP

If you're attending a card show looking to sell to a dealer, remember they'll want to make money on your cards. Because of this, many dealers will offer to pay between 70 and 80 percent of a card's current value. Some will go lower, some higher. Expect to give your card's value a haircut to get a deal done this way.

Card Show Etiquette

We live in a society, so there are some unwritten rules of engagement when it comes to card shows. They aren't overly complicated and can improve the overall experience for buyers and sellers. More unwritten rules of the hobby are covered in Chapter 16.

Table manners

It's important to be respectful when interacting with dealers at card shows. We'll get to a healthy negotiation in a second, but proper manners start on the approach. Dealers will often offer a quick greeting and may ask what you're looking for. Something like "just browsing" is more than enough if you aren't ready to offer up a specific request.

Avoid putting your bag or carrying case on the table or glass showcase when browsing. Along with blocking the view of cards from other potential buyers, this can cause damage to the seller's setup. And *never* put food or drink near their cards. This is a simple show of respect for their space.

As we cover above, negotiations can be avoided altogether or, with prior price research, can be completed quickly. Feel free to pause and return later if you feel like you're not making progress. It's better to table discussions than force a deal that doesn't work for everyone.

Remember to make good faith offers that aren't far too low; hopefully, the dealer will do right by you with a counter that isn't too high. Working as a team toward a deal is better than a game of one-on-one.

Thank you for being a friend

Card shows are a great place to make friends — even with dealers. Get to know them, and they'll get to know you. Do you know what card dealers love more than a single slam dunk sale? Repeat customers. A great negotiation can turn into more down the line, and dealers may be willing to give you better deals if they know they'll have your business again.

Feel free to chat about who and what you collect, too. Few people understand the card market as deeply as some dealers, so they can often offer valuable insight into what you might be looking for. If you're lucky, they might even point you in the direction of what you're looking for — even if they don't have it — and may keep an eye out for you.

In general, it's better to have collecting friends than not, and your local card show dealers are no exception.

Plenty of fish in the sea

Sometimes, it's just not meant to be. It's possible that both the buyer and seller offer up fair prices, but a deal is hard to push past the finish line. It happens. Don't panic.

As a buyer, stick to your budget and don't overspend. Sellers also have their own goals and objectives for shows, so things may not always align. Don't burn a bridge over a failed negotiation. If you take anything away from the previous two sections, being nice and making friends is fun and extremely beneficial to your collecting experience. Ruining a relationship over a failed deal is seldom worth it.

It's also important to recognize early if a deal isn't possible. As much as we want to give other collectors the benefit of the doubt, some dealers may not be interested in making a fair deal. Plenty of dealers overprice cards and are only interested in massive profit margins. You don't have to engage with those sellers. If you approach a table with cards priced two or three times their current value, you might want to just walk away. They are hoping you haven't done your homework. If you're interested, ask if they "have any room" and see what they say. It's not uncommon for dealers to bring items they don't exactly want to sell but will for the right price, and they may be marked especially high. Inquire if you wish, but don't break your budget. Something similar *will* come around again.

Chapter **11**

Finding or Building a Community

The sports card hobby can be fun solo, but it's often much better when collecting with your friends. For many collectors, some of their earliest memories of the hobby are ripping packs and trading with their friends. A fun network makes it more likely that you'll stay anchored in the hobby for the long term, and it's also a great way to learn and grow your collecting knowledge. You can learn much on your own, but it is easier when you and your pals are pooling resources. A great friend group is also a great way to make sure that the hobby stays fresh and dynamic even if the overall market isn't great or new products aren't inspiring. Your buddies will almost definitely have something cool to share to get you back into the groove.

In this chapter, we cover how to find hobby friends online, network in person, and start your own community when you want to take the lead.

Using Social Media to Find Your Community

For many, sharing their collection with others is their favorite part of the hobby. Who doesn't love seeing new and interesting cards, after all? And it's hard to argue that there's an easier way to share your collection with more people than with social media. Sure, it may seem a bit colder than enjoying things in person, but the reach is undeniable. You're likely already on social media, but consider creating a profile to share your collection if you aren't already. It likely won't be long before you start interacting with like-minded collectors and making some new friends.

Best platforms to get started

While each major social media platform tries to be a one-stop-shop for all things entertainment, some are simply better than others for certain things. Below, we cover some of the most popular platforms within the sports card hobby and briefly explain what makes them special.

Instagram

By nature, the visual aspect of Instagram makes it a perfect match for card collectors. Scrolling through a truly endless sea of cards is wonderful — you'll almost certainly stumble on something you've never seen before. It's hard to know for sure, but anecdotally, it seems like Instagram is the most popular platform for collectors at the time of this writing. One cool feature is Instagram Live, which allows users to stream publicly and allows others to join. A couple of the primary drawbacks to Instagram are that you can't organize your posts into public collections because they are just in sequential order, and you're mostly on your own finding and communicating with others.

Facebook

While Instagram is a photo powerhouse, Facebook does a better job of community building with written discussion. You can certainly share plenty of photos — that's highly encouraged — but Facebook provides a variety of groups and pages that you can join for regular discussion. Facebook and Facebook Marketplace are also places to buy, sell, and trade. There are pages and groups dedicated to this and a host of other hobby topics for specific sports, eras, teams, and more.

Twitter/X

Where Instagram and Facebook have clear concepts they're good at, Twitter/X splits the difference to a certain extent. Plenty of photos exist, but the platform is less visual than Instagram. It's meant to have lots of discussions, but Facebook might be a little bit better at creating groups and communities. Twitter/X also regularly has buy/sell/trade threads organized by trusted collectors.

TikTok

Strictly meant for video, TikTok was late to the party but quickly became extremely popular with the card community. Privacy concerns have made the platform controversial, so feel free to ignore this section if the app isn't still standing when you're reading this.

Discord

The most niche of the major platforms we cover, Discord is great for discussions and audio/video calls. Discord is also a common place for hobbyists to sell their cards with various buy/sell/trade groups. There also are both free and paid Discord servers. If you're going to pay for access, be sure it's on the recommendation of a trusted friend to avoid wasting your time and money.

Reddit/Forums

Collectors can also find interesting and niche communities on platforms like Reddit. Some pages are dedicated to collecting individual sports like baseball, basketball, or football. The Blowout Cards Forums — a community associated with the trading card retailer — has also been an incredible resource for the hobby for years. Some members of the Blowout Forums are among the savviest in the hobby and have helped illuminate scams and other issues in the space.

How to safely communicate online

We won't bog this section down with the basics of general social media safety, as there's a certain level of personal responsibility involved here, too. If this is your first time with social media, we recommend searching for specific resources about online safety. But the hobby does have some nuances to watch for, and we focus on those instead. More tips about staying safe in the hobby in general can also be found in Chapter 13.

Avoid oversharing

You should avoid sharing information that isn't necessary, especially when it comes to personal details and anything to do with children. The hobby is filled with kids learning to collect, and they inevitably want to join social platforms to share their collections. Tread carefully here, especially if you're a parent or guardian overseeing a young person.

Navigating a transaction

Buying, selling, and trading online is common, though social media offers some challenging hoops to jump through. In some cases, buyers or sellers may prefer to do transactions through social media to avoid the additional fees and taxes that large marketplaces require. We highly recommend using a tool like Facebook Marketplace that already has e-commerce infrastructure or using business options through digital payment services like PayPal or Venmo.

WARNING

These protections are important because you'll have the chance to get a refund if things go wrong. Too many collectors are scammed by sellers accepting payment and disappearing without recourse because the buyer wanted to save a few bucks by making a Friends and Family payment instead of a Goods and Services payment.

Avoid drama

At this point, we all know that the Internet is the perfect place to start a fight without any recourse, and unfortunately, the hobby is no different. Try to avoid fights, bullies, and other drama. Although being informed of scams and corruption is good, that shouldn't be what you look for in the sports card hobby. Plenty of people enjoy stirring the pot, and you don't need to get caught in the scuffle. If someone's content is off-putting or not in line with your values, you can unfollow, mute, or block them. Your mental health will be better off this way.

Find your group, but avoid toxic tribalism

The hobby is made up of humans, and humans have a basic tendency toward uniting around common interests. We cover earlier the benefits of finding a group of friends you can relate to, grow with, and trust, but far too often, those tribes can become toxic and start projecting their own preferences, pet peeves, and unwritten hobby rules onto others. Don't fall victim to this trap. If your tribe spends more time criticizing things than talking about what originally brought you all together, your recent acquisitions, or your next purchases, it's time to find a new one.

Starting a community when you can't find one

You'll likely struggle to find a hobby topic that *doesn't* have a community at this point, but in the rare chance that you do, you can take things into your own hands and start one yourself. There are pages, groups, and Discord servers for all kinds of topics, and creating one more doesn't hurt anyone. Want to share your love for Andre Drummond cards? Start a Facebook group or page and share it with your friends. Love collecting Stadium Club image variations? Start a new Instagram account dedicated to just that. You can have as many accounts as you want and start as many pages or groups as you want.

We can't promise that many people will participate, but you should consider how many other collectors you know that might be interested in the topic before you get started. Fire away even if you don't have collaborators, but it helps if you know a few collectors with that shared interest. And there's truly no shame in having a small but engaged group on niche topics. In fact, those social groups can be some of the most rewarding and fulfilling.

Networking at Events to Grow Your Community

Though social media and other online tools have better reach, there's nothing quite like sharing stories or trading cards in person with your friends. Whether it's hanging out at your local card shop, wandering through a card show, or connecting with friends at a trade night, in-person events are the lifeblood of the collecting community and the highlight for many.

Event etiquette

We've said it before: Don't be a jerk. It's really that simple. It doesn't matter if you're buying cards in your local shop or attempting to iron out a trade — be friendly, and good things will happen. We cover how to navigate a card show more in Chapter 10, but one point that's worth doubling-down on is that there doesn't need to be a clear winner or loser.

TIP

If you can't make a deal work, maybe it's not meant to happen. Step back and make a second attempt later, or simply move on. It's possible to be friends with someone you couldn't make a deal with, and not every interaction needs to involve a transaction.

Show up to events prepared to chat about your favorite cards and the players or teams you collect most, and you'll often find that you have a lot in common with most other collectors. Most hobbyists are friendly people excited to tell you about their collections and equally excited to hear about yours in return.

Why all events aren't created equal

Card shows and events like trade nights at local card shops are the most common hobby events, but others are worth noting. The National Sports Collectors Convention (NSCC) is more of an experience than just a card show and is worth attending at least once in your collecting journey. An event like the National is great for the pure volume of unique items, but many will attest that better deals can be found online or at smaller shows.

The cost of travel and lodging for such a popular event might also be a deal-breaker for the regular collector, though the show does move around to different cities in the Central and Eastern US, providing some opportunity to go at least once.

There are also industry events that companies like Topps or Beckett have typically put on. These events are great for shops and business owners but might not be the best fit for a regular collector. Industry events often have panels and workshops that are helpful for businesses to attend but probably aren't as interesting to the typical collector. Consider attending if that's the side of the hobby you want to see, but don't feel left out if you skip them. You likely aren't missing much.

Chapter **12**

Resources to Grow Your Hobby Knowledge

You'll inevitably run into collectors who seemingly know *everything* about the hobby. They don't, of course, but hobby rookies won't know much better. Often, some of the most knowledgeable collectors out there get that way by accident. Simply existing in the hobby for long enough will make you seem like a pro to the newbies. Collect. The combination of time and dedication will turn you into a sports card sponge. It's difficult, but we can help you get there.

In this chapter, we offer up resources that will turn you into an expert on every upcoming set and direct you to other tools and publications to get you caught up on everything you missed from the past.

Free Industry Resources

The sports card hobby is about spending money, so getting about anything valuable for free is big. There are plenty of high-end resources you can subscribe to, but we lead this chapter with some free ones. In fact, some of the best tools are completely free, and the major companies and manufacturers are basically begging you to use them. You just have to know where to look.

Set and product details

You should do a good bit of research on sealed products before you buy them, and a lot of the key details are delivered to you right from the manufacturer. We extensively cover the importance of set details in Chapter 4, so flip to that if you've skipped it. Along with helping you find the right fit for your next purchase, these resources will also keep you updated on what's fresh. From a set detail standpoint, the two best resources are checklists and the sell sheets — and they are both completely free.

Checklists

There's no better way to see if a sealed product has what you want than skimming the full checklist. You can typically find these on the manufacturer's website, though sites like Beckett (www.beckett.com) and Cardboard Connection (www.cardboard connection.com) make them a little more digestible for new products as they are released.

TIP

For older product checklists, Beckett is also a great resource, as are Trading Card Database (TCDB) at www.tcdb.com, Baseball-cardpedia at http://baseballcardpedia.com, and Check Out My Cards (COMC) at www.comc.com.

Naturally, the more of these you go through, the more you'll understand about the hobby and the key cards to chase. Unfortunately, the checklist details don't always come out until close to (or even after) a product is released, which can make pre-orders even more of a gamble. The checklists also won't have images of all the cards in the product. Knowing what a card design or the photos look like for the specific players matters.

Sell sheets

Manufacturers put together sell sheets and send them to major retailers and hobby shops. These provide basic breakdowns of the product and what the collector should be chasing. For hobby shops, these are basically advertisements for a product they should consider carrying. For collectors, they are a gold mine of information. Sell sheets will typically highlight all the new additions to the set (if there are previous iterations) and can sometimes provide information on the print runs of the key cards. If nothing else, you can get a visual preview of some of the cards. Sell sheets aren't generally made public by the manufacturer, but retailers like Blowout or Dave and Adam's Card World will often post these on the product pages. Dig through these as they come out, and you'll quickly catch up to some hobby veterans.

Authentication, grading, and auctions

Grading companies and auction houses want you to spend money. That's the bottom line. But to help convince you to do that, these companies provide a ton of free resources that can boost your hobby knowledge. Whether it's trying to convince you to grade your cards at all or explaining why a card is a *must* for your collection, these companies will jump through a lot of hoops to provide you with as much information as possible. Be a sponge when this is offered, even if you don't plan on buying. They did all the leg work, and you can benefit.

Grading and authentication

Various grading companies are fighting to evaluate your cards, and a certain amount of transparency is sometimes offered to help convince you that one process, track record, or area of expertise is better than another. Dig into these resources and you'll learn a lot about the overall grading process. Images of cards that qualify for certain grades are extremely helpful for your own future evaluations. Examples of anything from miscuts to trimmed or recolored cards can be helpful, too.

TIP

Population reports can also be great resources, and you can find them individually on each grader's website or compiled into a universal report through a website like GemRate (www. gemrate.com).

Every card has a story

Major auction houses provide various services that we cover more in Chapter 9, but for this section, we want to highlight the background information for individual lots. Although low-dollar items may have only basic facts or attributes listed, high-end items often offer additional background details to help drive you toward bidding. Many high-end items have a specific story that helps make them so valuable.

Whether it's background on why the set or player is important or an interesting journey with past collectors, auction houses spend significant time telling the whole story. Understand it as advertising, but take advantage of this regularly, and you'll learn about some of the industry's most iconic cards and memorabilia.

Community Content and Other Media

Beyond the major manufacturers, grading companies, and auction houses, some of the best resources come from collectors themselves. From data analysis to hobby watchdogs and investigative research, dedicated collectors often spend a great deal of time talking about the cards they love and end up educating others in the process. Paid resources are also easy to find, though they vary in quality and price.

Pricing data tools

You could argue that the improvements to price transparency during the hobby's Ultra-Modern Era have been the most important and influential in decades. Specific tools are covered across Part 4 of this book, so we'll keep this area brief. We also want to keep the self-promotion of our own data tool to a minimum, so flip to Chapter 16 for more about specific applications. The main takeaway, for now, should be that more information is always better, and accurate pricing data helps everyone. Even if a paid option isn't right for you, seeking out additional pricing data is necessary if you're spending significant money on cards.

Picking the right creators

If the number of educational resources from manufacturers, graders, or auction houses is overwhelming, it's fair to consider what individual collectors produce virtually limitless. From social media posts to YouTube videos, you could spend the rest of your collecting life constantly consuming, and you'll never be without something new.

The quality of the content is highly variable, however, and you'll almost certainly align yourself with specific individuals, themes, or styles that you like more than others. Bias aside, we strongly believe the Sports Card Investor accounts are great resources for all collectors. A channel like Chasing Cardboard can provide great entertainment and education, and Ryan Johnson and his Card Collector 2 brand can take you inside running a card shop.

Investors or collectors

Most of the content you'll find can be considered financially focused or collector-driven. Both types are valid and important to the hobby, but they are very distinct from one another. Creators will also typically fall into one or the other, though some juggle both effectively.

With financially focused content, you'll typically see deep analysis around prices, player performance, and other factors that impact a card's value. Collector-focused content may instead highlight why a card is interesting from a design or historical standpoint.

Analysts or storytellers

When diving deeper into how creators express themselves, you'll often see financially focused content be extremely data-driven with various charts and price analyses. The collector content may be more narrative-driven with a great storyteller.

TIP

Again, the best of the best can juggle both effectively, but don't be surprised if you find a YouTube channel almost completely focused on buying and selling for profit while another is all about mail days and interesting finds. Consider consuming both types regularly, even if one isn't your thing. You never know what you might learn; the two are intimately linked, no matter what some claim.

Magazines and more

Most of the content around today's hobby is found online, but once upon a time, it was all about magazines. For many, snagging a collecting magazine was just as important as any card when they visited their local hobby shop. The landscape has changed, however, and there are fewer print products you can physically hold. Along with current magazines, consider picking up old issues if you stumble across them, as they remain great resources for hobby history.

Beckett Magazine

Any discussion about hobby publications starts with Beckett Magazine (see Figure 12-1). Founded by Dr. James Beckett in the 1980s, the Beckett Price Guide spent years as the definitive way to value your cards. The use of the magazine has faded as price transparency has increased over the years, though Beckett Media still provides great resources like interesting stories, news, and checklists.

Courtesy Goldin Auctions

FIGURE 12-1: 1990 *Beckett Basketball Card Magazine*

Tuff Stuff

Like Beckett Magazine, Tuff Stuff was a hobby publication focused on stories and card prices for two decades. The final Tuff Stuff issue was released in 2011.

PSA Magazine

Formerly known as *Sports Market Report*, *PSA Magazine* is published by the PSA grading company. The publication typically focuses on interesting cards and sets and why they've become so popular through the years.

Other media

Outside of the major publications, there are a variety of other more niche resources you can dive into. Basketball Card Fanatic Magazine comes out monthly and, as expected, emphasizes basketball cards and their stories. Plenty of other books besides this one also exist, though we'll let you decide which is the best for your own taste. The Society of Baseball Research (SABR) even has a blog focusing on sports cards.

Chapter **13**

The Dark Side of the Hobby

I f you take away nothing else from this book, we hope that you at least know that the hobby is filled with awesome cards and incredible people. But the reality is that, as with anything, there are bad actors who want to take advantage of anyone and everyone. From basic scams where a card is never delivered to sophisticated alterations, danger comes in all shapes and sizes, and you need to be prepared to navigate it. Luckily for collectors, dedicated hobbyists and improved technology have helped curb some of the biggest issues.

In this chapter, you learn about the dark side of the hobby, avoiding its most common scams and spotting fakes, alterations, and more.

Too Good to Be True

Like with anything in life, if it seems too good to be true, it likely is. If a price seems way too low, there's probably a reason — either a defect that's been carefully hidden or the card may never arrive. If a vintage card is simply too clean and crisp, there's likely been some adjustments done to make it that way. Use common sense when operating in the hobby and do a little digging if something seems off. Below, we'll break down many of the hobby's most unethical or immoral actions while highlighting nasty tricks to watch for.

Spotting fake cards

Fake cards have gotten increasingly sophisticated over the years, and that's a major reason why the authentication process that reputable grading companies perform is more important than ever. As you can imagine, many of the most popular, most expensive, and rarest cards in the hobby are also some of the most faked cards. We don't cover many specific cards here, but you should consider researching common mistakes the counterfeiters make when attempting to pull a fast one. Some of the most popular cards have interesting tells that can make spotting a fake easier than you think. You'll be happy you did some research if you're considering spending thousands of dollars.

TIP

If you're a newer collector, we recommend that you don't buy expensive cards that aren't authenticated and slabbed by a major grading company to protect yourself early on.

TIP

For additional guidance on fake cards, consider reading Ryan Nolan's 2021 book, *Spotting Fakes: Examining the Top 50 Fake Sports Cards.*

Physical red flags

If counterfeiters believe they can make money, they'll fake a card. When making any purchase, you should always consider why a card isn't graded if it's worth a significant amount of money. That makes sense if the card has clear damage that would hold back its value. An extremely clean, ungraded card is at least a yellow flag, especially regarding vintage cards. Assuming you've researched the specific card, the next step is to go down the checklist of common mistakes the counterfeiters may make. A common mistake for Michael Jordan's 1986 Fleer is an incorrect Fleer logo. For Wayne Gretzky's 1979 O-Pee-Chee, there's a print defect on the original card that fakes might not copy.

A little research can also be necessary when dealing with cards from specific eras. The printing process has evolved over the years, and if you have the eye for it, you may spot a modern process on a card allegedly from the 1960s.

With vintage cards, pay close attention to the edges, corners, and quality of colors. These are typically in poor condition compared to modern cards, and unethical collectors may attempt to alter the cards by trimming or recoloring. It seems odd, but some trimming techniques have gotten so sophisticated that graders can spot them because the cuts are too clean. Pay close attention to the colors across the card and attempt to spot any differences in texture or vibrance. Many hobbyists attempt to recolor with paints or markers that don't match the original.

Some cards are also outright faked — meaning that card never even existed. Common examples are cards with autographs that aren't meant to have them. Scroll through the product's checklists and confirm that the card even exists.

WARNING

Some hobbyists will swap out the memorabilia patch often seen with ultra-high-end memorabilia cards for a more attractive one. A multicolor patch is much more attractive than a plain white napkin patch. In some cases, that can be the difference between "That's a nice card" and "Congrats on finding your new home." Many of the cards targeted for this scam are serial-numbered, so check past auctions or listings for the exact example you're looking into and confirm that nothing has been changed. It's better to be safe than sorry.

While the authentication and encapsulation done by grading companies can provide peace of mind when making a purchase, those companies have also been known to make mistakes. Although rare, the grading companies have also had their slabs counterfeited by scammers. Always check the certification number against the company's population report and inspect the slab for anything that looks or feels off. The savviest of fraudsters will also make sure certification numbers match — this is where buying from a reputable seller is important, as they will often make things right.

TECHNICAL STUFF

It's worth noting that some artists make major alterations to cards by adding new designs, patches, or autographs. These are commonly referred to as *custom cards* and are commissioned by specific collectors. We won't lump these artists with counterfeiters as they are transparent about adding desirable items to cards that don't have them.

Smell

It may seem silly, but one of the easiest ways to spot a fake vintage card is by the smell. Older cards, by nature, smell exactly how you'd expect. If a card from the 1950s doesn't smell like it's 70-plus years old, it probably isn't. This test isn't perfect, but it's an easy way to get started.

Avoiding scams

Scams are, unfortunately, aplenty in the sports card hobby, especially with the rise in young collectors in recent years. Be vigilant as a parent or guardian if you're supervising a young collector, and consider listening in on a trade between an adult and a younger collector if it isn't being supervised. It takes a village. Unlike spotting fakes and alterations, spotting and avoiding scams is a bit easier. As we mentioned earlier, a too-good-to-be-true price is likely just that, and you might want to stay clear. When operating online, consider asking for other collectors to vouch for the character of the person you're doing business with.

WARNING

Make sure that when conducting in-person deals, like at a trade night event, you always keep an eye on your cards. A signature con tactic is to have one person inquire about specific cards while another person snatches one or more of your other cards when you're not looking. Young collectors tend to be targeted for this, so be vigilant as a parent or guardian and ensure the children in your care keep their cases closed and that there is only one set of hands on their cards at a time.

TIP

We also highly recommend never using payment options meant for friends and family if they aren't between friends and family. While the transaction may be cheaper than one that includes buyer protection, such as PayPal Goods and Services payments, you don't have any insurance if the deal goes bad. Potentially paying and never receiving a card is never worth saving a few extra bucks in taxes or fees.

You can certainly spend your money how you like, but we'd caution against repackaged products often sold online unless you know or trust the seller. Repacks will typically advertise a chance at a massive hit. However, the purported hit often is not included, and the cards you get will be junk.

Not all repacks are scams, but many are, so be vigilant and research the seller if you're committed to the chase.

One final thing to consider is recording yourself opening any packages you receive. Before you ever make a cut or tear into the packaging, set your camera up to ensure you have proof of what's inside. This helps protect you against cards that may arrive damaged, missing, or swapped with entirely different cards. This is also smart whenever opening any sealed products in case the manufacturers fail to include guaranteed hits or if the product was re-sealed with bogus packs or cards.

Shill bidding

Few unethical practices have become as common during the online marketplace era as shill bidding. A quick glance around social media might make you believe that someone has been shilled in almost every lost auction, but that's not the case. In fact, the vast majority are legitimate, but some players and specific cards are targeted more than others. Most commonly, this will happen if a once-popular player has experienced a significant price decline, and the people holding those cards are trying to preserve the perceived value artificially.

A common way to spot shill bidding is to look at the bid history on an item for a couple of red flags. Look for new accounts with low or zero feedback that are aggressively bidding on an item. We all start with a low feedback rating, but shill bidders often use new accounts so their real accounts aren't banned. Shill bidders can often have multiple throwaway accounts for this process alone. Multiple accounts battling in a very systematic manner can be another red flag. It's worth mentioning, however, that two accounts fighting it out aren't always shill bidding. Two people can battle, after all. Timestamps that show a bid one second and another bid the next second may seem fishy, but it can also be the marketplace auto-bidding a user's high bid. For example, you can set a high bid at $150, and another collector may walk their price up slowly, from $100 to $110, and then $120 to $130.

Your high bid will automatically take over in this case, making the timestamps and bid history seem odd. One last tip is that while buyer usernames are masked on eBay, you can still click the bidder's link to see their bid history, including how often they bid with a certain seller, the overall number of items they've bid on, how many items they've won, and how many bid retractions they've had. These can all be useful data points to deduce any questionable behavior patterns.

Online etiquette

Follow through on a transaction; it's that simple. If you sell a card, ship it to the buyer. It doesn't matter if the card is worth $1,000 and the buyer won the auction for $20. As much as you may want to, resist the urge to cancel the transaction. We don't condone the behavior, but actions like this are an easy way to get your profile posted on social media with a giant "SCAMMER" title attached to it. The money you saved canceling that transaction might not make up for the money you'll lose when no one wants to do business with you anymore.

On the other end of the spectrum, don't refuse to pay, and don't ask the seller to cancel your winning bid. We'd consider this an option in only the most extreme circumstances. Buyers will also use every excuse under the sun, some of which can be so absurd that they could fill an entire comedy special. Mistakes happen; kids can grab phones or computers and make bids you aren't unaware of. Consider it the cost of having a child — and, more importantly, failing to supervise them around a sensitive device. It hurts, we know, but your mistake shouldn't result in the seller being punished. Even if you think you may be the victim of shill bidding, you should still be committed to paying the final hammer price.

Drama queens

We mention simply being nice to other collectors several times in this book, and this is no different. Unfortunately, the hobby does have the occasional troublemaker who likes to stir the pot unnecessarily, and some of them end up having large followings online of like-minded people with a penchant for bullying. We emphasize *unnecessarily* stirring the pot because there is a big difference between calling out a scammer with abundant evidence versus lobbing accusations at others without evidence to damage their reputation.

TIP

Don't give in to the drama. It's best to avoid interacting with these people and to move on if they engage with you. The overwhelming majority of collectors are nice people, and rarely will negative interactions happen in person. Beware of the Keyboard Warrior and Armchair Character Assassins, and either move on quickly or consider blocking them if the harassment continues.

Pumping and dumping

Taken originally from stock market analysis, pumping and dumping involves a person of influence talking positively about something they already own to convince others to buy into it (the pump). This talking up will potentially inflate the value so the person of influence can then quietly sell what they own (the dump) for a profit.

We can objectively say this tactic is extremely unethical and immoral. Pumping and dumping has been a common accusation in the hobby, though it likely happens much less than people think. While it does happen, the term is often inaccurately attributed when anyone of influence talks about anything positively. Being excited about something is acceptable, but unfortunately, some will assume the worst.

There's absolutely nothing wrong with sharing why you love a specific card, variation, or product. And if the person doing that happens to have a large following, that doesn't mean they are conducting a pump-and-dump scheme. Unless you have proof that they are liquidating the same cards they previously hyped, don't make the accusation or buy into it when others go there.

Personal Responsibility and Managing Your Budget

For all the bad actors you may encounter in the hobby, the person who can do the most damage to your collecting experience is *you*. The decisions you make as a collector are yours and yours alone, and while it may be easy to point the finger at everyone else, this is your hobby, and you must take responsibility for all of it. It's easy to get caught up in the advice of others and blame others if something doesn't go the way you envisioned. Whether a recent purchase went sideways or you made a trade you regret, it's all on your shoulders.

What is and isn't out of your control

Taking personal responsibility for your actions is important, but part of understanding your mistakes is identifying what is and isn't within your control. A player breaking their leg during a game shortly after you make an investment in their cards isn't within your control, for example. Purchasing that player's cards *was* in your control, but you need to separate the two. You took a risk that unfortunately didn't work out, but many others did as well — you aren't alone in a terrible moment. There's also a difference between doing all the proper research before buying and having an injury derail the purchase compared to not doing enough research, only to find you bought at the top with no money to be made. One of those instances is unlucky and out of your control. The other happened because you didn't pay attention to the card's price history and the probabilities of its future trajectory.

It's also common in the hobby to blindly listen to "experts" who might directly recommend buying or selling cards. Tread carefully here, especially when they are making direct recommendations. It's one thing to speculate that a player could go up or down in value, but it's another thing to declare it for others to follow. If someone else's analysis inspires you, the next step isn't to blindly buy — do your own research. If you agree with their theory, maybe it's a good purchase. If not, feel free to skip.

REMEMBER

A certain amount of regret is also normal, especially when making a purchase or trade. Keep that regret in perspective, and remember that you can sometimes fix things, so be patient. If there's regret, and the decision isn't reversible or salvageable, consider it as paying tuition toward the next purchase. You messed up, but you're learning from it. The next one will be better.

Setting a budget and staying on target

Few things are more dangerous to a collecting journey than straying from the budget you set. If you haven't established a card budget, we highly recommend doing so, and we cover that more extensively in Chapter 14. Financial responsibility when collecting should be one of the biggest takeaways from this book. How much you spend is up to you, but make sure it's acceptable based on your income, expenses, and other personal responsibilities. If you're single, feel free to spend more if you can afford it. A collector who is married with kids may need to be more careful. Opening sealed products specifically can be extremely addicting. Ripping packs can be extremely fun for many, but the parallels to gambling are very clear. This also applies to box breaks, which can be exhilarating but also an expensive and addicting habit. Don't stretch your life thin financially so you can open another box of cards — we promise it's not worth it.

REMEMBER

Sticking to your budget can be frustrating because it's possible that cards you *need* in your collection pop up and you've already used your allowance for the month. Be vigilant about staying on target, as it's easy to overextend yourself financially more often after you've done it once. Don't make exceptions, and remember that the key cards for your collection will come up again. Sports cards aren't something worth going into debt over.

4

Flipping, Investing, and Turning a Profit

Chapter **14**

Investing in Cards While Attempting to Turn a Profit

While most of this book is dedicated to collecting cards for fun and enjoyment, we'd be doing you a disservice if we didn't talk about the financial side of the sports card hobby. We are under no illusion about the controversial nature of this chapter and, for that matter, about including the word "investing" in this book's title.

The financial aspects of the hobby are undoubtedly the most polarizing. Collecting purists will often say that investing in cards to make money has no place in the hobby. They'll say collecting is strictly meant for fun, and people who try to make money from it only hurt everyone around them. They'll even argue that there is no such thing as investing in sports cards, splitting hairs over semantics while ostensibly denying the reality that cards are — and have long been — about money for many people.

Everyone is entitled to their own opinions about collecting, but the reality is that people have been buying and selling cards to make a profit for about as long as the cards have existed. Selling cards to fund one's own personal collection is also incredibly common. There's *nothing* wrong with selling what you don't want and putting that money toward something you do, be it more cards or something else entirely.

The sports card business is *big*, so we must cover that side of the hobby in this book. Feel free to skip this part if you don't think you'll ever be interested in selling your cards; it'll be here if you change your mind later.

In this chapter, we cover the basics of sports card investing and call out some beginner mistakes many of us had to learn from the hard way.

The Basics of Sports Card Investing

We're going to make one thing clear: it can be *extremely* difficult to buy and sell cards regularly to make a profit. Like playing the stock market, macro and micro economic forces can and do change with little notice. Understanding the market and when to buy and sell is a skill developed over time, and you'll absolutely make costly mistakes when you first get started. We like to call it the price of tuition. Truthfully, selling sports cards for a profit requires more time, effort, and money than it may be worth for some hobbyists. That said, trading sports cards instead of stocks does offer a different type of excitement that many sports fans prefer, and many hobbyists who have dedicated themselves to the research and patience necessary have turned it into a viable source of income and, in some cases, even a legitimate career.

WARNING

Understanding the difference between flipping cards for short-term profit and investing in cards for long-term appreciation is important. Both can make you money but in entirely different ways. Flippers tend to buy cards of younger active players who they think are about to get hot and shoot up in value. Flippers never want to hold onto any card for very long. It's a high-risk, high-reward way of trying to profit from cards. Long-term investors tend to favor cards of well-established superstars or all-time greats. These won't fluctuate in value as much in the short term, and the hope is they will slowly but steadily appreciate over time. Long-term investors favor scarcity when selecting the cards they invest in and often try to obtain iconic cards in as high of a grade as possible.

One critically important concept to understand is the idea of floor versus ceiling. The price floor for a card is the lowest price a card has been (past tense and factual) or to which it could descend (future and theoretical). For example, we may think of the future floor in absolute terms — as in the long-term trajectory of the card — or in the short-term, to describe the floor for a card in the upcoming season. In this example, the ceiling would describe the card's highest price.

REMEMBER

Having comprehensive and accurate historical data for a card you're evaluating as an investment is indispensable, which is where a data tool like Market Movers (or others we mention in Chapter 16) comes into play. To fully understand where a card can go, you need to understand where it has been and where other similar cards have been. In the following sections, we give more examples of how to think about the floor and ceiling.

Some important disclaimers

Before we go any further, we need to cover a few things. First, we aren't offering financial advice in this book. How you spend your money is between you, your loved ones, and maybe your financial planner. This book won't offer specific recommendations on what to buy. Even if we wanted to, recommendations can't be made because the card market landscape can very well change between now and when you started reading this paragraph. Speculating about which cards can appreciate is also very different from making direct recommendations. Through speculation, we can theorize what a card's market may do based on data that *has* happened. By making a recommendation, we'd be, in some aspects, committing to a belief that something *will* happen.

Second, the concepts we mention in this part of the book should only be considered broad strategies that can help get you started. We can't and won't spend money for you — and you shouldn't want us to either. Instead, this part is aimed at helping you identify trends and other aspects that can make a card a good investment candidate. This is important to understand because nothing is foolproof. Even if you've done the research and purchased the right cards at the right price, it's impossible to predict a torn ACL or personal conduct issues that can end a player's career.

REMEMBER

Remember, even if everything on the field is working, your cards are tied to human beings who can (and typically do) get hurt playing their sports. For every megastar with a valuable lineup of cards, *thousands* of athletes could have had incredible careers had it not been for that one critical injury.

Third, it's important to understand that most cards will lose value over the course of their existence, no matter what. For most cards, the value will never be higher than the moment they are pulled from the pack. Demand is often highest right after release, and copies are constantly added into circulation as packs are opened.

In addition to a growing population of cards, most players simply underperform relative to early expectations. Plenty of data tells us that only a few players from each generation across the major sports see their cards appreciate in value over the years. We're talking two, maybe three players from each generation. Think Magic Johnson and Larry Bird, Mickey Mantle and Hank Aaron, Joe Montana and Jerry Rice. Other former MVP winners like Derrick Rose may eventually be largely forgotten, just as players like Dave Cowens and Moses Malone have been (by most). Plenty of players who have won a handful of titles or multiple MVPs have virtually zero hobby relevance and nearly zero long-term value outside of key cards from some of the hobby's most iconic sets. Great for your personal collection? Certainly. But expecting anything more from their overall market just isn't realistic.

TIP

Last — and this is critical — we can't overemphasize the need for personal accountability. If you make a financial mistake with cards of any kind, taking ownership of your own actions is essential. Nobody else is forcing you to buy or sell anything. (If they are, contact the authorities.) Many of us in the hobby like to listen to other opinions, insights, and ideas. We rely on close, trusted networks to be sounding boards. Yet, at the end of the day, we're the ones making our own decisions and taking our own actions. So, if you make a mistake, own it as the price of tuition. Learn from it, share your learnings with others, and move forward.

Key concepts to follow

With the warnings and disclaimers out of the way, we can finally dive into some specifics when it comes to what makes a card investable. Again, we won't make specific recommendations for you here. You can find plenty of those online if you wish, but this isn't the space for those. Instead, we'd rather offer insight into why certain cards are considered valuable so you can apply those concepts for yourself. In the next chapter, we cover the different types of investments, including the various timelines.

Major stars and top prospects

It may seem like a no-brainer to strictly focus on a sport's top stars when buying cards to sell for profit later, but the reality is that some of the biggest financial gains often come from buying under-the-radar players before they win awards or set records. Buying a proven MVP or Hall of Famer may have a higher floor (or be safer from sharp price declines), but it also typically offers a lower ceiling (less upside). This is where many hobbyists enjoy the art of prospecting, especially when it comes to baseball.

There is certainly a prospecting aspect to sports like football and basketball, but the most prominent in the sports card hobby is baseball. While basketball and football largely rely on college sports for most prospects, baseball has both the collegiate level and all levels of the minor league system, which creates a much larger pool of players to evaluate. The larger pool of players makes evaluation more complicated but offers a better chance to buy into players early before others catch on.

The most highly sought-after prospect cards come from Bowman products and feature a "1st" designation (see Figure 14-1) on the cards, denoting their first licensed card. There is plenty of money to be made buying current MLB-level players, though many hobbyists dedicate a significant portion of their card budget to buying prospects during baseball's off-season to sell them for a profit as they are called up to the majors. Some consider this the easiest way to profit from selling cards, while others feel there is generally too much research or too much risk required.

Courtesy of Goldin Auctions

FIGURE 14-1: 2009 Bowman Chrome Draft Prospects Refractor Autograph Mike Trout

Active versus retired players

Playing status also plays a major role in how cards are evaluated and how prices can fluctuate. All card values are fluid — even cards widely considered the best investments will see their prices fluctuate regularly. While many cards are considered valuable or investable because of their physical attributes, some are considered valuable because they feature active players doing notable things right now. A big game in one week can make prices go up as hype builds, but a bad performance can have the inverse effect.

Because of this, the cards of active players are typically considered more volatile than those of retired players. In addition to big and bad games, a player's regular news cycle and current popularity can also be big factors in their card prices. The narrative is largely set for retired players from a statistical standpoint. We know what those players did during their careers — and that isn't changing. Retired players typically see less price volatility without active performances to shift public perception. These players are often considered safer investments than active players, though they often offer less upside.

Retired players may not have current highlights to rely on for pricing changes, but they still have major events that can impact them. Often referred to as *sell markers*, the major events for retired players are typically the announcement of making the Hall of Fame (if applicable) or, unfortunately, a death. These moments push players back into the news cycle, and collectors — seeking nostalgia — can drive prices up temporarily.

WARNING

It is worth noting that selling during the "death bump" is controversial and viewed by many to be disrespectful and insensitive.

With few sell markers after their playing days, retired players can often see their prices extremely reflective of the current economic climate. Cards are nonessential items, and a healthy economy can raise prices, while a recession can hurt even the greatest and most established superstars.

Rookie cards, autographs and more

Beyond the players themselves, it's important to remember that the desirability of different cards is highly variable. Players like Michael Jordan or Mickey Mantle may be considered valuable and important players, but their cards aren't all the same. This is where it's extremely important to understand the different types of cards and why certain attributes may be more valuable than others. You can find more information about the different types of cards in Chapter 4.

For many players, their most valuable cards will be their rookies. There are plenty of notable exceptions, though. Mickey Mantle's 1952 Topps (see Figure 14-2) is considered by many to be the most important sports card of all time — but it's not his rookie card. Mantle's 1951 Bowman (see Figure 14-3) is his key rookie, while his 1952 Topps is beloved for a variety of other reasons. Some collectors refer to it as his "Topps rookie" and place increased value on the Topps brand, while others consider the 1952 Topps Baseball set to be the birth of the modern sports card. In addition, the Bowman 1st prospect cards often command higher prices than the same player's corresponding rookie cards.

Courtesy of Heritage Auctions

FIGURE 14-2: 1952 Topps Mickey Mantle, PSA 1

Courtesy of Heritage Auctions

FIGURE 14-3: 1951 Bowman Mickey Mantle, PSA 6

Cards that feature autographs or memorabilia are also considered extremely valuable, with Rookie Patch Autographs often being the most desired from an investment standpoint (see Figure 14-4). Securing a card with an autograph, some memorabilia, and the rookie designation is ideal, but there are plenty of instances where the autograph and memorabilia are considered more valuable than most rookies. Outside of a player's rarest or sought-after rookies, it's common to find autographs and memorabilia selling for significantly higher prices. Again, not all cards are created equal, and the quality of the autographs and memorabilia plays a major role. You can read more about autos and patch cards in Chapter 4.

Courtesy of Goldin Auctions

FIGURE 14-4: 2017 National Treasures Holo Gold Patrick Mahomes

Short-printed cards

If you've been paying close attention, you may have noticed as we move through this section that cards featuring all the best attributes are getting increasingly rarer. Trying to pair a top-tier star with a rookie card featuring autographs or memorabilia isn't easy. Overall, some of the most investable cards have very low print runs or small graded populations. We'll talk more about graded cards shortly, but cards that are harder to find very often sell for higher prices. It's a simple supply and demand scenario — or, more specifically, a scenario of scarcity — the intersection of rarity and demand.

Short-printed cards are essentially cards with a lower print run than regular cards. Serial-numbered cards, in particular, are good places to start, while cards with autographs or memorabilia tend to have shorter print runs, too. While often not numbered, case hits and other super short-printed cards can be extremely valuable, even if they aren't rookie cards. Panini's iconic Kaboom! and Color Blast inserts are case hits and some of the most desirable and iconic modern cards on the market.

Graded cards

We talk about graded cards in this book across almost every chapter because grading has become a major part of the sports card hobby, especially in recent years. You can read about grading and card condition more in Chapter 7, but there are several key reasons why graded cards are often more desired when it comes to the investment side of the hobby.

First, a major value of graded cards is the authentication process. Much of the hobby gets caught up in the number grade assigned to illustrate condition, but authentication is just as important as anything. In fact, you should consider the authentication aspect to be *the* most important part because the most valuable cards are also among the most faked cards. The hobby's rarest and most valuable cards are tough to find, which means they are the most common targets for fraud and manipulation. Even if a card is real, it's not uncommon for iconic cards to receive alterations to clean up the condition — a single point in the number grade can account for thousands, if not millions, of dollars in value in some cases. Card graders aren't perfect, but the most reputable companies put as much effort into ensuring cards are authentic as anything else.

The encapsulation process during grading also adds significant value to key cards just because of the protection provided. You want your investments to appreciate; they can't do that if they are susceptible to damage. Finally, the grading scale assigned to assess condition is also incredibly important. Not every PSA 9 is the same, especially when it comes to vintage cards, but it does help create a baseline for condition. Small differences may add up to a PSA 9, but you can generally expect most 9s to be of similar quality. Of course, this isn't guaranteed, but it's a good place to start.

TIP

When it comes to vintage cards specifically, eye appeal plays a major role. Two cards can be graded PSA 5s but have very different levels of eye appeal. In these cases, one card may have less damage but dull colors, while the other may have softer corners but a bright, vibrant image. Though they arrived at the same grade for different reasons, one may be more attractive.

Many of the best investments are low-population cards, but that doesn't mean high-population cards can't be valuable. The terms "high pop" or "low pop" often reference a card's graded population being high or low, with low pop being objectively better than the other.

REMEMBER

It should be noted that population counts require more context than simply being high or low, however. The COVID-19 pandemic introduced millions of additional collectors into the hobby, which resulted in many more cards being graded. Some collectors may consider a card with more than 1,000 PSA 10s to be high pop, but what's more important is whether the card's population can meet its demand.

For some cards, especially during the pandemic, a PSA 10 population of 5,000 wasn't meeting the market demand. Investing in high-population cards during that specific time was viable simply due to the overwhelming demand. Of course, this doesn't mean that high population cards are always viable investments — far from it, actually — but it's important to consider context. That trend of grading every card under the sun, by the way, has since faded for many reasons — another testament to the complex and ever-evolving nature of the sports card hobby.

While many high-pop cards may lose their luster over time, it's also important to consider that not all low-pop cards are investable or valuable either. The term simply means that there aren't many of them. This is where *rare* and *scarce* once again become important distinctions. Rare simply means not many exist, while scarce means the supply doesn't meet the demand. Rare may seem nice, but scarce is what matters. Rare doesn't matter if there aren't others looking to own the card. In fact, when it comes to investing, the term "low pop" can be more misleading than "high pop." High pop at least implies that enough people were excited about the card to get it graded. A card can be "low pop" because no one cares to grade it at all.

TIP

Use each card grader's website to find the population count, or search online for print runs to see how rare your non-numbered card truly is. The terms high or low pop can certainly be a good place to start, but tread carefully, as the context behind *why* they are high or low is the most important.

Overall, the value added with grading is undeniable. If you're looking for a ready-to-sell card, something already graded is a good place to start. If you're looking to maximize value, buying raw and then grading yourself is an option, too. Not all investable or valuable cards are graded, but many are, and you should seriously consider that part of the hobby if you're serious about this as a business.

How, when, and where to sell your cards

Because nothing is ever easy, picking the right time and place to sell cards is just as important as anything else during the process. You can buy the right card of the right player at the right price and have all that work undone by ending your auction at the wrong time or using the wrong marketplace or auction house. We'll cover fatal mistakes to avoid more in the next section and more about selling your cards in Chapters 15 and 16, but there are some key concepts to know when it comes to selling your cards that we should briefly cover now.

Sell markers

We mentioned sell markers earlier in this chapter in reference to major events around players, and these are the windows where you should be targeting to sell. Popular sell markers for active players can be anything from winning an award or, even better, a title. In fact, in many cases, it's best to sell a particular player's card *right before* those events happen, as the general population is confidently buying *in anticipation* of an award or title. Price boosts can come after big games, too, though the performance needs to be truly exceptional or largely unexpected, and getting your card listed quickly enough to capitalize may be difficult.

KNOWING WHEN TO HOLD'EM AND WHEN TO FOLD'EM

As we cover with baseball prospecting, the period right after a player gets called up to the majors or is announced as having made the MLB roster during Spring Training is a key time to sell. For retired players, the announcement of making the Hall of Fame or, unfortunately, a death can be key markers.

Sell markers come in a variety of forms, but the key is knowing when those could happen before you buy the card. Remember that moment when you buy the card and stay committed to it. You're better off missing a little profit by selling a little too early than waiting too long and missing your window completely. Selling for even a small profit still has you moving forward, while selling for a loss will set you back. We recommend having a strategy for every card you purchase for investment purposes, including a target sell price. When the card hits that price, consider moving it, and don't look back.

Right place, right time

There's a right time to sell when it comes to broad concepts like a prospect call-up or winning a title, but there's also a right time to sell in terms of minutes and hours. Deciding when your auction will end can be as important as anything. Searching for auctions ending at weird hours is a great way to score a deal, so try to avoid falling into that trap as the seller.

There's a reason why the major auction houses end their top items on weekends during the evening, so you should take a hint there. Avoid early mornings or something in the middle of the week if possible.

TIP

More information about the major marketplaces can be found in Chapter 9, but it's just important to know now that they come in all shapes and sizes and are also incredibly important to your ideal outcome. If you're looking for broad exposure to as many buyers as possible for a low- to mid-tier investment, your card may perform best on a platform like eBay or COMC (www.comc.com).

If your investment is super high-end and may only be a fit for a handful of buyers, you may want to consider a major auction house like Goldin, PWCC, or Heritage. There are several other great options as well, some of which specialize in specific kinds of cards and have clientele actively seeking those cards. These companies specialize in getting your card in front of the *right* people more than anything else and can also offer additional resources like marketing and promotions.

Also related to timing, make sure you're selling your card when the time comes. You can do all the research in the world, have the best strategy, and "hit" on the correct player and card, but if you fail to get your card listed to strike while the iron is hot, it will have all been for naught. This is one of the most common mistakes, by far, for people looking to speculate on cards over short time frames.

Know your sell window and sell markers, and don't fail to sell the card.

Auction listing formats

Using the right selling format for your investment is also extremely important. A seven-day auction is common on marketplaces like eBay, while auction houses may put high-end items up for an entire month to get as many bidders as possible.

Some may consider any auction high-risk, high-reward, so something in the Buy It Now (also known as fixed price) category may be better for your card. Set your item at the desired price and see what happens. Some hobbyists even like to put their items at an extremely high price and accept offers on them instead. You might be pleasantly surprised when a collector smashes the Buy button for a card they must have in their personal collection. This may be the best option if you can wait for your investment to sell, while auctions may be better if you want your investment timeline to end quickly.

Selling on eBay

For those looking to sell on eBay specifically, we can offer a few additional tips:

>> First, don't use a reserve price. It aggravates prospective buyers who already have no way of knowing if their max

price is higher than other interested buyers. Subjecting them to the additional mystery of a hidden reserve price is cruel and unusual punishment. Instead, set your opening bid at the price you're comfortable with. It creates better price transparency and increases the odds of you selling your card.

>> Secondly, never — and we *do* mean *never* — cancel an item you sold if you feel it sells for too little. Always respect the "contract" of an auction and ship the card once paid. Far too many buyers feel entitled to bid up cards and never pay for them, which drives sellers crazy. The flip scenario is sellers not getting what they wanted for the card and refusing to let it go for the final hammer price.

>> In that same vein, our final tip is never to shill bid to manipulate the market. Shill bidding is fraud. The hobby has a lot of people who police for this kind of activity, and you could very easily find yourself on the outside looking in — if not also facing legal consequences.

Fatal mistakes to avoid

A major reason why investing in sports cards is so difficult is that so many things can go wrong during the process. In fact, you can do just about everything right, and one mistake could undo all of it. It's not for the faint of heart, but there are, of course, mistakes that are more common than others that we can put on your radar now.

Research is key

One of the most common mistakes is not doing enough research from the beginning. Whether it's buying a player who doesn't have a strong history of price growth or purchasing sealed wax that isn't a popular product, many of the most problematic mistakes beginners make are self-inflicted by a lack of research.

REMEMBER

Truthfully, the sports card market changes so quickly that you're attempting to hit a moving target. Don't make things more difficult by purchasing cards that didn't have a great chance of working out to begin with because you didn't spend enough time researching them. Time is money; in this case, you'll cost yourself a lot of cash because you didn't dedicate the time.

Giving into FOMO

When you first get started, there may be pressure to do more than you're financially capable of from fear of missing out (FOMO) — but you must understand your budget and stick to it. It's normal to feel pressure to buy bigger cards when looking at other collections on social media, but you mustn't give into FOMO and stretch yourself too thin. Blowing up your budget isn't the right move if you're taking this seriously as a business, and it's even worse if this is something you're doing on the side and it's impacting your personal life.

Fees and taxes

The hidden expenses of the hobby can cut into your bottom line. Depending on your selling volume, these hidden expenses can truly add up. Buying and selling fees on platforms like eBay are things you need to consider — sales tax adds up, and you can expect all the major online marketplaces to take a cut of your profits with selling fees. Consider the selling fees when you're shopping around where to do business. This is also a major reason some dealers prefer to sell in person, though taxes also apply there.

WARNING

We also can't stress enough how important it is to keep a detailed sales log for tax purposes. Even if you handle mostly cash, you must keep track of your sales and pay the proper taxes.

Building Your Business from Scratch

Buying and selling sports cards for a profit can be something you do alongside your day job, but improvements in things like pricing transparency and e-commerce have made it easier to turn it into a legitimate business. It's extremely difficult, but it can be done with time, effort, and patience.

Turning the hobby into your full-time job isn't for everyone, but we've included a few tips below for you to consider if you believe this could be in your future.

Making your first deals

Even if your budget allows for bigger purchases, it really is smart to start small and progress into bigger cards when beginning. You'll make mistakes, and it can take hundreds, if not thousands, of transactions to get really good at buying and selling. It's also important to understand that there's a major difference between a good deal on a card for your personal collection and a good deal on a card you intend to sell for a profit later. A 5 or 10 percent discount on a card can be great for your collection, but your business may need discounts closer to 20 or 30 percent to be effective. There is much less room for error, and you'll want to play it safe until you are confident with bigger purchases.

Building on a budget

Major improvements to pricing transparency with tracking apps have made it a lot less likely that you might overpay for a card, but it's also made it a little more difficult to find great deals in many cases. We cover how to find deals more in Chapter 9, but one really stands out when you're attempting to buy inventory to sell later.

If you're taking this seriously as a business, you should really consider buying in bulk if possible. To get your own discounts, you often need to offer your own value proposition, and in this case, it's that you're willing to purchase more than other people. When negotiating on a single card, you might be able to create a 5 or 10 percent discount with the dealer. If you're offering to buy a larger number of cards, you can increase that discount to 30 percent or even higher. The final day of a card show is a great time to strike these deals because sellers may prefer to take less inventory back home.

When to take a loss

The sunk-cost fallacy can be fatal to businesses, and this industry is no different, especially when you've invested a lot of money or time into finding a card. However, it's critical to have a good handle on the market. Sometimes, when you make a mistake, limiting the damage is best. Every professional sports card dealer makes mistakes, but the best ones are great at limiting how much they lose.

Understanding when to take a loss as a seller is arguably the most important and difficult thing to learn, but it'll make a difference down the line. If a recent purchase has started to tank in value, consider offloading it quickly and investing that money into something different. Rather than think of this as a financial loss, try to imagine it as a second chance to bet on yourself and find another deal. You'll often be better off putting that money into something new — even if it's less money — than trying to wait out the decline. Many of the most successful dealers operate within a very short window, which helps prevent massive dips in value.

Creating realistic expectations

Like traditional collecting, it's important to set goals and operate with realistic financial expectations when investing in cards. Set your budget and stick to it with no exceptions. You mustn't overextend yourself financially, even if you think it can be worth the risk. There are other ways to make aggressive moves than going beyond what you're financially capable of. Overextending your budget is an easy way to dig a hole that can remain with you long after your attempt at investing ends.

DON'T LET MONEY BE YOUR ONLY MOTIVATOR

Although there isn't anything inherently wrong with participating in the sports card hobby purely with monetary motivation, it's not what we recommend. Many, if not all of us, have a collector gene, and what makes the hobby so fulfilling is the thrill of building and sharing an incredible personal collection over time. One of the main reasons card prices and population reports exploded during the COVID-19 pandemic is that many people came in motivated purely by money, similar to the NFT and cryptocurrency crazes simultaneously.

And where are those people today? Well, many of them have since left. Many of them, unfortunately, didn't come out on the winning side of the financial equation. There are a great number of ways to invest your hard-earned money. Investing in sports *can* be profitable, but you'll be way more satisfied with investing your *time* into the hobby if you can enjoy it — at least part of the time — as a collector.

Chapter **15**

Three Ways to Profit

We cover the basics of sports card investing in Chapter 14, but now it's time to get more granular with specific strategies. Unless you already have a strong grasp of how to get started, we highly recommend reading that chapter before diving into this one.

Most cards' investment timeline typically falls into one of three categories upon purchase: a quick flip, a short-term speculation, or a long-term investment. To be fair, cards can fall into any of the three timelines depending on your goals, but most cards will be better suited for one or two at a given time.

As in Chapter 14, we don't offer specific cards for you to purchase. Instead, we rather arm you with the tools needed to make your own decisions. In this chapter, we break down the three different types of investments and the types of cards successful investors typically target for each.

The Quick Flip

The fastest and most common timeline for investments is the quick flip. Although the term "flip" can simply be used to describe purchasing a card and then selling it later, it's also often used to describe a shorter timeline.

Typically, "flips" are cards purchased and sold within a few days, a couple of weeks, or maybe a month. An investment's overall timeline is relative to the collector themselves, but quick flips typically don't describe cards that are held for more than a few months at most.

WARNING

Of the three methods outline, the quick flip is the most controversial. It's the game within the game. Not everyone is a fan of "flippers," so don't be surprised if you're trying to flip cards at a show and get met with resistance by some. The sports card community is composed of passionate, tribal, and highly opinionated people, many of whom condemn flipping.

Flipping has been around for a long time and certainly isn't a new phenomenon. As we cover in Chapter 14, we highly recommend cultivating a personal collection in addition to whatever investment approach suits your fancy.

Spotting flipping candidates

When it comes to flipping a card quickly for profit, the ideal cards are the ones that can see explosive price growth. Because of this, many quick-flip candidates are cards of active players rather than retired ones. Active players can have big performances that boost their prices on a day-to-day or week-to-week basis, allowing you to purchase a card, see it rise in price, and quickly sell within a short window. That selling window is often so short because many of these cards are just as likely to drop in value as quickly as they rose. The tricky part is predicting that window, finding the right deal, and then selling for a profit before the card regresses in price.

More than anything, the quick flip is about understanding human psychology and forecasting hype cycles. If you're plugged into card show scenes, social media, Discord servers, and web forums, you'll pick up on which players are getting a lot of early buzz and be able to jump in before their prices take off. When paired with buying cards in a sport's offseason, you've already locked in two of the most important strategies.

Cards of retired players are certainly options, too, but they typically have fewer sell markers for you to target. It's possible to buy a player before they are announced for the Hall of Fame, for example, and flip the card right after the announcement as the player rises in the news cycle.

Whether you're working with cards of active or retired players, the key is identifying your sell marker and timing your purchase around that. Some of the most successful dealers who flip cards regularly are also committed to holding those cards for a short period and exiting at a certain point, even if the card would sell for a loss. In this scenario, they cut their losses and reinvest their money into a different opportunity. If the price growth hasn't been there, they simply move on to something new after a few weeks or months. Buying and selling this way allows them to *hopefully* capture a big bump in price or exit quickly with a smaller loss.

Graded cards are also popular targets for quick flips. We cover the extensive benefits of graded cards in Chapter 7, but the grading process can be especially important here because many buyers prefer graded cards when spending any significant amount of money. Plenty of collectors prefer raw cards, but raw cards can vary greatly in condition — which can be difficult to agree on and trust when buying online — while graded cards offer a basic baseline for conditions that can easily have a price attached to them.

REMEMBER

It's worth noting that it's perfectly fine to flip raw cards, but it's often a little too difficult to buy raw and grade for a quick flip. The grading timeline can be cumbersome unless you opt for an express-level service, which can take a massive chunk out of your profits. Because of this, most cards that are quickly flipped are bought and sold as-is.

When it comes to the quick flip, liquidity is king. You typically want to target cards from flagship products that sell often. If you buy an obscure card of a player in an obscure grade, and there are no other sales at the time of your intended flip, you'll struggle to move the card. Target cards that transact weekly, if not daily, because these are the ones people buy first when prices begin to spike.

REMEMBER

If you're looking to flip a card for profit, the price you paid is every bit as important as what you can later sell it for. Savvy flippers often set up at card shows and offer to buy cards from attendees with cash at 60 or 80 percent of the card's value. Others use social media to look for similar deals. Buying cards under market value is key to later selling them for a profit.

Targeting the right timeline

The card itself largely determines the right timeline for your quick flip. There's no universal answer here, so you'll need a strong grasp of the overall market and some of its regular trends. Prospecting season, for example, typically aligns with baseball's offseason — particularly November and early December. Many collectors dedicate time to finding the top players for the next season and purchasing their key Minor League cards in those months. These cards are bought and flipped when the player is announced as part of the MLB roster during Spring Training or when they are called up to the majors during the regular season. Prices for prospects are rarely higher than at the call-up.

This concept applies to other sports as well. The hype for key players is rarely higher than right before a season starts, so many flippers target the offseason as the buying season and sell right as the regular season begins. In this scenario, you avoid having poor play affect the prices negatively. You might not make as much profit as you would if the player has a strong start, but you don't risk a big loss either.

Whether you're targeting the start of a season, a call-up, or the beginning of a playoff run, it's important to keep that target in mind and avoid holding those cards too long.

Using data to make the right moves

You should be using data when it comes to all things investing. This doesn't mean you have to pull up a price chart for every decision, but you should know what an acceptable price is going into a deal. Before buying a card, check to see what recent sales have been and what the card's historical highs or lows have been to project its floor and ceiling. Using a data tool like Market Movers (see Figure 15-1), you may use price charts to determine whether a deal is good. A card currently selling for $100 might seem like a good deal, but historical data could show that it's never sold for more than $110. Unless the card features a prospect with a longer growth runway, it might be best to avoid it, as there's little historical evidence that the price could get much higher.

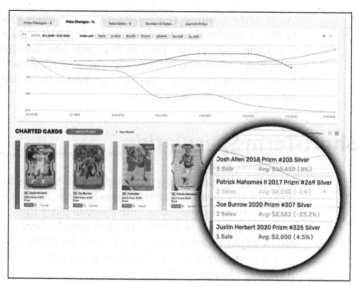

FIGURE 15-1: Market Movers data tool

Price charts are also extremely helpful to spot a card's lows. You can often spot seasonal trends if a card has been tracked for long enough. These could help you hold off on buying a card in the offseason because, historically, it's dipped lower in price. You can also use data tools to extrapolate historical patterns of a similar player from prior years to forecast what the "next guy up" might be poised to do.

Other tools to help

Outside of pricing data tools, you can use several other resources to make quick flips easy. The rise in vaulting services has made flipping easier than ever. When purchasing through certain marketplaces, you can sometimes opt to have your card vaulted rather than have it sent to your home. You own the card, but it's not in your possession. Some collectors don't love the idea, but it's helpful when buying cards you know you will sell.

Rather than paying shipping fees, you can vault a new purchase and immediately post it for sale and sell it directly from the vault. The turnaround time is much faster than posting your own listing and then prepping it to be shipped. Vaults aren't for everyone, but they are great tools for a quick flip and long-term, secure, and fully insured storage.

While some vaulting services typically only allow graded cards, COMC, a marketplace we cover more in Chapter 9, allows raw cards, too. With COMC, you can buy cards and have them mailed as a group rather than individually. This also allows you to use the vault-style service as a seller to post various cards and list them for sale when the time is right.

Short-Term Speculation

Beyond quick flips, short-term speculation has a longer timeline and typically involves different types of cards. More specifically, a quick flip when prospecting with baseball likely involves a player right on the cusp of joining an MLB roster. Short-term speculation might target a player who's only in Single-A or Double-A. These players often need another year or two of development, requiring a longer timeline.

Cards that need a little more time to appreciate than a quick flip but have faster growth potential than long-term investments often fall into this category.

Expectations and timeline

Again, the timeline for sports card investments is relative to your individual goals and expectations, but short-term speculation often falls between a few months and a few years. You can, of course, have a short-term buy turn into a quick flip if the market makes that available to you, but generally, these cards don't see that type of growth often.

Short-term investments can often be more high-dollar cards than quick flips. Expensive cards can be flipped quickly, but the more expensive a card gets, the fewer buyers are available to purchase in most cases. You might, for example, see cards that sell for less than $500 as great candidates for a quick flip, but short-term investments might be between $500 and a few thousand. There aren't exact price thresholds set for these timelines, but some prices are better fits for certain types of investments than others.

Grading or selling raw

Buying high-quality raw cards to grade and sell is one of the better ways to make a profit in sports cards, provided that you become very adept at identifying which raw cards have the potential to get a perfect grade. Unlike a quick flip, a short-term investment allows you to grade a raw card without using one of the fastest and most expensive submission levels. A regular submission level generally takes a few months before returning to the owner, so you must understand that your investment won't be sellable during this time.

TIP

You can cut down on the grading time if you opt to use a vaulting service. In some cases, you can even buy a card and then have it graded and either vaulted or put up for auction by the same marketplace. These marketplaces don't generally have better turnaround times, but it does streamline the shipping process.

When considering whether to grade a raw card, consider the value proposition of the process. As we discuss in Chapter 7, grading a card can add a significant amount of value. In some cases, however, earning a 9 or lower could be catastrophic and might decrease its value. Like it or not, some cards may sell for more in raw condition than in a PSA 9. This is a risk you have to be willing to take, and there's the possibility that the card's price goes down during the grading process. Maybe the player gets hurt or has a stretch of poor games. Those are all things that can happen and can be completely out of your control.

In addition to evaluating your cards yourself for condition, we recommend studying population reports to understand gem rates (the rate that a card scores a Gem Mint across all copies graded) to determine whether it has a good chance at the top grade. If a card only has a 38 percent Gem rate across all graded copies, chances aren't great that yours will score a Gem Mint, even if you think your copy is a good one. It's worth noting that gem rates may be more relevant for modern cards, as vintage items typically grade much lower.

TIP

Remember those potential sell markers you targeted when purchasing the card? Take those into consideration when opting to grade. Rather than buying and grading a card in-season, consider buying a raw card at the beginning of the offseason, so you have a multi-month window for it to come back from grading. Using the offseason window also makes it less likely that something unfortunate happens with the player and drastic declines roll in.

Buying and selling seasons

Speaking of the offseason window, the offseason is a prime buying season for many savvy collectors. Cards are certainly bought and sold throughout the year, but some seasons are better for investment purposes than others. When looking to turn a profit, buying during the offseason when casual fans and collectors aren't paying attention can be a solid strategy. Casual collectors are more likely to buy cards as a player enters the news cycle.

Outside of the offseason, buying when a player isn't participating in the playoffs can be a solid option, too. Popular players often see sharp price declines once eliminated, and scooping cards up is a valid strategy.

The selling seasons typically occur in the gaps when you're looking to buy. For investment purposes, the start of the regular season, the end of Spring Training, or the middle of a playoff series can be good targets. It can be easy to get caught up in strong performances for active players, but price declines often come even faster than price increases.

During the NBA Playoffs, for example, you may see a steady rise as a player and their team advance round by round. It may be safer to consider selling in the middle of a playoff round rather than risking a playoff loss. Price transparency has shown us that a team going down even just one game in a series can have an impact, and selling for a profit before a steep decline may be best, depending on your risk tolerance. Teams going down even just one game can also result in non-paid items. Unfortunately, buyers having second thoughts after a tough loss can be more common during the postseason.

While it's relatively safe to assume that offseason, regular season, and postseason benchmarks are safe sell markers, the true test is to look at a player's individual pricing data and zoom out as far as possible. If you can, compare several of their most popular cards and see if there are regular peaks and valleys. Assuming that these come at certain times isn't quite as good as knowing for sure.

Long-Term Investments

While quick flips — and even short-term investments — are generally where collectors can see explosive price growth or decline (price volatility), the typical long-term investment is more of a slow burn. And that's the whole point. Long-term investments are the cards you plan to hold the longest because, while they may appreciate slowly, they ideally offer much less volatility. Long-term investments can come in a variety of price points as well, though the most high-end cards out there can often fall into this category and may only change owners a few times over the decades.

What makes a great long-term hold

The name of the game here is safety and a proven track record of demand. The best long-term investments are the equivalents of blue-chip stocks in many cases. If Visa or Microsoft were athletes, who would they be? If the S&P 500 was an iconic set, what set would it be? Those are typically the players and sets that are the best fit for long-term investments.

REMEMBER

Long-term investors look for scarcity and eye appeal when selecting the cards they invest in. These cards are rare, feature the best players of all time, are in high demand, and often come in high grades.

Retired players are common targets because long-term holds often require less volatility. Their statistics are set, and they typically only have a few sell markers to target. This means there will be fewer price bumps, but prices also won't go down because of a bad season. Sometimes, the prices of these cards may also be more reflective of the economy's overall health than anything specific about the player or card itself.

These players often are also the best of the best. And we don't just mean an MVP winner or single record holder. We're talking about generational talents. If you're looking at an individual sport like baseball, basketball, or football, there may only be a dozen or two dozen players that could fit this mold — if not fewer. These blue-chip players for a sport like baseball include stars like Mickey Mantle, Babe Ruth, Hank Aaron, Jackie Robinson, and Willie Mays (see Figures 15-2 and 15-3). In basketball, Michael Jordan comes to mind, and for football, Tom Brady has cemented himself in most people's minds as the greatest ever. Not all the cards for those players are valuable, of course, but their rookies and other key cards are typically among the most expensive cards on the market at any given time.

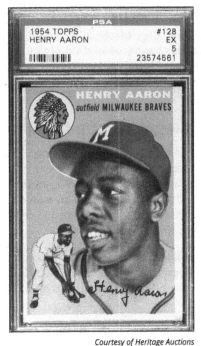

Courtesy of Heritage Auctions

FIGURE 15-2: 1954 Topps Hank (Henry) Aaron, PSA 5

Active players can fall into this category, but the list is short. As of this writing, active athletes like LeBron James, Stephen Curry, Lionel Messi, and Patrick Mahomes (see Figures 15-4 and 15-5) can be among the safest long-term holds. Their status among the all-time greats is largely set. They are widely popular and have plenty of high-end or rare cards that any collector would be excited to own. That list could include more players, but it illustrates the level of superstardom required. Despite being considered relatively safe, these players aren't immune to massive price drops. In fact, players of this level, with some of the most expensive cards on the market, can see some of the biggest drops because their prices managed to get so incredibly high.

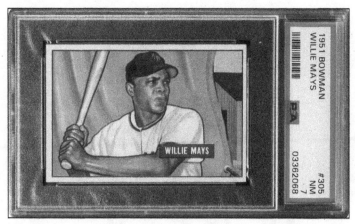

Courtesy of Heritage Auctions

FIGURE 15-3: 1951 Bowman Willie Mays, PSA 7

Courtesy of Goldin Auctions

FIGURE 15-4: 2009 Topps Chrome Stephen Curry, PSA 8

Courtesy of Goldin Auctions

FIGURE 15-5: 2004-05 Mega Cracks Lionel Messi, PSA 10

For athletes below that level, cards considered the most ultra-high-end are often the targets. Ask yourself, if you could own *one* card of a non-generational talent, what would it be? Those are the cards that long-term investors may consider.

TIP

Blue chip sports cards have a long history of being predictably stable alternative investments over the long term. In many cases, they have outpaced other traditional investment vehicles. The main thing to watch out for is not buying a blue-chip caliber card during a period when it is experiencing unusual hype. Instead, be patient, look for deals, and when you find one, act.

Why vintage has been considered a good investment

Plenty of card categories can make great long-term investments, but vintage cards remain relatively safe in an overall volatile market. Again, we're talking key cards of top players here, but the point stands. Vintage cards of retired players have shown the ability to grow in price slowly but surely and have declined in price at a slower rate than other eras like modern or ultra-modern.

This value growth likely happens for a combination of reasons. First, when it comes to long-term investments, many of the most popular vintage cards check the boxes we cover — key players and their most important or rare cards. Vintage cards also feature players that have long been retired. Cards made before 1980 are generally considered vintage. The players depicted on them are no longer playing, so their legacies are set. There are occasionally major changes in consensus, but they're not often. Sometimes, a long-retired player has a passionate group of supporters that shifts public opinion, especially when it comes to Hall of Fame candidates, and that can apply to the card market, too. A player can see their prices rise when a vocal group of hobbyists collectively shout, "This doesn't make sense."

By nature, vintage cards are often rarer or harder to come by in great condition. Many of the sets produced before 1980 didn't have the same print runs as today's ultra-modern products — and come nowhere near the print runs of the Junk Wax Era — and collectors have collectively gotten better about protecting cards.

There are horror stories of Mickey Mantle rookies living in a child's bicycle spokes or a Hank Aaron rookie being glued to the inside of an album. While cards were beloved as collector's items, few envisioned them as eventually being worth any significant amount of money. And that's a major reason why some of the hobby's most expensive and rare cards are expensive and rare. They began as ordinary cards before neglect and apathy depleted the population of mint condition cards. Thankfully, we've mostly learned from the mistakes of past collectors, though that lesson may result in fewer cards becoming ultra-rare. Today, it's not uncommon for collectors to take great care of any player who has even the most remote chance of being good.

Pairing an old-school superstar with a rare or condition-sensitive card also makes many of the most popular vintage investments extremely expensive. This is where some of the stability comes in. Though it's easy for a $50 card to jump up to $100 or down to $25, it's less likely a card that normally sells for $5,000 or $10,000 will see similar percentage changes. The investment is much more expensive, but there's overall less volatility.

REMEMBER

It's worth mentioning before we move on that there has been concern about the vintage market's stability as we continue to get further and further away from those stars and their playing days. Although it's normal to appreciate a player like Willie Mays through highlights, it's more difficult when that's all you've ever experienced. It's harder to connect with a player you never saw play live or even on TV during their playing days. As generations of new collectors come into the hobby, it's fair to wonder how much they'll care about a player — even if he's considered one of the greatest of all time — if their only experience is seeing them through highlights while being told they were great.

Chapter **16**

Properly Valuing and Selling Your Cards

ven the sharpest negotiators can be undone by a lack of research, and with card prices going up and down daily, you must use all the tools at your disposal to be as prepared as possible. Being a great seller is more than the dollars, though. Sure, making money is the idea for selling, but the hobby's best sellers also provide a service for the sports card community. The hobby's best sellers make money while also providing buyers with great deals, and they are often some of the best resources for information and guidance.

In this chapter, we break down how to use data tools to properly value your cards while guiding you toward becoming a top-flight super seller.

Sales Data Matters, but There's More to the Story

Gone are the days when card prices were determined by a heavily speculated number in a publication like *Beckett Magazine*. While *Beckett* was a cornerstone of the hobby for years, there's simply more transparency around card prices than ever before, and there's a variety of tools to help you determine *exactly* what a card has been selling for recently. We introduce you to some data tools that can provide additional depth and resources shortly, but the most basic form of creating a price comparison, also known as a *comp*, is to look at recent sales data. The easiest way to do this is to search for your card on a marketplace like eBay and sort the listings by "sold." Instead of active listings, the list will show items related to your search query and the price paid.

Sorting auctions by "completed" listings will also display all auctions that have ended, even if the item wasn't sold. While this is the easiest way to comp a card, it should be noted that additional noise can slip into the data presented. For example, eBay does not — by default — show the true price when a Best Offer is accepted on a card. In addition, a card may have "sold" for a certain price, but the key thing is whether the item was paid for. An auction can end, but the buyer never paid for the item. Unfortunately, this happens far too often and is one of the major pain points of trying to sell cards and trust sales comps. This is not how business should be done, but it happens.

TECHNICAL STUFF

Your search results may include items that aren't quite what you're looking for. They'll often be close, but the simple fact that humans create the listings means mistakes in the listing titles and other descriptions can happen. That 2019 Zion Williamson Prizm Silver PSA 10 (see Figure 16-1) may have been a 2019 Prizm Base PSA 10 (see Figure 16-2) that was listed incorrectly. What's more, sellers rarely put the word "base" in their listing titles. As such, to refine your search, you typically need to exclude every other possible match from the set to whittle down to just the base cards. Adding a modifier like "-silver" to your search will remove items that have the term "silver" in them. Use this to eliminate anything from reprints of vintage cards to cards from certain grading companies. A trusted data tool can help do some of this for you.

While comps matter, they're far from guaranteeing that your card will sell for the same or more. In fact, a card rarely sells for the same price from one sale to the next — even if it sells within a few minutes of the last sale. The value of a card is a complex mélange of scarcity, exposure, timing, and the overall state of the economy.

Courtesy of Goldin Auctions

FIGURE 16-1: 2019 Zion Williamson Prizm Silver, PSA 10

REMEMBER

Comps serve as a useful baseline for valuing cards, but the bottom line is that a card, simply put, is ultimately worth whatever someone else is willing to pay for it. The goal is to find the seller willing to pay the most.

Trusted pricing tools

A quick Internet search for "sports card price guide" or something similar will deliver many sites and tools claiming to have correct card pricing. They likely don't, and it's safe to assume that most free tools have serious holes in what they can provide.

REMEMBER

You get what you pay for, and how to price your cards probably isn't the place to cut corners.

Later in this chapter we cover some trusted data tools that are also available in a variety of price tiers.

Courtesy of Goldin Auctions

FIGURE 16-2: 2019 Zion Williamson Prizm base, PSA 10

Market Movers

For full transparency, the authors of this book created and built Market Movers, so we're admittedly biased. However, we believe in the product and can attest firsthand to the work that has gone into making it over the years.

This book isn't meant to serve as an ad for Market Movers, but the major selling point is its robust set of analytics tools built atop a database that features millions of cards with carefully curated search queries to ensure that the data points you're sifting through are trustworthy. Data is also pulled from all the hobby's leading online marketplaces, ensuring that comps for cards of all price points are available (see Figure 16-3).

TIP

Market Movers is a paid tool, but if you're looking for something free to get you started, check out the Sports Card Investor mobile app instead.

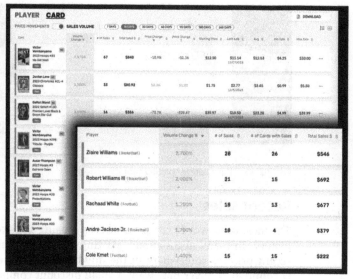

Courtesy of Market Movers

FIGURE 16-3: Market Movers pricing tool

Card Ladder

Featuring both a free and paid option, Card Ladder is another data tool in the hobby that tracks sales from various auction houses and marketplaces (see Figure 16-4). Card Ladder was acquired by Collectors Universe, the parent company of PSA, in 2020.

130 Point

130 Point is a free resource that asks users to do some of the heavy lifting when crafting specific card searches. It's essentially a sales comp look-up tool — a step up from eBay sold searches. It also offers resources like checklists and a release calendar.

Important price points, trends, and more

Regardless of your pricing tool of choice, there are some key concepts to understand when breaking down the data. A chart doesn't mean much if you aren't reading it correctly, and a variety of items to sort through play a factor in deciding what you should sell your card for.

Courtesy of Card Ladder

FIGURE 16-4: Card Ladder pricing tool

Recent sales

The most basic way to comp a card is by looking at its recent sales history. In many negotiations, starting things right at the most recent price or somewhere in the middle of several recent sales is common. A buyer may want a small discount compared to the most recent sales, while a seller may be more focused on a comfortable price relative to how much money they have invested in the card.

WARNING

We cover more about the do's and don'ts of negotiating in person in Chapter 10. Please beware of recent sales outliers, as some sellers have been known to intentionally manipulate prices a day before card shows to artificially inflate their card values. Use common sense and, if applicable, look at 7- or 30-day averages instead of single last sales.

Trend lines

Beyond looking at the most recent sale, the trend lines for prices are important indicators of a card's immediate future. If a card has seen steady growth over the last 60 days, you may want to ask for slightly more than the most recent sale because the card has shown a recent history of price growth.

The strength of the trend line matters here, too. Has the card seen a few outlier sales that have the price chart shifting up and down drastically? Or does it have a steady climb or decline over that same period? Once again, outlier sales should always be excluded when negotiating prices — for both the buyer and the seller.

A hotly contested auction ending 30 percent above the previous sale may be legitimate but may not accurately indicate the market for that card. On the other end of the spectrum, an auction that ends late at night or very early in the morning can have the inverse effect. Prices that fall within a steady trend line are typically considered better indicators of a card's true market, but outlier sales often include an additional variable that impacted the sale.

Highs and lows

A card's past price highs and lows should greatly impact when you decide to buy or sell. From a selling standpoint, the highs may be the most important indicator. If a rookie card of a star player has never gone above $200 at any point over the last three years, it may be safe to assume that it won't now or in the future, barring that player's emergence as a true superstar.

Highs and lows are often tied to the seasonality of every sport as well. The card market for each sport often heats up leading up to the start of the season and again in the playoffs for the players making deep playoff runs. You see many price highs during these periods. For example, the football card market is typically hottest in late July, August, and early September and again in January for players in the playoffs. Those months are often the best time to sell to maximize your sale price. The card market for each sport often cools down in the early offseason, which leads to price lows, so you may want to avoid selling during that period.

Things can change, of course, and that's where your instincts and knowledge of the players and their specific sport are important. The overall health of the market plays a part as well. A card's lows are also important benchmarks for the buying season. Use the card's previous peaks and valleys to indicate when a card may best be bought and sold.

Sales volume

While price changes are certainly important, one can argue that volume is just as strong of an indicator of a card's market. Ideally, a card's sales volume will be paired with its recent price changes to paint a complete picture.

Sales volume typically increases in one of these scenarios:

>> Right after the card first hits the market and interest is high
>> When a card is starting to truly heat up, and everyone is trying to get a piece of the action
>> When a card is tanking, and sellers are trying to liquidate

Sales volume typically slows in one of these scenarios:

>> As a card reaches its peak price
>> When the card has crashed so much in price that sellers refuse to come down, and buyers lose interest
>> When hobbyists choose to keep the card in their collection long after the initial release

A card with a lower overall price may not seem flashy to some sellers, but it could be worth consideration if it sells at an extremely high volume. Lots of successful sellers focus on cards that sell for less than $50 but sell often. The profit per card is lower, but the volume makes up for it.

Cards with a lower sales volume can be great investments, too, but it's important to understand why they sell less often. An extremely rare card will have lower sales volume because there just aren't many in existence. From a price standpoint, extremely expensive cards will also have a smaller pool of potential buyers to work with, which often causes fewer overall sales. Auction houses can be used to sell these types of cards because they are often better at getting items in front of the *right* buyers. You're likely looking at a dud if the card doesn't sell often and it isn't expensive or rare.

Price growth

Getting caught up in things like price growth when using data tools is easy, but cutting through the noise doesn't take much effort. Many data tools will offer things like a price percentage change view of a card, and that's dangerous to take strictly at face value.

A card that has gone up 100 percent in price may seem great on the surface, but that doesn't mean much if the card went from $4 to $8. Additionally, cards that transact daily can often have a random sale that dips 15 percent below the prior sale while another goes 15 percent higher a week later. That can look like a massive increase between two sales, but the average price of the card across all sales for that period is a much better representation of its value.

Price percentage changes are a great tool, but a card's overall dollar amount is also critical. A card may only jump 10 percent in value, but that's significant if 10 percent is $1,000.

TIP

Consider that the raw dollar amount sometimes tells the real story when looking at price percentage changes.

Becoming a High-Quality Seller

We mention it several times in this book, but we're doubling down again because it's that important. The best sellers provide a service to the hobby community. Full stop. It's not just about flipping cards for a profit. The best of the best make money while still offering great deals to buyers. They help deliver grail cards to their forever homes. And they serve as great resources for information to those looking for help.

TIP

Think of the sports card hobby as a relationship; healthy relationships require you to give just as much as you take. It might be time to rethink your process if you're making money in this hobby and don't think you're contributing much to its overall good.

A personal touch

Although many sellers do most of their business online, many do just as much, if not more, in person at card shows. Outside of the initial setup of your space, the process for selling in person is possibly a little easier than online. Things can move more quickly, and you likely aren't shipping anything. We cover navigating card shows as a buyer more in Chapter 10, but here are a few tips to get you on the right track as the seller:

>> **Be friendly.** Just be nice. This isn't difficult, or at least it shouldn't be. We all have bad days, and some card show attendees can be off-putting, but it's not hard to be nice. Consider offering a short greeting when a potential buyer

arrives at your table. A smile or a quick nod can be just as good. How you treat people in person can play a big part in how successful you are as a seller, and it's not hard to understand that some of the more abrasive sellers may struggle to make sales. Buyers are more likely to return to you if their experience was pleasant, and you may be a little more likely to have a one-and-done sale if the buyer doesn't feel things went well.

» **Be a hobby ambassador.** Along with being a friendly face, it's important to remember that card show dealers can be seen by many as ambassadors for the hobby. For many young collectors, card show dealers are some of their first interactions with the space, and those experiences must be good ones. The best sellers are also generally the most educated about the industry and can offer advice and guidance.

» **Sort and price your cards fairly.** One of the best ways to ensure that buyers keep walking right past you is to be completely disorganized or lack clear pricing. Sure, it takes work to sort everything and even more work to update prices before each show. But if you're serious about moving inventory, it's worth it. Fairly pricing your cards shows buyers you're serious about making a deal. If you have a subset of your inventory that you're not overly eager to move and are holding out for top dollar — like rare grail-type cards — consider putting those in a section of your showcase either labeled accordingly or verbally communicated as such. You're in control of your pricing, but transparency helps. Dealers don't like it when buyers waste their time, so don't waste theirs.

» **Arrive willing to negotiate.** You'll likely arrive at a card show with ideal prices in mind, but those typically won't stand. It's natural for buyers to want a good deal, and one way to work with that is to build in some negotiation room to your prices. This is why you may see high prices across the board when shopping at card shows. Prices are high because they are meant to come down a little. Be willing to work with your potential buyers to come to a deal both parties are happy with.

TIP

As we mention in Chapter 9, the best deals don't involve winners and losers, and sellers play as much a part in that as the buyers. If you don't have what the buyer is looking for, consider pointing them in the right direction if you know another seller who can help. A small gesture like that can go a long way.

Maintaining a good standing selling online

Having a great reputation selling at card shows is great, of course, but it's not hard to argue that your online reputation is more important than anything else. It's not uncommon to see apology posts across social media when sellers fail to stick to shipping times, and anything less than a stellar feedback rating on eBay seems like a massive red flag for buyers. When it comes to selling online, a negative interaction can end up being so much bigger than that single transaction — even one instance of negative feedback can sit atop your profile for all to see, and prospective buyers may decide to avoid the risk.

However, maintaining a flawless reputation online isn't as difficult as it seems. You can do plenty of things to ensure a positive experience, even when something goes wrong.

Communicate

A little communication can go a long way, especially when dealing with people online. Consider a short message when a buyer makes a purchase, letting them know that their order has been received and when you anticipate shipping. Marketplaces like eBay often allow a short window to pay for or ship items, and while immediately completing the task is ideal, some transparency for anything else gives buyers more confidence.

REMEMBER

Mark your account as Away if you'll be out of town for some time. This lets buyers know that you cannot ship their items immediately.

Communication also means being descriptive in your listings. Consider using a standard and consistent listing title syntax for all your listings. For example, you can list out the details of the card in the following sequence: Player, Year, Set, Card Number, Variation, Serial Number, Grading Company, Grade, Rookie, and Team.

This helps make browsing your entire store easier for a buyer. Beyond the identifying aspects of the card itself, you can add notes and comments in the item description, especially any notable defects in the condition of the card. Also, consider a note about which type of shipping you plan to use. Sports cards are often expected to be shipped in a bubble mailer with a tracking number — a simple abbreviation of BMWT (bubble mailer with tracking) will be enough.

Ship quickly

Fast shipping doesn't necessarily have to mean immediately, though plenty of buyers will expect that. In general, a good benchmark is to get items shipped right before or after the weekend. A three-day window after the sale is the general expectation. Anything sold during the week should probably be shipped by Friday or Saturday, and anything sold over the weekend is probably best shipped on Monday.

Leave feedback

Strongly consider leaving feedback for transactions that go well. Receiving positive feedback as a seller is extremely helpful, so it's only fair that you do the same for a buyer who paid quickly or left their own feedback. Selling online helps you reach more potential buyers, but it also limits the first impression. Your feedback rating is your first impression, for better or for worse, and it's your responsibility to keep it pristine.

Handle with care

Along with a crisp, descriptive card listing, the best way to make your transaction great is by providing high-quality shipping. This isn't difficult and mostly just requires a little time and effort. It also doesn't have to be expensive, though most buyers will be willing to spend a little more on shipping expenses if they know their cards will arrive safe and secure.

Supply basics

You'll need to make sure you have a few supplies on hand before shipping your cards — assuming you want them to arrive safely and receive positive feedback. If you've purchased cards before, you'll know that the packaging comes in all different shapes and sizes. The various supplies may all look different, but in general, many collectors prefer a specific order of operations.

The basics are penny sleeves, Toploaders or semi-rigid holders, plastic team bags, and some painter's tape. These items aren't super expensive and will go a long way toward making your buyers happy.

How to pack

First, the card needs to be placed in a penny sleeve and Toploaders. Semi-rigid holders are acceptable alternatives for Toploaders. Make sure that these all fit properly, as buyers won't appreciate their card being stuffed into something a little too small or too big. In addition to potential damage, no one likes fighting with the packaging to retrieve their item.

If your card is secured in a Toploader, consider placing it in a plastic team bag with the top sealed. You can also use a small piece of painter's tape to secure the opening. Painter's tape is preferred as it doesn't leave behind residue. Don't use scotch tape to seal a Toploader shut. Doing so is a major hobby faux pas that ruins Toploaders and aggravates buyers.

Using a budget shipping option like eBay's Standard Envelope might be the maximum protection you can use before the mailer becomes too thick to ship properly. Cards under $20 are eligible for the Standard Envelope, and it is not recommended that you use this shipping option for cards over that value. This shipping option is meant for budget cards, and buyers will rightly be frustrated if a more expensive card is shipped this way so you can save a few dollars.

If you're shipping with a bubble mailer, technically, you can simply place the card into the package and seal it. However, the best practice is to secure the card between two pieces of cardboard cut to the same size as the Toploader or graded slab. This shows that you really care about ensuring the card reaches the buyer in the same state it left you.

Protect yourself with insurance

Things happen with the mail, which may include an item you shipped being stolen, misdelivered, or simply damaged during transit. This is extremely unfortunate for both parties, but in most cases, the seller loses the most. You aren't a big-box store that can simply ship out a replacement or consider the loss spillage. In scenarios like this, buyers can rightfully request a refund and get their money back, and the seller is likely eating the loss. This is why you need to consider additional shipping insurance for anything you aren't comfortable taking as a complete loss.

TIP

Fighting with the marketplace, delivery service, or even worse, the buyer over these things isn't ideal. Your best course of action is to ensure that your items are properly insured so you can simply provide the refund and move on. The best sellers are often prepared for the worst, even if major issues are extremely unlikely. We recommend that all sellers decide what price threshold makes sense to insure cards and stick to that. It's an upfront cost to protect against larger potential losses.

WARNING

It's also important to note that USPS insurance can be somewhat of a hassle to make a claim on. Make sure you have proof of the purchase made, and even then, the USPS will sometimes refuse to pay out the claim if the card shows as delivered but was stolen. As an alternative to insurance from the couriers themselves, collectible insurance companies (who can be used to insure your entire collection) sometimes offer a one-time insurance service if you're shipping high-dollar cards and need total peace of mind.

5

The Part of Tens

Chapter **17**

Ten Unwritten Rules Every Collector Should Follow

The sports card hobby has rules. You likely won't get in trouble by ignoring them, but some rules make the collecting experience better for everyone. Be good to the hobby, and it will be good to you.

In this chapter, we explore tips and tricks for being a good collector while making your hobby experience great.

Have Fun and Collect What You Love

Sports card collecting is a hobby, after all, right? It's certainly possible to make money or a career out of sports cards, but it's important to remember that having fun is why most people participate.

Having fun is also easiest when you're filling your collection with cards that bring you happiness. Sure, there may be unique cards or rarer or expensive cards out there, but do they bring you joy when you see them?

Ask any longtime collector about some of their favorite cards, and you'll often be presented with at least a few items that hold little value to most but mean everything to their owner.

Don't Let FOMO Drive Your Decisions

One of the biggest mistakes a collector can make is giving in to the fear of missing out (FOMO). Longtime collectors have all done it — paid too much money because a card was popular at the time, only to see it drop in price a month or even a few weeks later.

Remember the tip about collecting what you love? The fear of missing out is an easy way to buy a card you don't love or pay too much for something that will almost always pop back up later at a better price.

One of the best ways to avoid making FOMO purchases is to have a list of cards you're targeting so that other cards won't become regrettable purchases.

TIP

Take a step back, do your research, and consider whether buying that specific card at that specific moment is the best decision for your collection.

Set a Budget and Stick to It

Sports card collecting is an expensive hobby. Even for the richest of the rich, there are cards out there with prices that could make Jeff Bezos flinch.

This principle doesn't apply only to buying singles on the secondary market either. Ripping packs can be addicting, and those trips to your local shop, show, or retailer can add up.

REMEMBER

This is a hobby. Don't overspend and put yourself in a tough financial position for a piece of cardboard.

Respect How Others Collect

As we cover in Chapter 8, there are all kinds of ways to collect. Some may have clear goals and themes for their collection, and others may buy a wide variety of different cards. Either way, it's important to respect all collectors.

At its core, the hobby is about having fun, and no one gains anything by being negative toward someone else's collection. Even if you don't like their cards, you should appreciate the fact that it makes them happy.

REMEMBER

Though some would have you believe otherwise, there's no such thing as "true collecting."

Be Reasonable When Trading

Trades in professional sports are often evaluated with a winner and a loser. That doesn't have to be the case in the hobby.

Sure, it's always nice to get back more than what you put in, but don't put too much effort into being the clear winner. Do your best to agree on the value of cards and make a trade that all parties are happy with. It's also acceptable to walk away if you can't find a fair agreement.

REMEMBER

Trades will almost never be perfect, but one side coming out as the clear winner isn't worth the other side being a clear loser.

Ship Cards Like You'd Want Them to Be Shipped

It doesn't take long scrolling hobby posts on social media to run into a horror photo of a poorly packaged card from an online purchase. Don't be that seller.

We cover how to package and ship your cards when selling in Chapter 16; the process isn't difficult. Properly packaging your cards doesn't have to be expensive either, so it's mostly about time and effort.

Cards deserve protection during transit but shouldn't require a chainsaw to open. Imagine how you'd like to receive your cards, and the right way to do it likely isn't far off.

Understand the Cost of Doing Business

Negotiating the cost of cards is a major part of the hobby. In fact, it's highly encouraged to negotiate whenever possible. But be respectful and understand the cost of doing business, especially when it comes to your local card shop and dealers at shows.

This doesn't mean that sellers should get a free pass to overcharge — that's far from the case. But consider that making deals in person is a major convenience for the buyer, and it costs money to set up as a dealer at shows or run a shop.

TIP

The best show dealers and shop owners are almost always willing to make deals and provide a service to the buyer. Consider this when making your next deal. As with trades, try to find a deal without a clear winner or loser.

Support Your Local Card Shop

Speaking of local card shops, do your best to support them when possible. Local card shops are the lifeblood of the hobby. The best shops provide great deals or services and can often be the hub of your local collecting community with trade nights and other events.

This doesn't mean supporting shops that you don't enjoy, of course. These places and people need to earn your business; not all shops are created equal.

TIP

Stop by your local card shop often, even if you just browse. You never know; you might just make a new collecting friend or two.

Look to Pay It Forward

A little kindness can go a really long way in the collecting world. From tossing in a few extras when shipping something out — be thoughtful, don't just send junk — to always leaving the last pack in the store, you can really make another collector's day with a small gesture.

Consider a Random Act of Kindness (RAK) when the opportunity arises. Did you befriend an Atlanta Falcons fan at your local card shop? You never know what someone is going through, and receiving some of your Bijan Robinson cards might make a difference.

Never Stop Learning

Whether you've been in the hobby for three months or 30 years, there's always more to learn. The world of sports cards and collectibles is so vast that even the smartest hobbyists have a lot to learn, and it's important to be willing to grow with the hobby. The hobby is always evolving in terms of products, trends, technology, and more.

REMEMBER

Be open to meeting new people and hearing and respecting their points of view. The hobby is filled with all kinds of wonderful people, and there's something to learn from every one of them.

Chapter **18**

Ten Tricks to Building a Great Collection

B uilding a collection that they are happy with and proud to display is a major goal for many hobbyists. Some start small and build over the years, while others immediately dive in hard and amass an impressive collection.

In this chapter, we explore how to take your collection to the next level while working at a pace that's perfect for you.

Find a Collecting Theme, Identity, or Style

A major key to building a great collection is identifying your collecting identity, which we cover more in Chapter 8, and building around that theme. If you're a big Los Angeles Dodgers fan, consider dedicating a large part of your collection to your favorite Dodgers players. You can take this even further by collecting those players in your favorite sets, too. If you remain focused, you'll likely quickly assemble a collection of cards you're proud of.

However, it's important to note that while picking specific themes and sticking to them is a great way to collect, it's not always necessary. Many collectors are interested in dozens of players, teams, and sets. In the end, collect how, why, and when you want. Focusing on a specific theme may help build your collection, but it's always acceptable to do something else if a themed collection isn't how you want to do things.

This is your hobby — collect how you want.

Set Realistic Goals, but Dare to Dream Big

It's likely that, even if you're just starting your collecting journey, you have an idea of what kind of collection you want to have. Maybe it's extremely valuable, and you're proud to pass it down to your children. Maybe it's a lineup of cards that display well in your home office. Either way, you should take time to set collecting goals so you can always see the path toward completing them.

It's also extremely important to set realistic goals. Most of us would love to have a 1952 Topps Mickey Mantle in our collection, but is that realistic for your budget? You should have a list of grail cards that may take years to assemble, but don't commit to tracking down things you can't realistically acquire.

The most effective goals and grails are the ones that take time but are reachable.

Be Patient and Play the Long Game

Speaking of goals and grails that take time to acquire, it's critical to be patient when collecting. As we cover in Chapter 17, don't let fear of missing out (FOMO) impact how you collect. The fear of missing out is an easy way to overpay for cards or even buy cards you don't want at all.

Being patient still applies to cards you are certain you want, too. Unless you're dealing with an ultra-rare item that you rarely see, you can be sure it'll pop up again. You might be able to grab that card now, but it's sometimes possible to snag a variety of other cards on your wish list instead. Remember this because "now" isn't always the right time or place.

Use saved searches on marketplaces that have a saved item or wishlist functionality. Also, consider posting your "want list" on your social media profiles to let others know what you're trying to acquire.

Use Data and Other Resources to Find Great Deals

Being patient is a lot easier when you know the exact price and scarcity of an item going in. We cover pricing data in Chapters 9 and 16. Paid tools like Market Movers are great resources for making sure you're paying what something is worth. It's not hard to say no when the price isn't right.

It's also important to research important cards ahead of time. Even if a card isn't serial numbered, it can be extremely rare or difficult to find in great condition. It's important to use things like checklists, sell sheets, and graded population reports to make an educated decision. The most recent sales price should have an impact, but a variety of other factors should be considered.

Curate Your Collection Periodically

Buying what you love is a great way to assemble a collection that brings you joy. The problem, however, is that your interests may change over time. Maybe you've finally given up on rooting for the Detroit Lions and no longer want to collect Barry Sanders. Likes and desires can change, so it's critical to be willing to curate your collection when needed.

Consider regular collection audits where you move on from cards you no longer want or need. You can often sell these items and put them toward something you'll be happy with instead. Cards you no longer love have no use sitting in storage, so consider moving them for something better.

Consolidation Can Help Win Holy Grails, but It Isn't for Everyone

Regular collection consolidation is also a great way to score your grail cards. Collectors often "trade up" by trading or selling several small cards for one expensive card. This concept is also commonly used to get better examples of a card. The owner of a 1933 Goudey Babe Ruth PSA 3 may look to combine that card with others to "trade up" into a PSA 4 copy.

Collection consolidation isn't for everyone, however. Quality over quantity works for some but not for others. Plenty of collectors would prefer several cheaper cards over one more expensive. Hobbyists looking to "trade up" need a partner in the transaction, after all.

Go Off the Beaten Path and Search for Hidden Gems

Although adding some of the hobby's most iconic and popular cards to your collection is a great way to impress others, consider going off the beaten path, too — you'll often find hidden gems your collecting circle doesn't know about.

TIP

Next time you stumble across a great card, try searching for that set to see what you find. You might just run into new players to collect or discover similar designs you need in your collection. These hidden gems can often get even better reactions from your collecting friends than the typical lineup of iconic cards.

Develop a System to Store and Display Your Cards

For most hobbyists, admiring their collection is a major source of joy, and you should consider the best way to display yours. Whether in your home office, at your desk at work, or on a social media account, there are plenty of ways to show off your cards. Don't overdo it, though, especially if your chosen space is shared. You may love your collection, but maybe your family doesn't.

Consider developing a great system for storing your cards outside the typical bookshelf, stand, or other display. Displaying them is great, but protecting them is most important. (Displaying and storing your cards is covered more in Chapter 9.)

If cards aren't on display, you should have a system in which they are safely stored and can be easily found. You never know when you may need to retrieve something quickly.

WARNING

Don't forget about what light can do to cards, especially autographs. Keep these cards away from direct sunlight, and consider putting them behind UV glass to prevent fading over time.

Find Hobby Friends and Collecting Groups

The hobby is almost always better when you have a group of friends to share it with. Of course, you can go into the hobby solo, but you might just have a better time sharing the hobby with others. A great collecting group is also the best way to discover new cards or learn new things.

Start with trade nights or local card shows if you want to meet other collectors in person. Try social media and online forums for greater reach. Whether you collect Dallas Cowboys cards or Topps Finest refractors, a community of people with similar interests would likely love to have you.

Learn from Your Mistakes

Everyone makes mistakes, and the hobby is no different. We call it the price of tuition. Maybe FOMO got the best of you, or maybe you made a poor choice trying to flip a card and lost money. Mistakes happen, but what's important is that you learn from them.

When it comes to building your collection, mistakes are all relative, and you'll find new ways to buy and sell over the years.

REMEMBER

How you collect on day 1 will be much different than how you collect on day 1,000. Never stop learning, and your collecting mistakes will become far less common.

Chapter **19**
Ten Iconic Cards Every Collector Should Know

The sports card hobby is filled with incredible cards. Then there are *these* cards. These are the trendsetters, the record-breakers, and the most sought-after grails. In one way or another, each of the following ten cards has left an impact that won't be forgotten.

Below, we explore the hobby's most important cards in order of release.

In this book's color section, you can see color versions of all the cards shown in this chapter.

TIP

Cards and collectibles are incredibly subjective, so don't forget that this list is what *we* believe are 10 of the most iconic cards of all time. Your list may be completely different, and that's what makes this hobby great.

REMEMBER

1909–1911 T206 Honus Wagner

Arguably the greatest shortstop ever, Honus Wagner is also considered one of the best baseball players of all time. One of five players inducted into the inaugural Baseball Hall of Fame class in

1936, Wagner led the National League in batting eight times, runs batted in five times, and stolen bases five times.

On paper, it makes sense that one of baseball's all-time greats lands on this list. The history of Wagner's T206 card is more complicated, though.

Issued by the American Tobacco Company from 1909 to 1911, the T206 set features one of the most recognizable designs in the hobby and is often synonymous with the term "tobacco card." While most cards from the T206 set aren't generally considered rare, Wagner is an exception. Printing for his card was halted early, leaving what is believed to be between only 50 and 60 copies in existence. The story behind the stoppage isn't clear, though common reasons are that Wagner didn't feel he was being compensated properly or didn't want to be associated with a tobacco product. Either way, his T206 is one of the scarcest cards in existence.

An SGC 2 example of the T206 Wagner (see Figure 19-1) sold through Goldin Auctions in 2022 for $7.25 million — a record at the time for any trading card.

Courtesy of Heritage Auctions

FIGURE 19-1: 1909 T206 Honus Wagner, SGC 2

1933 Goudey Babe Ruth

Issued by the Goudey Gum Company in 1933, this set reshaped the bubblegum card era while delivering four stunning Babe Ruth cards (see Figure 19-2). Featuring beautiful colors and bright portraits, 1933 Goudey also stands out due to its size. These cards are wider and slightly taller than old tobacco sets but smaller than modern cards.

All four cards of Ruth from 1933 Goudey are individually important, though the four cards collectively make this set exceptionally important. The 1933 Goudeys are far from Ruth's only important cards — his 1914 Baltimore News rookie is one of the hobby's all-time greats, too — but it's hard to argue against the overall impact this set and these Ruth cards have had on card collecting.

Courtesy of Goldin Auctions

FIGURE 19-2: 1933 Goudey Babe Ruth, PSA 7

1948 Leaf Jackie Robinson

Although some cards land on this list with help from an odd series of events that helped create an interesting story, this card's history is rather straightforward. Jackie Robinson's 1948 Leaf rookie (see Figure 19-3) lands here as the most important card for one of the most important athletes of all time, regardless of the sport.

Robinson broke baseball's color barrier in 1947, and Leaf produced this gem a year later. This card is helped by the fact that the 1948 Leaf release featured an impressive lineup of Hall of Fame rookies. Along with Robinson, collectors can find rookies for Stan Musial, Warren Spahn, Ralph Kiner, and Satchel Paige.

Courtesy of Goldin Auctions

FIGURE 19-3: 1948 Leaf Jackie Robinson, PSA 7

1952 Topps Mickey Mantle

One cannot discuss the most important cards without mentioning the 1952 Topps Mickey Mantle (see Figure 19-4). And much like the T206 Honus Wagner, this card's shocking history has helped make it the treasure it is today. It's important to note that this is not Mantle's rookie card — that's his 1951 Bowman. However, the 1952 set is known as the birth of the modern sports card for many.

Looking to make a design splash, Topps released its 1952 set with a larger card size and featured bright colors on the front and player stats and notes on the back. After strong initial success, interest in the set fell off as football season closed in, and stores and shops struggled to move inventory despite Mantle's inclusion.

Pallets of 1952 Topps were piled onto garbage barges and dumped into the Atlantic Ocean to create warehouse space, and suddenly, an unknown number of Mantles were sinking in the water. The destruction of these cards has helped keep the overall population of 1952 Mantles relatively low, with only three perfect PSA 10s in existence.

Despite being a second-year card, Mantle's first Topps release has become arguably the most important trading card ever behind the set's iconic design and a wild story. In 2022, an SGC 9.5 example sold for $12.6 million through Heritage Auctions, setting a record for any trading card.

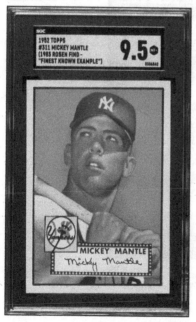

Courtesy of Heritage Auctions
FIGURE 19-4: 1952 Topps Mickey Mantle, SGC 9.5

1979 O-Pee-Chee Wayne Gretzky

The greatest basketball, football, and baseball players are often hotly debated. The greatest hockey player ever isn't. Wayne Gretzky stands atop the sport, and his 1979 O-Pee-Chee rookie card (see Figure 19-5) also lands among the greatest cards — ever.

Gretzky's iconic rookie has both O-Pee-Chee (Canadian release) and Topps (US release) variations, though the O-Pee-Chee is considered more valuable. There are just four total PSA 10 examples across both O-Pee-Chee and Topps (two each) due to quality control issues and its bright blue border.

In 2021, one of the O-Pee-Chee PSA 10s sold in a private deal facilitated by Heritage Auctions for $3.75 million, a record for any hockey card.

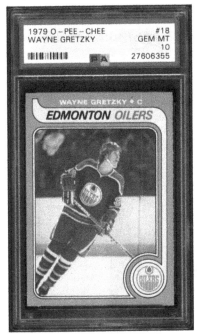

Courtesy of PSA

FIGURE 19-5: 1979 O-Pee-Chee Wayne Gretzky, PSA 10

1980 Topps Bird/Erving/Johnson

A rookie for one of basketball's all-time greats is fantastic, but how about two? The 1980 Topps set featured a unique three-panel layout; in this case, collectors got rookie cards for Larry Bird and Magic Johnson simultaneously (see Figure 19-6).

Each panel can be separated thanks to perforated edges, though cards from this set are only considered complete when all three panels are intact. There are just 23 PSA 10 examples at the time of this writing, and that number likely won't go up much anytime soon.

A beautiful design in a unique format that features three of basketball's greatest lands, this card is among the best created.

Courtesy of Goldin Auctions

FIGURE 19-6: 1980 Topps Larry Bird/Julius Erving/Magic Johnson

1986 Fleer Michael Jordan

The 1986 Fleer Michael Jordan card is, without question, the most important card for basketball's most influential player (see Figure 19-7). Whether this is his true rookie card is up for debate.

If the year 1986 seems off to you, it's because Michael Jordan's rookie season was in 1984. Without traditional basketball releases from Topps, stars like Jordan didn't have a flagship rookie card during their actual rookie season. It wasn't until Fleer's entrance in 1986 that Jordan and a host of other Hall of Famers got their first traditional cards — despite the late release, many consider these their rookie cards.

Many collectors consider Jordan's 1984 Star his true rookie, however. While the 1984 Star set featured Jordan's first NBA-licensed cards, these were distributed in team sets and aren't considered rookies by many collectors.

Both cards are extremely valuable, though the 1986 Fleer has largely won the battle for rookie status and features a stunning action shot of Jordan dunking. Some sports cards may be more valuable or rare, but few feature a better photo or design.

Courtesy of Goldin Auctions

FIGURE 19-7: 1986 Fleer Michael Jordan, PSA 10

1989 Upper Deck Ken Griffey Jr.

This is arguably the most important card from the entire Junk Wax Era. Of course, this isn't to say that Ken Griffey Jr.'s 1989 Upper Deck rookie is junk — that's far from the case. Featuring a clean border and timeless design, this rookie features a portrait of Griffey Jr. sporting the same legendary smile that captivated fans for years. This card also happens to be the most graded card in history, with nearly 100,000 examples from PSA alone.

Hoping to bring luxury to the hobby, Upper Deck delivered a revolutionary set in 1989 with cards printed on higher-quality card stock with a glossy finish. Griffey Jr. at card No. 1 was the perfect start to the checklist.

Few athletes have been as universally beloved as Griffey Jr., and pairing a beautiful rookie card with a revolutionary set helps land it among the greatest cards ever.

Figure 19-8 shows this iconic card.

Courtesy of Goldin Auctions

FIGURE 19-8: 1989 Upper Deck Star Rookie Ken Griffey Jr., PSA 10

2000 Playoff Contenders Rookie Ticket Autograph Tom Brady

In a hobby dominated by baseball and basketball, the 2000 Playoff Contenders Rookie Ticket Autograph Tom Brady delivers this list's only football card (see Figure 19-9). Before the first pack-inserted autographs debuted in 1990, stars were often stuck with base cards as their key rookies. That's far from the case for Brady.

While his rookies from Topps Chrome and Bowman Chrome are important, too, these on-card autographs helped usher in a new era of collecting in which the top rookie cards often featured autographs and memorabilia.

In 2021, the Championship Ticket parallel of this card, numbered to just 100, sold for $3.1 million through Lelands Auctions. The sale at the time was a record for any football card.

Courtesy of Lelands

FIGURE 19-9: 2000 Playoff Contenders Championship Ticket Autograph Tom Brady, BGS 9

2003 Exquisite Collection LeBron James

Not unlike several other cards on this list, the 2003 Exquisite Collection LeBron James Rookie Patch Autograph (RPA) was a right place, right time type of moment (see Figure 19-10). In this case, Exquisite Collection made its revolutionary debut as an ultra-high-end set as James entered the NBA.

Originally selling for $500 per pack, Exquisite Collection gave some collectors pause. Years later, the price seems like a bargain when you consider the value of the cards from this set. In addition to on-card autographs and game-used jerseys from top rookies like James, Dwyane Wade, Carmelo Anthony, and Chris Bosh, Exquisite Collection also featured high-end cards for Michael Jordan, Kobe Bryant, and other megastars.

In 2021, a BGS 9 example of this card, numbered to just 23, sold for $5.2 million in a private sale brokered by PWCC. The sale at the time tied the record for any trading card and was a new high for any basketball card.

Courtesy of PWCC

FIGURE 19-10: 2003-04 Exquisite Collection LeBron James Rookie Patch Autograph, BGS 9

Glossary

Acetate: A transparent plastic that is sometimes used to make trading cards. This material is known to yellow over the years.

Allen & Ginter: A tobacco company founded in the late 1800s that was known for including trading cards in packs of cigarettes. A&G exists today under the Topps brand.

Alteration: Changes made to a trading card, usually with the intent to increase its value. Common alterations are trimming and recoloring.

American Caramel: A tobacco company founded in the late 1800s that was also a major producer of early trading cards.

Arena Design: A design company best known for producing popular inserts for companies like Fleer and SkyBox during the 1990s.

Art cards: Licensed cards that typically feature a creative spin on a traditional design by a professional artist. Popular modern examples are cards from the Topps Project 2020 and Topps Project 70 sets. Vintage art cards like Donruss Diamond Kings and Goal Line Art football cards are also quite popular.

Authentication: The process in which third-party grading companies confirm the legitimacy of a trading card or other collectible.

Autograph: A signature, typically from an athlete, that can be found on trading cards. These can be signed directly on the card, or the autographs may be on transparent stickers that are placed on the cards during production.

Base: The cards that make up a product's base set. These are generally the most common and least valuable.

Beckett: A popular hobby company founded by Dr. James Beckett. The brand is best known for its series of price guides and the Beckett Grading Services (BGS).

Blaster box: A retail configuration of sports cards that is often available in stores like Target and Walmart. These boxes generally contain fewer packs than hobby boxes and offer worse odds of finding the best cards in exchange for a lower price.

Border: The area of space that separates the main photography from the edges of a sports card. Borders are typically white or black. Some cards feature full-bleed photos or designs that eliminate the typical border.

Box break: The process of opening a box of trading cards. Is also used to describe what is expected from each individual box. For example: one autograph and one memorabilia card.

Bowman: A confectionary company that began producing trading cards in the 1920s. The company has a long history of producing some of the hobby's most iconic sets. It is most associated in the Ultra-Modern Era with prospect cards.

Cabinet cards: One of the earliest formats for sports and trading cards. These typically featured a photograph attached to a cardboard backing and were large enough to display in cabinets. The Allen & Ginter brand has produced modern versions of these classics.

Cardstock: The material that sports cards are printed on. Paper and chromium stock are common materials for popular sets.

Case: A sealed collection of boxes containing trading cards. Cases typically contain anywhere from 2 to 20 or more boxes. A case hit also describes a type of card that appears only once, on average, per case.

Cello pack: A retail configuration that features packs of cards wrapped in cellophane.

Centering: One of the major categories grading companies use to evaluate a card's condition. It describes how well-positioned a card is top-to-bottom and left-to-right.

Chase: Describes a card that may be considered more valuable or popular in a product. These cards are typically the reason a collector purchases a product.

Chrome: A reflective finish most associated with refractors and sets like Topps Chrome and Panini Prizm.

CGC: Abbreviation for Certified Guaranty Company, a third-party grader with extensive experience in the comic and coin categories.

Condition: The overall physical quality of a trading card. Categories like centering, edges, surface, and corners make up a card's condition.

Configuration: The format for a trading card product. Blaster boxes, hobby boxes, and cello packs are all considered different configurations.

Cracker Jack: A company that produced popular snacks as well as trading cards in the early 1900s. The Cracker Jack brand has been brought back several times over the years by Topps.

Custom cards: An unlicensed card created by an artist or collector that typically features creative designs or memorabilia. These items may also include major alterations to what was originally a licensed card.

Die-cut: A card that has additional cuts made during the manufacturing process to create a nonsquare or nonrectangle shape.

Donruss: A confectionary company founded in the 1950s with a long history of producing trading cards. Donruss was acquired by Panini in 2009 and is best known for its Rated Rookie cards.

Edges: The surface area that defines the outside of a card. Edges are also one of the major categories grading companies use to evaluate a card's physical condition.

Eye appeal: Describes how physically appealing a card is to look at. Cards with high eye appeal may still be extremely attractive despite having damage. This is extremely important when evaluating vintage cards.

Fanatics: A major manufacturer of sports-related apparel and other merchandise that acquired rights to produce trading cards for leagues like the NFL, NBA, and MLB. Fanatics later acquired Topps to help manufacture trading cards.

Fleer: A confectionary company credited as the first to make bubble-gum. Fleer began making trading cards in the early 1920s.

Full-bleed: Describes a card with photography that stretches to the edges. Full-bleed cards don't have borders.

Game-worn: Refers to pieces of memorabilia that were used during a game.

Gem Mint: Describes a card of the highest physical quality. Cards that earn a PSA 10 or BGS 9.5 are considered Gem Mint.

Goudey: A chewing gum company that is best known for producing trading cards, including the iconic 1933 Goudey set.

Grading: The process of a third-party company evaluating the physical condition of a card.

Group Break: An event where a group of collectors shares the contents of a box. Participants divide the cards by paying for the rights to categories like specific teams or individual players before the box is opened.

Flipping: Refers to a card bought and sold quickly, ideally for profit.

Hit: Similar to a chase card, it describes the best cards you can pull from a pack.

Hobby box: A configuration of products sold through hobby shops or directly from the manufacturer. Hobby boxes typically contain the best pack odds for the product's top chases and are usually more expensive than retail boxes.

Insert: A card that isn't part of the base set. Insert sets typically follow a uniform theme and feature players fitting the theme.

Junk Slab Era: A period of time during and after the COVID-19 pandemic when collectors submitted massive amounts of trading cards to grading companies. Many cards would go on to sell for less than the cost of grading.

Junk Wax Era: A period of time during the 1980s and 1990s when manufacturers greatly overproduced trading cards, leading to a loss of interest in the hobby for many collectors.

LCS: Abbreviation for local card shop.

Leaf International: A confectionary company that produced several important trading card sets in the late 1940s.

Leaf Trading Cards: A trading card company founded in 2010 by Brian Gray. It has no association with Leaf International.

Licensed: Refers to cards with official licenses using player names and team logos from a professional league. Companies like Topps, Panini, Upper Deck, and Fanatics pay exhorbitant amounts for exclusive rights to use player names and team logos on its products.

Memorabilia: Pieces of jerseys, bats, balls, sneakers, and other items that are placed into trading cards.

Modern Era: The era of trading cards between 1980 and 2012. The Modern Era saw a variety of design innovations that remain important today.

National Sports Collectors Convention: Often simply called "The National," this is the largest sports cards and collectibles show in the world. Typically takes place in late July or early August. It rotates locations every year.

Numbered: Short for serial-numbered cards. These come with stamps indicating the total print run as well as the card's placement within that total run. Ex: 9/10.

O-Pee-Chee: A Canadian confectionary company that is best known for collaborating with Topps for trading card releases. Upper Deck currently uses the O-Pee-Chee brand to produce hockey cards.

On-card: Refers to a type of autograph signed directly on the card by the player.

One-of-One: A card with just a single copy made. These are typically stamped with "1/1" or "1 of 1."

One-Touch: Also called magnetic holders, One-Touch holders are hard plastic card holders held closed by a magnet.

Panini: A trading card company formed in Italy during the 1960s. The Panini America brand has been a major producer of trading cards, especially for the NBA and NFL, during the Ultra-Modern Era.

Parallel: Refers to cards with additional designs or color variations. Popular examples are gold, silver, black, mojo, shimmer, or cracked ice. Modern products often include a dizzying array of parallels for every base card.

Penny sleeve: A thin plastic sleeve that is typically used as the simplest form of protection for a trading card. Penny sleeves are used before placing a card in a top loader.

Personal Collection: Refers to cards a collector will likely never sell. Some of these cards may have high value to the owner but little value to anyone else. Often informally abbreviated as "PC."

Player-worn: Describes a piece of memorabilia that was put on by a player, typically at an event. These items are not worn during games.

Population report: The total number of graded examples of a specific card. Each of the major grading companies produces its own population report.

Pop: Describes the graded population of a specific card. For example, "Pop 1" means only one copy of a card exists with a specific grade.

Pre-War Era: Refers to cards produced before the start of World War I.

Prospecting: The process of collecting cards of players before they become stars or even join a top professional team. The term is most associated with minor league baseball players and the modern-era Bowman sets.

PSA: Short for Professional Sports Authenticator, a third-party grading company. PSA became the most popular grader during the Ultra-Modern Era, specifically during and after the Covid-19 pandemic.

Rainbow: Describes the full lineup of parallels for a card. Rainbow collectors have become more common with the rise of parallels during the Ultra-Modern Era.

Refractor: A chrome card with a rainbow-like shine. The first refractor was featured in 1993 Topps Finest Baseball.

Recoloring: An alteration used on trading cards to make the colors appear brighter or more vibrant. Recoloring can also be used to fill in areas where color is missing. Mostly associated with vintage cards.

Relic: A term that often refers to the pieces of memorabilia placed in trading cards.

Rookie Patch Autograph: These cards are autographed and contain a piece — called a "patch" — of a jersey from a player's rookie year. These cards are some of the most desirable in the hobby. Often abbreviated as RPA.

Semi-rigid holder: A plastic holder that's thicker than a penny sleeve but not as sturdy as a Toploader. Cards are held in place but are easy to remove when needed.

Shill bidding: The unnaturally driving up an item's price at auction with illegitimate bids.

Short print: Refers to any card that has a shorter print run than the base variations. Abbreviated as SP. An SSP (super short print) is a card printed in even smaller quantities.

Slab: Slang for the plastic holder used to encapsulate cards during the grading process.

SGC: Abbreviation for Sportscard Guaranty Corporation, a third-party grading company most associated with its vintage-era card expertise.

Sticker: A collectible that is meant to be peeled and placed in an album. Stickers are similar to trading cards but have a more passionate following in Europe than North America. The term sticker can also refer to an autograph that was signed and then placed onto a card later.

T206: An iconic set of tobacco cards that features the Honus Wagner card. The T206 Wagner is considered by many to be the most important trading card in history.

Tobacco cards: Cards typically associated with the late 1800s and early 1900s. These cards were placed in packs of cigarettes both as collectibles and to provide physical support to the cigarettes.

Toploader: A rigid plastic holder for trading cards. Toploaders are more rigid than penny sleeves and semi-rigid holders but less rigid than one-touch holders.

Topps: A confectionary company founded in the early 1900s with a long history of producing trading cards. Most associated with its unprecedented run as the primary brand of baseball cards.

Trimming: The process of altering a trading card with a cut, typically to increase its value. Trimming is often done to improve the edges or corners of a card and is largely considered fraud by the hobby.

Variation: Describes a type of card that is anything other than the base version. Variations can be refractors, parallels, or other short-printed versions.

Vintage era: An era of trading cards that typically describes anything made before 1980. Specific eras that are considered vintage include tobacco, Pre-War, and Post-War.

Ultra-Modern Era: An era of collecting from 2012 forward. Panini, Topps, Upper Deck, and Fanatics have dominated the Ultra-Modern Era.

Upper Deck: A trading card company that began producing cards in 1989. The first cards were considered premium releases and had a major impact on the industry.

Index

C

active vs. retired players, 216–217

announcements to Major Leagues and, 119

authentication, benefits of, 139–140

autographs, 217–219

becoming high-quality seller

high-quality shipping, 254–256

online reputation, 253–254

personal touch, 251–253

building business from scratch, 226–228

on budget, 227

making first deals, 227

realistic expectations, 228

taking losses, 227–228

disclaimers, 213–214

flipping cards quickly, 229–234

candidates for, 230–232

timeline for, 232

using data tools, 232–233

graded cards, 220–222

long-term investments

characteristics of good holds for, 237–240

vintage cards, 240–242

major stars and top prospects, 215–216

mistakes to avoid

fees and taxes, 226

FOMO (Fear of Missing Out), 226

lack of research, 225

overview, 211–213

psychology behind, 12

rookie cards, 217–219

selling cards

auction listing formats, 224

on eBay, 224–225

sell markers, 222

timing, 223–224

short-printed cards, 219–220

short-term speculation

buying and selling seasons, 236

expectations and timeline, 234

grading or selling raw, 235–236

valuing cards, 243–251

past price highs and lows, 249

price growth, 250–251

pricing tools, 245–247

recent sales history, 248

sales volume, 249–250

trend lines, 248–249

investors, 195

J

Jackson, Joe, 23

Jackson, Reggie, 32

James, LeBron, 281

jersey swatches, 83–84

jeweler loupe, 135

Johnson, Earvin "Magic," 92, 277

Johnson, Ryan, 195

Jordan, Michael, 92, 277–278

Junk Slab Era, 39–40, 287

Junk Wax Era, 13, 287

football player cards, 102–103

history of, 33–35

K

Kaboom! cards, 77, 219

King of Collectibles show, 166

L

The Last Dance documentary, 94

LCS (local card shop), 167, 262, 287

Leaf International, 26, 102, 287

Leaf Trading Cards, 112–113, 287

left to right (L/R) centering, 129

Lelands, 167, 280

Library of Congress, 10, 20

licensed cards, 111–115, 287

local card shop (LCS), 167, 262, 287

logo cards, 83

long-term investments

characteristics of good holds for, 237–240

flipping cards vs., 212–213

vintage cards, 240–242

lots, 162–163

loupe, 135

low-population cards, 221–222

L/R (left to right) centering, 129

M

M designation, 116

magazines, 195–197

Beckett Magazine, 196

PSA Magazine, 197

Tuff Stuff, 196

Magic Photos baseball card set, 27

magnetic (One-Touch) holders, 173, 288

Mahomes, Patrick, 103

mail-in autographs, 157

Make an Offer feature, 170

Manning, Peyton, 100

About the Authors

Geoff Wilson founded Sports Card Investor, the largest YouTube and content network in the sports card hobby, and Market Movers, the leading price guide and collection tracking platform. Geoff enjoys collecting cards and visiting card shows with his sons, Reaves and Harrison, and his daughter, Emilia.

Ben Burrows is the collectibles editor at *Sports Illustrated* and the former content director for Sports Card Investor. Introduced to collecting at age 5 by his father, Ron, he has since dedicated his collection to his favorite Atlanta Braves players and anyone who attended his alma mater, Syracuse University.

Tyler Nethercott's career has spanned roles in finance, innovation, data management, and software development. With a life-long love for sports, a penchant for collecting, and a deep interest in human behavior, his professional expertise meets his personal passion as vice president of product development at Sports Card Investor.

Acknowledgments

Like many journalists, writing a book has been on my bucket list for about as long as I can remember. I wasn't sure what that first book would look like, but I can safely say that I never imagined it would be with such a great publisher and brand like Wiley and the For Dummies series. I'm unbelievably fortunate to have been surrounded by an incredible group of people who made this entire project possible, and I can't thank them enough for their love and support during this process.

To my father, Ron, thank you for introducing me to collecting nearly 30 years ago and for always reading anything I wrote. To my mother, Susan, and my sister, Ashley, thank you for always being my biggest fans when I've needed you the most. To my partner, Rebecca, this book would have never been possible without your unwavering love and support. To our editors, Rick Kughen and Adam Gray, and the entire Sports Card Investor team, thank you for your kindness and guidance through such a challenging process.

This book would have never been possible without the help and support of an incredible community of people.

—Ben Burrows

I've bought many For Dummies books over the years to learn real estate investing, football coaching, computer programming, and more. So, it was an incredible honor when I was asked to write this book! Thank you to everyone at Wiley for giving me the opportunity!

This book was the work of many, especially my co-authors Ben Burrows and Tyler Nethercott. Ben and Tyler are great collectors who want everyone to have an awesome experience with the hobby, and they both poured countless hours into this book to make it a valuable resource. I cannot thank them enough.

I'm lucky to have a great team at Sports Card Investor and Market Movers, who have helped me immensely with my collecting pursuits. My journey in cards would also never be possible without the strong support from my wife, Kim, and my kids, Reaves, Harrison, and Emilia. There is no greater thrill than sharing my collecting journey with my children. I hope you get to experience the same.

—Geoff Wilson

Writing this book has been incredibly challenging and incredibly rewarding. Someone asked me at the time of its announcement, "How can you write 320 pages about sports cards?" The hard part wasn't having enough to say but how to consolidate more than a century of history and passion into one book!

I'd like to thank Geoff Wilson for allowing me to work in the best hobby industry in the world. Thank you to my wife Natalie for supporting my interests and especially for giving me the nudge to contact Geoff Wilson via Discord four years ago. I'd like to say a huge thank you to Ben Burrows for his writing, editorial leadership, and expertise throughout this process. Thank you to Adam Gray for being a great friend and our technical editor. Your passion for sports cards is truly unmatched, and your positive attitude is a model for all in the hobby. Thank you to Jeremy Lee of Sports Cards Live and TAG grading and Aaron Lapointe of Lapp3r30's Hockey Card Flips for providing expertise on hockey cards.

It was an incredible privilege to be a part of writing this book for the sports card hobby. We take this responsibility seriously and hope that all readers, regardless of their experience level, will be entertained, educated, and proud to share it with a friend.

—Tyler Nethercott

Publisher's Acknowledgments

Acquisitions Editor: Jennifer Yee

Project Manager: Rick Kughen

Development Editor: Rick Kughen

Technical Editor: Adam Gray

Production Editor: Tamilmani Varadharaj

Cover Image: © Hunter Martin/ Getty Images